DISCARD

THE SMOKE OF SATAN

THE SMOKE OF SATAN

CONSERVATIVE AND
TRADITIONALIST DISSENT
IN CONTEMPORARY
AMERICAN CATHOLICISM

MICHAEL W. CUNEO

New York   Oxford
OXFORD UNIVERSITY PRESS
1997

Oxford University Press

Oxford   New York
Athens   Auckland   Bangkok   Bogotá   Bombay
Buenos Aires   Calcutta   Cape Town   Dar es Salaam
Delhi   Florence   Hong Kong   Istanbul   Karachi
Kuala Lumpur   Madras   Madrid   Melbourne
Mexico City   Nairobi   Paris   Singapore
Taipei   Tokyo   Toronto

and associated companies
Berlin   Ibadan

Copyright © 1997 by Michael W. Cuneo

Published by Oxford University Press, Inc.
198 Madison Avenue, New York, New York 10016

Oxford is a registered trademark of Oxford University Press

Chapter 3 is a significantly revised version of the author's "Life Battles:
The Rise of Catholic Militancy within the American Pro-Life Movement,"
in Mary Jo Weaver and R. Scott Appleby, eds., *Being Right:
Conservative Catholics in America* (Bloomington:
Indiana University Press, 1995), pp. 270–99.

Library of Congress Cataloging-in-Publication Data
Cuneo, Michael W.
The smoke of Satan : conservative and traditionalist dissent
in contemporary American Catholicism / Michael W. Cuneo
p. cm.   Includes bibliographical references and index.
ISBN 0–19–511350–0 (cloth)
1. Catholic Church—United States—History—20th century.
2. Conservatism—Religious aspects—Catholic Church—History of doctrines—20th century.
3. Dissenters, Religious—United States—History—20th century.
4. Catholic traditionalist movement—United States—History.
5. Independent Catholic churches—United States—History—20th century.
6. Mary, Blessed Virgin, Saint—Cult—United States—History—20th century.
7. United States—Church History—20th century.   I. Title.
BX1407.C76C86   1997
282'.73'09045—DC20   96–34719

1 3 5 7 9 8 6 4 2

Printed in the United States of America
on acid-free paper

to DANIEL CHRISTOPHER CUNEO

SATAN'S SMOKE
HAS MADE
ITS WAY INTO
THE TEMPLE
OF GOD THROUGH
SOME CRACK.

POPE PAUL VI (JUNE 29, 1972)

CONTENTS

ACKNOWLEDGMENTS

I AM ENORMOUSLY INDEBTED, first of all, to the many women and men (not all of whom make appearances in this book) who agreed to speak with me of their spiritual disaffections and longings as Catholics thirty years after the Second Vatican Council. While virtually all of them were gracious and forthcoming, I especially profited from the perceptiveness of William Doino, Jr., Monica Migliorino Miller, John Cavanaugh-O'Keefe, Theo Stearns, Sr. Michelle of the Infinite Love community, Alphonse Matt, Jr., and E. Michael Jones. Of the many friends and colleagues who offered me assistance and counsel along the way, I would like to express particular gratitude to John J. Shea, S.J., James R. Kelly, Roger O'Toole, Robert Cuneo, Bill Baumgarth, Jean-Guy Vaillancourt, Jeffrey L. Gray, John Macisco, Rosemary Santana Cooney, Gregory Baum, Stewart Guthrie, Bruce McCullough, Kathie Lowes, Gerald Shattuck, Jim Lowes, and Lloyd Rogler. The book could not have been written without the hospitality and unceasing support of the Jesuits at Fordham, or the earlier support of John H. Simpson, Ronald Sweet, Paul Gooch, and Jane Dammen McAuliffe of the Centre for the Study of Religion at the University of Toronto. Mary Jo Weaver, R. Scott Appleby, and the Lilly Endowment provided both the encouragement and the means for undertaking part of my research, and my research associate Richard P. Cimino contributed indispensable (and immensely skillful) help at almost every turn. My debt to William Dinges for his pioneering work on Catholic traditionalism will be obvious to anyone familiar with the field, and the same is also true for Sandra Zimdars-Swartz and her utterly splendid work on Catholic Marianism. I owe a special word of thanks to Joe Muriana for his wise and patient advice on some of the manuscript's earlier sections, and also to Rebecca E. Cuneo and Shane D. Cuneo for subjecting the entire work to sharp critical analysis. I have counted heavily on Margaret J. Cuneo for literary and philosophical advice throughout, and whatever coherency the final product enjoys is at least partly a reflection of her talents. I am grateful, finally, to Cynthia Read of Oxford University Press for helping me find my stride at the outset and shepherding the work to completion, and also to the press's anonymous reviewers for their astute suggestions and criticisms.

iNTRODUCTION

AMERICAN CATHOLICS ON THE WHOLE today don't seem a particularly tormented group. Many of them enjoy a standard of living that their grandparents could only have dreamed of, very few doors are closed to them in either public or private life, and they seem for the most part as easily at home with democracy and political liberalism as anyone else in contemporary America. As longtime residents of suburbia, moreover, many of them are connoisseurs of consumption and comfort, and even their religion seems tailored for personal convenience. Long gone are the days when being Catholic in America implied close (or, at least, closely pretended) adherence to a rigid system of doctrine, morals, and ritual. Today it is enough merely to affirm oneself as Catholic, and to take from the church whatever one needs, whenever one needs it.

Not that there still isn't occasional complaining. Many American Catholics undoubtedly wish that their church were even looser than it now seems, especially in the area of personal morality. Although widely ignored, and practically never enforced, church rules against divorce and extramarital sexuality are an annoyance to some simply for remaining on the books. And the rules against abortion, the ordination of women, and contraception certainly strike many Catholics as embarrassingly archaic. There are other complaints as well—insipid priests and dead-on-delivery homilies, arrogant bishops and overcrowded pews at Easter—but nothing serious enough to incite widespread rebellion. All things considered, being Catholic in America today seems a winning proposition: with its easygoing combination of affluence and affability, it's as good a deal as one is likely to find anyplace else.

Such, at least, is the view from the surface. Once one digs a bit deeper, however, it becomes apparent that not all Catholics in the United States share this positive assessment of the current situation. In small pockets scattered throughout the country, there exists a sort of Catholic underground made up of people who are in rebellion against the new comforts and freedoms of American Catholicism. Far from being a place of legitimate faith, in the view of such people, the church in the United States today is an outright disaster zone. Its theologians are traitorous, its bishops derelict in defending traditional truth, and its schools breeding grounds of heresy. Pampered and complacent, its laity are mostly ignorant (or altogether dismissive) of fundamental doctrine and morals. Its once-great ritual life is enfeebled and disgraced, and many of its priests seem enamored less by the sacraments than by the prospects of gay sex and left-leaning political action. The martyrs and saints of yesterday, in short, have been pushed aside; and American Catholicism today draws its inspiration instead from the phony allures, the cheap salvations, and the discounted commitments of the modern world.

Many who belong to this underground look upon the 1950s as a lost Golden Age of authentic Catholicism: Paradise before the Fall. The fifties was a time, in their view, when the American church was still proudly Catholic, defiantly true to its own past and fully committed to the business of saving souls. It was during the 1960s, when the Second Vatican Council tried to make the church more relevant to the modern world, they claim, that the decline began. Before long the American church was suffering from an epidemic of relevance, and the very idea of what it meant to be Catholic had become endlessly negotiable. In trying to be all things to all people, the American church seemed perfectly willing to dispense with everything that had once made it distinctive. Latin and incense and cassocks rapidly gave way to Bob Dylan and blue jeans, candles and statues disappeared almost overnight from parish churches, and eventually even such long-standing requirements as priestly celibacy and personal chastity came to be regarded as little more than yesterday's hang-ups. And today, these critics claim, the transformation is virtually complete. In the space of just three decades, the American church has been reduced to a solemn superfluity—a vaguely pious adjunct to the secular culture. The institution might still be standing, in other words, but the spirit has long since abandoned the premises.

Although I've thus far spoken of it in the singular, this Catholic underground actually consists of several more or less distinct factions, each with its own specialized world view, its own spirituality, and its own particular take on what must be done to save authentic Catholicism in the United States from outright extinction. The first of these factions, which I designate here as *Catholic conservatism*, is mostly made up of disaffected laypeople who are committed to revitalizing the church through a campaign of moral militancy. Fiercely loyal to Rome, and just as fiercely opposed to the moral flabbiness of the broader culture, Catholic conservatives want to create a newly masculinized Catholicism: a Catholicism that's tough and defiant, stripped down and ready for battle. And the prime testing ground for this toughened-up Catholicism is on the frontlines of America's current abortion wars. Fighting abortion, in the conservative view, is far more than simply a political undertaking. It's the final frontier of faith, the last opportunity for Catholics in the United States to recapture the zeal and spiritual prowess of their religious ancestors.

As much as they deplore its current condition, conservatives still hold out hope that mainstream Catholicism in the United States can be restored to some semblance of its former self. *Catholic separatists* (as I refer to those who belong to the underground's second major faction) are considerably more pessimistic. For the past thirty years, according to separatists, the institutional church in America and elsewhere has undergone a process of almost complete spiritual meltdown, and its prospects for recovery seem exceedingly bleak. In Rome no less than in America, they claim, the institutional church has become mainly a sham of faith; and trying to reform it from within is no longer a viable strategy. Indeed, the only strategy worth pursuing today is one of strict isolationism. If authentic Catholicism is to be kept alive, Catholics still loyal to the traditions of the past are compelled to withdraw altogether from the institutional church and create alternative communities of their own. It's only within such alternative communities (or theological utopias-in-exile), separatists claim, that a newly sanctified Catholicism—completely unadulterated by the perversities of the historical present—can be nurtured into being.

While conservatives seek redemption through moral purification, and separatists through radical isolation, *Catholic Marianists* turn instead to the more exotic realm of miraculous apparitions and mystical prophecy. In these desperate times, they contend, the Virgin Mary has re-entered history with new messages of hope (and warning) for the suffering faithful. These messages, transmitted directly by the Virgin herself to specially appointed seers, spell out the precise steps that must be taken for Catholics to attain salvation, and also the punishments awaiting anyone foolish enough not to take heed. For Catholic Marianists, the messages and their accompanying apparitions are more than just a spiritual consolation; they're also a powerful vindication. In an age that treats virtually every expression of religious passion as a laughingstock, here's live-wire evidence that miracles still happen and that forces greater than nature and the human will still rule history. And for anyone who persists in scoffing, the Vengeful Virgin will be back on the scene soon enough to set matters straight.

Of these three factions, it's Catholic conservatism that has thus far had the greatest public impact. For the past two decades, conservatives have been at the forefront of anti-abortion protest in America, frequently taking the lead in civil disobedience and other militant forms of street activism, and doing their utmost to keep the abortion issue in the public limelight. Catholic separatism is fascinating primarily as a case study in the ironies of religious protest: distressed by the breakdown of authority and unity within Roman Catholicism since the

Second Vatican Council, separatists have responded by—what else?—trashing the authority of Rome and entering into schism from the institutional church. Catholic Marianism is a classic expression of what I would describe as colloquial Catholicism. Of the underground's three major factions, it's the most egalitarian, and also the most accessible to ordinary believers. Neither moral purity nor doctrinal virtuosity is part of the admission price here; all that's required is personal devotion to one's favorite apparition and personal trust in the power of magical nostrums to cure evil and set everything right.

———————

THE CHAPTER THAT FOLLOWS BRIEFLY DESCRIBES the tremendous changes that have taken place within American Catholicism since the 1950s, and chapters 2 through 5 offer a guided tour of the Catholic underground that has come into being largely as a result of these changes. As tours go, however, this one is considerably less than comprehensive. Rather than exploring every nook and cranny of the underground, my goal has been to introduce readers to some of the rather more engaging (and representative) organizations and personalities of its various factions. And this has occasionally meant going beyond the strict geographic confines of the United States. As Catholicism in America has become increasingly modernized over the years, some of the Catholics with whom this study is concerned have felt compelled to look elsewhere for spiritual consolation, and two of the places they've looked with particular interest (as we shall see in chapter 5) have been St. Jovite, Quebec, and Fort Erie, Ontario. A final chapter attempts to place the overall story in broader social and historical perspective.

While all of this is unquestionably a Catholic story, it's also an inextricably American one. For all of its technological sophistication and technocratic sophistry, the United States remains a hugely hospitable place for religious and political sectarians, with their wildly varying dreams, conspiracies, and atavistic visions. More often than not, America's sectarians are content to stay tucked out of view in some corner of the nation's thick cultural underbrush, and it's usually only scandal or catastrophe that catapults them to occasional public prominence. It shouldn't take a Waco or an Oklahoma City, however, to make us realize the importance of understanding those whose vision lies far outside of the mainstream. Given time and opportunity, the protest of the disaffected seems almost always to result in consequences beyond itself.

OUT OF THE GHETTO

CHAPTER ONE

IN 1899. Pope Leo XIII issued a letter of condemnation against an intellectual movement that he identified, quite simply, as Americanism. As noted by Dennis McCann in his provocative book on the topic, the encyclical letter *Testem benevolentiae* took direct aim at the innovative views of Isaac Thomas Hecker, an American Catholic convert and founder of the Paulist fathers.[1] At a time when the Vatican was still implacably opposed to the twin principles of democracy and religious freedom, Hecker had argued that in their American context these principles had actually proven beneficial to the Catholic faith. Not only had the church in the United States enjoyed impressive institutional growth despite holding neither religious monopoly nor legal privilege, according to Hecker, but it had also been enriched spiritually through prolonged exposure to the American democratic ethos, with its tolerance for diversity and its characteristically experimental approach to truth. As a consequence, Hecker had argued, there was emerging within the American church of the late nineteenth century an unprecedented respect for religious liberty and a corresponding confidence in the capacity of a laity nurtured in democracy to find its own way to Christian virtue. Indeed, it was Hecker's view that American Catholics, sustained by the presence of the Holy Spirit within their community, were authors of an entirely new chapter in Catholic ecclesiology.

It was scandal enough to the Vatican that Hecker and his supporters would so avidly endorse a political arrangement in which Catholicism was denied favored status. In an earlier encyclical, *Immortale Dei* (1885), Leo XIII had declared it essential not only that the modern state be professedly Christian but also that within its boundaries Catholicism be accorded preeminent legal standing. But even more vexing was the theological creativeness that the so-called Americanists seemed to claim for their national church. Taking their lead from Hecker, a number of influential prelates within the American hierarchy, most notably John Ireland and Cardinal Gibbons, had proposed that by virtue of their openness to the Holy Spirit and their experience of democracy, Catholics in the United States were in process of developing a spirituality dynamically in tune with the cultural conditions of the modern world.[2] While the Americanists said nothing explicitly at variance with Catholic dogma, and it was clearly not their intention to challenge the authority of Rome, the progressive role they envisioned for the American church, coupled with their positive assessment of individual spiritual experience and democracy, seemed to the Vatican dangerously presumptuous. Moreover, the enthusiasm with which Hecker's ideas had been received among Catholic liberals in France served to increase Leo XIII's suspicion that Americanism was yet another attempt, not so very different from the Gallicanisms of the past, to assert the independence of a national church from Rome. It was with concerns such as these in mind that the pope in *Testem benevolentiae* decried the efforts of Hecker and others to reconcile the American church with its political and cultural environment.

> But in the matter of which we are now speaking, Beloved Son, the project involves a greater danger and is more hostile to Catholic doctrine and discipline, inasmuch as the followers of these novelties judge that a certain liberty ought to be introduced into the Church, so that, limiting the exercise and vigilance of its powers, each one of the faithful may act more freely in pursuance of his own natural bent and capacity. They affirm, namely, that this is called for in order to imitate that liberty which, though quite recently introduced, is now the law and the foundation of almost every civil community.[3]

There seems little doubt that *Testem benevolentiae* had substantial impact upon the evolving self-identity of American Catholicism. As if repentant for the theological deviations denounced in the encyclical, the American church retreated in the years following its release into a cultural ghetto, effectively shutting itself off from the ideological enticements of the broader society. And within this enclosure was fostered a piety that left Catholics palpably different from their fellow Americans, a piety undergirded, in the words of Dennis McCann, by "unquestioning loyalty to Rome, a veneration of the Blessed Virgin and the saints that at least bordered on the superstitious, clerical authoritarianism, and a consciousness of sin that made all these other differences seem not just plausible but indispensable."[4] There seemed little point in venturing beyond the ghetto in pursuit of truth, it came to be assumed, when all the truth that really mattered was already there, certified by Rome and available for instant consumption.

Within this all-embracing Catholic subculture, there was no structure more prominent, or more a symbol of intellectual confinement, than the parochial school. Since the Third Plenary Council of Baltimore in 1884, when it was mandated that every Catholic child should receive a Catholic education, the building of schools had been a priority of the highest order for the American church. So important was the parochial school to American Catholics that in many communities its construction preceded by several years that of the actual parish church. Staffed mainly by nuns recruited and trained expressly for a teaching role, these educational bastions of the Catholic ghetto instilled in the children of poor immigrants a dual loyalty to church and country, and in all of their students a basic literacy in Catholic dogma.[5]

Considering the immense financial sacrifice that went into its creation, and also the sense of fortified unity it provided their ethnically diverse church, the ghetto infrastructure of school, convent, and rectory—especially during the decades preceding the Second World War—was understandably an achievement of considerable pride for American Catholics. During the 1950s, however, as Catholics began their steady ascent into the occupational mainstream of American society, this infrastructure increasingly came to be seen as something of a mixed blessing—as tangible proof on the one hand of the dedication and resourcefulness of the church, and yet also a constant reminder of unfulfilled promise and spiritual vacuity. Particularly during this period for Catholics who had tasted secular success, the ghetto had become claustrophobic, its schools cramped and abandoned to mediocrity, its rituals meretricious, and its theology vacant and aloof. Even though dissatisfaction of this sort was not universally felt, it nonetheless reflected a certain restlessness within the American church on the eve of the Second Vatican Council.[6]

When painting with such broad historical strokes, we run a clear risk of oversimplification. While true that the American church of the pre-conciliar era was often seen (and sometimes also experienced) as a ghetto of oppressive sameness, it wasn't entirely devoid of excitement. In the political realm, for example, there were efforts by such coolly pragmatic priests as John Ryan, George Higgins, and Jack Egan to reform American society according to Catholic ideals of social justice. In the arena of social activism there was Dorothy Day and her Catholic Worker movement, with its anarcho-syndicalist vision for a transformed social order. In spirituality there was Thomas Merton, whose writings awakened a generation of Catholics to the mysteries of monasticism. And in theology there was, above all, John Courtney Murray, who spent decades dodging ecclesiastical censure while defending both religious liberty and the American constitutional principle of separation of church and state.[7]

But endeavors such as these were rare shafts of light upon an otherwise bleak intellectual landscape. Throughout most of the 1950s, American Catholic theology was an almost entirely endogamous affair, cut off from the wider society and also from much of the intellectual life of the church's past. Seminary instruction, based as it was upon neo-scholastic manuals produced in Europe, left students mostly unacquainted with the history of Christian thought; when priests thusly instructed took to the pulpit, the results were rarely edifying. The state of

9

Catholic colleges and universities prior to the council wasn't much better. In a sobering assessment published in the mid-fifties, the historian John Tracy Ellis observed that Catholic higher education of the day was distinguished by formalism, moralism, and authoritarianism—qualities hardly conducive to the pursuit of academic excellence. Even with a vastly improved economic standing, according to Ellis, American Catholics in the 1950s still remained intellectually very much second-class citizens.[8]

Nevertheless, even among its detractors it is sometimes conceded that the church of the 1950s could be a place of considerable enchantment. Writing in the early seventies, for example, Garry Wills confesses an abiding affection for the Catholicism of his childhood:

> We "born Catholics," even when we leave or lose our own church, rarely feel at home in any other. The habits of childhood are tenacious, and Catholicism was first experienced by us as a vast set of intermeshed childhood habits—prayers offered, heads ducked in unison, crossings, chants, christenings, grace at meals; beads, altar, incense, candles; nuns in the classroom alternately too sweet and too severe, priests garbed black on the street and brilliant at the altar; churches lit and darkened, clothed and stripped, to the rhythm of liturgical recurrences; the crib in winter, purple Februaries, and lilies in the spring; confession as intimidation and comfort (comfort, if nothing else, that the intimidation was survived), communion as revery and discomfort; faith as a creed, and the creed as catechism, Latin responses, salvation by rote, all things going to a rhythm, memorized, old things always returning, eternal in that sense, no matter how transitory.[9]

Grateful as he is for such cozy memories, however, Wills doesn't much regret that this "total weave of Catholic life" rapidly unraveled after the Second Vatican Council. For far too long, in his view, American Catholics had been prevented by the suffocating closeness of ghetto culture from realizing their true potential.

It's certainly possible that the unitary Catholic subculture depicted by Garry Wills might have come undone even had the Second Vatican Council not occurred. Or, as Andrew Greeley has suggested, perhaps the council merely hastened what was already an inevitable outcome.[10] Cracks in the ghetto wall, after all, had already developed a decade or so prior to the council, as Catholics increasingly reached beyond their immigrant roots toward full integration into the American cultural mainstream. Still, there seems little question that the council, in its own right, was a major influence behind the total overhaul of American Catholic life that would take place during the sixties and seventies.

†HE SECOND VA†ICAN COUNCIL

Thirty years after its third and final session was brought to a close in 1965, it can be said without exaggeration that the Second Vatican Council was an event of epochal significance for Catholicism worldwide. When Pope John XXIII announced his plans for the council in 1959, three years before it would formally convene, he envisioned it as a vehicle for renewing the church in terms relevant to the modern world. After generations of defiant insularity, Pope John observed, the church at mid-century was lethargic, self-absorbed, and without relevance to the world beyond its boundaries. It would not serve the purposes of evangelization, he was convinced, to repeat the condemnations of secularism and liberalism made famous by several of his pontifical predecessors. Rather, the moment had arrived for church and world to engage in mutually constructive dialogue. And in order that such dialogue might proceed fruitfully, Catholic teaching would have to be expressed in a manner more suitable to the cultural circumstances of the contemporary age. Thus, in his opening address at the council, Pope John advised the assembled bishops that their task was to reformulate Catholic doctrine "in such a way that it is adapted to our own times."

> For the substance of the deposit of faith or body of truths which are contained in our revered doctrine is not identical with the manner in which these truths are expressed, though the same sense and the same meaning must be preserved.[11]

If Pope John sought through the council to set the church on a course of renewal and modernization, he could not reasonably have anticipated just how dramatically change would occur. In the most perceptive account of Vatican II yet written by a sociologist, Bill McSweeney indicates the main directions that the council took in bringing about, almost overnight, a fundamental transformation of Catholicism.[12]

Above all else, according to McSweeney, the council was remarkably successful in breaking the long-standing monopoly of scholasticism over Catholic theology. Scholasticism, with its characteristic emphasis upon doctrinal clarity and conceptual precision, and its tendency to reduce faith to the passive reception of a body of exquisitely defined and immutable truths, was regarded by many council participants as a theological liability the church could no longer afford. What was required instead, it was claimed, was a radically new approach to Catholic theology, one better attuned to the dynamics of history and to the aspirations and experiences of women and men in a rapidly changing world. Moreover, advocates of such a new or progressive theology could claim support for their position by invoking the distinction, articulated by Pope John at the outset of the council, between the content of faith and its mode of expression. While the truths of revelation enjoy an infallible status, the pope had asserted, the language employed to communicate them must stand the test of cultural relevance. And it was precisely this test, contended the council's progressive faction, that the older theological language of the church had badly failed.

It is true, of course, that the older theology did not suffer total defeat at the council. It surfaces here and there in the council documents, in curious juxtaposition to the progressive theology by which it was otherwise replaced. The very fact, however, that the language of faith was so openly contested at Vatican II, under the scrutiny of the international media, signified the emergence of a new era of almost unlimited pluralism within the intellectual life of the church. While scholasticism survived, it did so now as but one theological voice among others of equal (and perhaps greater) claim to legitimacy.

Even more important than the decline of scholasticism at the council was the revolutionary potential of the new theology, or intellectual style, that came to ascendancy in its place. Indeed, there is considerable merit to Bill McSweeney's contention that the council implicitly endorsed several theological principles that the church previously had steadfastly opposed. Chief among these is the principle of the relativity of faith, by which is meant, in McSweeney's words, "that the meaning of any statement of doctrine is always open to interpretation, never finally captured in any particular form of expression for all times and for all cultures."[13] To a degree perhaps far exceeding what many of its participants intended, in other words, the council accorded legitimacy to the subjective interpretation of religious truth. Thus, for example, in a section dealing with the development of the church's tradition, the council's Constitution on Revelation states:

> This tradition which comes from the apostles develops in the Church with the help of the Holy Spirit. For there is a growth in the understanding of the realities and the words which have been handed down. This happens through the contemplation and study made by believers, who treasure these things in their hearts, through the intimate understanding of spiritual things they experience, and through the preaching of those who have received through episcopal succession the sure gift of truth.[14]

It is nothing less than remarkable that the council in this passage should so frankly acknowledge the important role of subjective experience in the apprehension of religious truth. For a full century prior to the council, after all, the Roman hierarchy had consistently rejected any such role for subjective experience, on the ground that it threatened relativizing consequences for the faith. There could be no assurance that truths arrived at experientially or intuitively would correspond with the official teaching of the church. Now, it's true that the foregoing passage, by seeming to grant final say on matters of faith to the episcopacy, stops short of endorsing a full-fledged subjectivism. But even so, here as elsewhere in the council documents, an impression of tolerance is conveyed toward theological approaches that previously were strictly prohibited.

Consider also what the council, in a related passage, taught regarding the inerrancy of scripture.

> Since everything asserted by the inspired authors or sacred writers must be held to be asserted by the Holy Spirit, it follows that the books of Scripture must be acknowledged as

teaching firmly, faithfully, and without error that truth which God wanted put into the sacred writings for the sake of our salvation.[15]

At first glance, this seems entirely unremarkable—not much more than a bland summation of traditional Catholic teaching. If we look again, however, a more complex scenario comes into view. The bible apparently teaches "without error," but only does so compellingly when dealing with matters vital to salvation. But which parts of the bible are invested with salvific truth, and which others deserve to be taken less seriously (or less literally)? Or, more simply, who is to decide (and by what criteria) what is essential for salvation? The practical effect of this passage, and others of similar inflexion, would be to provide Catholic theologians with an interpretive power over scriptural texts comparable to that already enjoyed by their Protestant counterparts.

Additional evidence of such ambiguity within the council documents could be adduced without difficulty, but it seems needless to belabor the point. While the council saluted traditional theological positions, it also suggested rich possibilities for theological innovation. This apparent split-mindedness undoubtedly owed much to the divergent perspectives of the council participants: on the one hand, Roman prelates and their supporters who sought to preserve as much as possible of the older order, and on the other hand, bishops and theologians from Europe and North America who saw Vatican II as the church's passport to the modern world.

In addition to shaking its theological foundations, the council went a long way toward realigning the church's relationship with the external world. Most striking in this regard was the conciliatory approach taken by the council toward groups, not to mention also entire historical developments, that the church had formerly treated with imperial disdain. Thus, for example, the council promoted greater ecumenical openness toward Protestants and Jews, and it also affirmed the intrinsic merit of non-Catholic religions generally throughout the world. Moreover, it defended religious liberty and other civil rights, and spoke approvingly of the pluralistic ideals of modern Western society. And in a quite remarkable declaration of support for what it termed the "new humanism," the council affirmed as well that men and women are defined foremost today by their shared responsibility for history and for one another. At virtually every turn, in fact, the council avoided negative judgment and opted instead to promote partnership between the church and the world beyond its boundaries.[16]

The transformative effects of Vatican II were felt in other areas as well. Perhaps most controversially, the council reformed the Mass—the centerpiece of Catholic worship—along more open and communal lines, and restricted the availability of subsidiary devotional practices. As for the ethical dimension of Christian life, the council affirmed the inherent dignity of men and women and highlighted the importance of conscience in moral decision-making. Still further, it fostered a spirituality of corporate responsibility in place of the traditional Catholic preoccupation with private piety and personal salvation. On a related front, the council dissolved, or at least softened, the age-long Catholic distinction between grace and nature, and emphasized instead the unity of the natural and supernatural orders, the goodness of creation, and the integrity of explicitly secular pursuits. Somewhat more tentatively, it imparted legitimacy to a more democratic or collegial form of church governance, and thus reopened the debate on papal infallibility which Pope Pius IX had attempted definitively to resolve a century earlier at the First Vatican Council. And in a similar vein, it reduced the distance in status between priests and laypersons and called upon all Catholics to participate in the essential functions of the church.[17]

Clearly, much more could be said about the specific contents of Vatican II, and there shall be opportunity in subsequent chapters for additional commentary. In any event, the revolutionary significance of the council owes more to the cumulative impact of its various decrees than to any one or another of them taken separately. In its entirety, and notwithstanding its occasionally vacillating tone, the council seemed to promise a new era of almost unlimited creativity for the church. The traditional postulates of the faith had been exposed as transitory and dispensable, and hence the future of Catholicism seemed to depend very much upon what Catholics themselves would make of it.

Vatican II and American Catholicism

Clifford Geertz once remarked that nothing alters quite like the unalterable, and the suddenness with which Roman Catholicism in the United States was transformed in the wake of the Second Vatican Council is a dramatic case in point. For several generations prior to the council, it will be recalled, American Catholics inhabited a tightly cohesive subculture that must have conveyed at least an impression of unalterability. By the late 1960s, however, it was apparent that American Catholicism was not nearly what it once was, and there was no telling what it would become. Traditional symbols of Catholic self-identity were discarded, almost without warning, as the church seemed determined to atone all at once for generations of cultural exclusivity. Nuns and priests abandoned the identifying attire of the religious vocation and frequently also the vocation itself, experimental liturgies celebrated more the possibility of cultural advancement than that of eternal life, and popular Marian devotions fell into desuetude. No longer content merely that their church possess supernatural truth, American Catholics in the aftermath of the council demanded as well that it be more accessible and more meaningful to the secular world.

Probably no aspect of the church's life has been more visibly altered since the council than its priesthood. Although numbers alone don't tell the whole story, they leave little doubt that the Catholic priesthood in the United States is an institution in steep decline. Not only have the ranks of the diocesan clergy been severely depleted in the thirty years since Vatican II, but the prospects for the future seem uniformly grim. Ordinations have plummeted in number to virtually half what they were in the mid-sixties, and efforts to arrest this decline in recruitment have been notably ineffective. The replacement rate for priests who leave the active ministry by retirement, resignation, or death averages only about 60 percent; and sociologist Richard Schoenherr projects that by the turn of the century, or shortly thereafter, almost half of all active priests will be age fifty-five or older, and only 10 percent or so will be age thirty-five or younger. Difficulties of this sort would be greatly alleviated, Dean Hoge and other sociologists have observed, if Rome were to authorize the ordination of women and married men. But this seems a remote possibility at best, and thus the American church will likely have to contend over the next several decades with a steady increase in priestless parishes.[18]

If anything, religious orders of women have been struck even harder by recruitment woes since the council than their male counterparts. Sociologist Marie Augusta Neal reports that the current population of nuns in the United States "is 60 percent of what it was in 1967 and the rate of entrance to religious communities as of 1984 was 15 percent of what it was in 1966." With so few young women having entered religious life since the council, Neal notes, the age distribution of American nuns has shifted alarmingly. "Whereas 22 percent of sisters were under thirty in 1967, only 1 percent are now. Fifty-one percent are over sixty now while only 20 percent were that old in 1967." Indeed, so diminished are they in size and vitality that orders of sisters have been forced to relinquish control of hospitals and schools and sometimes also to seek external funding for the care of aged members.[19]

In addition to their sorry record of recruitment, religious orders of both men and women have been decimated by defections since the council. Indeed, there have been few sights more disquieting to ordinary Catholics over the past thirty years than priests and nuns by the thousand rushing for the exits. Personal reasons, such as an expressed unhappiness with the requirements of celibacy and obedience, are part of the story here; but they're clearly not the whole story. That the demands of religious life should so suddenly be found unendurable by so many priests and nuns after the council must surely also have something to do with the council.[20]

Here, again, it's not so much any one of its particular teachings but rather the overall thrust of Vatican II that seems at issue. By according positive religious significance to worldly affairs—by sanctifying, in a way, the secular order—the council implicitly raised doubts concerning the purpose and value of an expressly religious vocation. Nuns and especially priests were previously regarded as chosen elites, spiritual aficionados elevated above the vicissitudes of the marketplace so as to reflect in their own lives, and for the benefit of the Catholic masses, the

lights of eternity. So clearly distinct was the role of priest or nun, and so ines-
timable was its importance, that there existed considerable incentive to attain it.
And once having done so, there was also powerful motivation to maintain it. By
virtue of being set apart from worldly distractions, the priest or nun was believed
capable of realizing a fullness of faith that somehow guaranteed or justified the
rather more circumstantial faith of the Catholic laity. The religious vocation was,
in other words, as much a community resource, an attestation of divine possibility, as it was an individual possession.

If only indirectly, however, the council removed much of this luster from the
religious vocation. If the secular world is alive with redemptive possibility and,
as the council also taught, political and scientific activity is a conveyance of faith,
what then is the point of subjecting oneself to the rigors of asceticism? The religious vocation seems somehow less obligatory, and its benefits less clear-cut,
when the world beyond convent or rectory is also thought to share in the advantage of grace. Even as it thus affirmed the continuing importance of the religious
life, the council lowered the incentive to stand apart from the world in fidelity to
vows of celibacy, poverty, and obedience.

The crisis of identity facing Catholic religious life after the council was further exacerbated by developments within the broader society. As feminism
became a potent cultural force during the sixties and seventies, and as traditional
authority in virtually every guise came under sustained attack, the rationale for
becoming (or remaining) a priest or nun was stretched progressively thinner. The
catch phrase of the day was "personal autonomy," and within this broader context
the discipline and docility of religious life came to seem positively freakish. Why
should priests be expected to submit automatically to the whims of their bishops
or religious superiors? Why should nuns be required to prostrate themselves
before the church's male-dominated authority structure? Many priests and nuns,
of course, decided against any further submitting or prostrating, and left the
active ministry altogether. And many of those who stayed were determined that
the rules of the game be changed. By the mid-seventies, accordingly, the non-
conformity and dissent that figured so prominently in the wider culture had
become institutionalized components of religious life itself. Priests could no
longer be counted upon to parrot the church's party line on sex or politics or anything else; and nuns were almost as likely to be found leading a workshop on
feminist spirituality or attending an abortion-rights rally as to be instructing
children in the mysteries of the rosary.

If the priesthood and sisterhood within the American church have fallen on
unmistakably shaky times since the council, the situation of the American
Catholic laity is decidedly more complicated. On the surface, at least, the vast
majority of lay Catholics in the United States seem to have adapted remarkably
well to the extraordinary changes that have taken place within their church over

the past thirty years. Theological dissent, endless liturgical experimentation, catechetical confusion, ritual iconoclasm: none of this has led to a massive exodus from the church, or to anything approaching a groundswell of opposition.

Here, again, numbers provide a useful starting point. During the two-decade span from 1966 to 1986, when other mainline Christian bodies in the United States suffered sharp declines in membership, the total population of American Catholics expanded from 46 million to nearly 55 million.[21] Perhaps more telling, the 15-percent defection rate among Catholics during this same period was not appreciably higher than the rate for the fifties and early sixties.[22] And what's more, on at least several counts (frequency of prayer and reception of Holy Communion, for example) the religious devotion of American Catholics seems actually to have increased throughout these two decades.[23] Catholic church attendance, it's true, declined markedly during the late sixties and early seventies, but since 1975, the percentage of American Catholics attending Sunday Mass has held fast at approximately 50 percent.[24]

If American Catholics remain heavily involved in their church, however, the terms of this involvement have shifted substantially since the council. Of today's regular churchgoers, 80 percent practice what Andrew Greeley has described as a "selective Catholicism," participating in the church's ritual life while ignoring whichever of its moral precepts they happen to disagree with. Forever lost, Greeley observes, are the days when the Catholic leadership could count on the compliance of the ordinary faithful.

> As humiliating as it may be to [the American bishops] it would seem that they have influence on their people only when their people decide to permit them to have such influence. The authority of the government apparently rests on the consent of the governed, not only in civil matters of the United States but also in ecclesiastical matters.[25]

The much-publicized controversy over artificial contraception in the immediate aftermath of the council provides perhaps the most definitive evidence of this shift from a comprehensive to a more partial or selective commitment. With the publication in 1968 of the encyclical *Humanae Vitae*, Pope Paul VI reaffirmed the traditional Catholic position that sexual intercourse should always be open to the possibility of conception. Instead of eliciting widespread assent, however, the encyclical was immediately dismissed by many American Catholics as an unwarranted intrusion into their private affairs. The full significance of this negative reaction to *Humanae Vitae* would unfold throughout the 1970s. As the survey research of Andrew Greeley and his associates consistently revealed, the sexual ethic of the church had somehow in the wake of the council lost relevance, not to mention legitimacy, for a substantial number of lay Catholics.[26]

The radically altered view of American Catholics toward premarital sex conveys very much the same story. Whereas disapproval of sexual intercourse prior to marriage was almost universal among American Catholics in the early sixties, today almost half the adult Catholic population in the United States thinks that premarital sex is not wrong at all. Among Catholics under the age of thirty especially, such traditional sexual prohibitions are increasingly felt to be anachronistic and personally insignificant. In a variety of other areas as well—divorce and remarriage, abortion, and homosexuality—the attitudes and practices of American Catholics thirty years after the council seem more attuned to prevailing cultural norms than to the teaching of their church.[27]

There seems little question, therefore, that the credibility of the church's sexual teaching has declined enormously among American Catholics since completion of the Second Vatican Council. What is rather less clear is the extent to which the council bears responsibility for this development. There are several factors worth considering here. First, while Vatican II said nothing explicitly at variance with the church's traditional sexual teaching, it did significantly alter the grammar of Catholic ethical discourse. In the tradition of the Catholic manualists prior to the council, morality was conceived in starkly legalistic and individualistic terms, with emphasis upon the objective definition of sins and the formal calculation of sinfulness. Within this all-embracing moral framework, norms of conduct were so precisely calibrated that Catholics knew what was expected—and not expected—of them in virtually every circumstance of daily life. With the Second Vatican Council, however, Catholic moral theology acquired a strikingly different tone. In place of the customary Catholic preoccupation with objective norms and obligations, the council affirmed the fundamental freedom of men and women and, accordingly, the primacy of conscience in processes of moral decision-making. And by conferring as such a certain presidency within the ethical realm to the role of conscience, the council implicitly gave legitimacy to a degree of dissent from the moral strictures, sexual or otherwise, publicly proclaimed by the church. Again, the point here isn't that the council in any way endorsed a turn to sexual permissiveness, but rather that in altering the terms of Catholic discourse about morality, it indirectly made such a turn easier to take.[28]

That this was the turn largely taken by American Catholics after Vatican II owes much also to factors beyond the council's control. As Andrew Greeley has tirelessly pointed out, the traditional pattern of Catholic life in the United States—wherein the laity obeyed (or, at least, pretended not to disobey) what their church taught—would not likely have survived the 1970s and eighties even had Vatican II not occurred. For it was during these two decades that American Catholics (not all of them, of course, but a great many nonetheless) emerged fully from the shadow of their immigrant pasts and attained a level of educational and occupational success the equal of virtually any other group in American society. And with upward mobility, or suburbanization, there came also a notable shift in ethical sensibility. Having transcended the ghetto materially, American Catholics sought to transcend it morally it as well—to fashion sexual lifestyles suitably commensurate with American values of personal autonomy and democracy. Or, to put it another way, the sexual ideals of their church were increasingly felt by Catholics finally "come of age" in the United States as not only personally unattainable but also—by virtue of the constraints they imposed upon individual freedom—as somehow un-American.[29]

And finally, it is undoubtedly of great consequence that the church through Vatican II encouraged a greater openness to the world at precisely a time when the world was in a state of considerable turmoil. More specifically, the cultural explosion commonly referred to as the "sexual revolution" was at full blast in the United States in the years immediately following the council; and American Catholics, so recently released from the confines of their religious ghetto, were perhaps the most exposed of American groups to its effects. The ethical and religious uncertainty that stemmed from the council, in other words, was compounded by the more general cultural volatility of the 1960s and seventies. In a cultural climate relentlessly hostile to the claims of traditional authority, the sexual teachings of the church—especially now deprived of the social support previously provided them by the Catholic ghetto—were bound to appear to much of the laity (and, for that matter, the clergy) as insufferably archaic.[30]

It's the combination of these various factors, then—their historical confluence, if you will—that must be held responsible for the rapid erosion of the church's authority over sexual matters since the Second Vatican Council. Still, it's not entirely clear why so many American Catholics remain actively involved with their church despite rejecting so much of its moral teaching. In Greeley's view, the relatively low rate of defection from the church is directly attributable to the emergence among lay Catholics of a new religious imagination; for the most part, he contends, American Catholics today envision God not as a stern judge but rather as a loving and tolerant spouse or parent who welcomes unconditionally their participation in the ritual life of the church.[31]

New religious imagination or not, it is unquestionably the case that the totalistic commitment of the Catholic ghetto has been largely replaced by a fragmented or sporadic commitment more consonant with American ideals of democratic freedom and personal autonomy. In a sense, therefore—and here this first chapter comes full circle—the ideas of Isaac Hecker have achieved nearly complete dominance within the American church almost a full century after their condemnation by Pope Leo XIII in the encyclical *Testem benevolentiae*. Indeed, Hecker's vision of a faith inseparably Catholic and American, one fully informed by individual spiritual experience and democratic values, has been realized to a degree that would scarcely have been imaginable at the turn of the century.[32]

ONCE AGAIN, NOTHING ALTERS QUITE LIKE THE UNALTERABLE. And it's not likely that many enterprises have passed more rapidly from a state of unalterability to one of radical change than American Catholicism after the Second Vatican Council. By no means, however, has this been an uncontested development. Over the past thirty years, a number of broad-based factions of resistance on the Catholic right have waged constant guerrilla warfare against the transformed Catholicism that has come into being since the council. The first of these factions of resistance—which I call *Catholic conservatism*—is the subject of the next two chapters.

CATHOLIC CONSERVATISM

ON SEPTEMBER 26, 1968, H. Lyman Stebbins, a retired stockbroker and Catholic convert, announced the founding of Catholics United for the Faith (CUF). At a press conference in Washington, D.C., Stebbins described his new organization as "a unity of lay men and women whose purpose it would be to bear corporate and public witness to the Faith, and to pledge fidelity to the Roman Catholic Church as the loving presence and authoritative voice of God among men, and to offer a rallying point for the multitude of Catholics who are bewildered by the surprising confusion of thought and clamor of voices within the Church itself."[1]

There was nothing accidental about either the timing or setting of CUF's unveiling. Just four months earlier, Pope Paul VI had touched off a storm of controversy in the American church with the release of *Humanae Vitae*, the encyclical most famous for its renewed condemnation of artificial contraception. American Catholics had widely anticipated that Paul VI would lift the church's ban on birth control, so *Humanae Vitae* was the target of intensive opposition almost immediately upon its release. And nowhere was such opposition more heated than in the American Catholic academy. In what was perhaps the most brazen gesture of protest, the theologian Charles Curran, of Catholic University in Washington, D.C., went so far as to publish a public denunciation of the encyclical, which was signed by six hundred (mostly liberal) Catholic intellectuals from across the country.[2] In addition to being almost wilfully wrongheaded on theological grounds, its detractors charged, *Humanae Vitae* contradicted the best moral instincts of culturally enlightened people everywhere.

In the view of H. Lyman Stebbins and CUF's other founders, this was nothing less than a declaration of war. By their public dissent against *Humanae Vitae*,

Catholic liberals had taken a dramatic stand for a fully Americanized Catholicism, independent morally and perhaps also spiritually of Rome. The time had clearly arrived for Catholics still loyal to the papacy to join together in battle, and there seemed no place better suited for launching a counteroffensive than the very city from which Charles Curran had rallied the forces of liberal dissent.[3]

In addition to counteracting dissent against *Humanae Vitae* from the Catholic left, CUF's founders were concerned with imparting a measure of order and discipline to the Catholic right. Already by 1968, just three years after the closing of Vatican II, there was a mounting sense of panic among many conservative-minded Catholics in the United States over the revolution that was brewing within their church. Cherished devotional practices were in process of being eliminated, priests and nuns were already deserting their posts, and even the Tridentine Mass, the historic centerpiece of Catholic worship, seemed threatened by imminent extinction. To many theological conservatives, all of this was unbridled lunacy: within just several years of the council (and probably as a direct result of it) the American church had ceased to be Catholic in any meaningful sense, and the situation seemed only to be getting worse. Indeed, in a letter of appeal sent to Pope Paul VI in 1967, just one year prior to CUF's founding, Gommar De Pauw, a Baltimore-based priest and onetime academic dean at St. Mary's Major Seminary in Emmitsburg, Maryland, had warned that Catholics of genuine faith would be forced to leave the institutional church altogether unless Vatican II and the reforms stemming from it were immediately revoked.[4]

Although deeply troubled themselves by the sudden collapse of traditional Catholicism in America after the council, CUF's founders utterly rejected the separatist course proposed by Gommar De Pauw. As desperate as the situation might appear, they argued, the institutional church still enjoyed divine protection against error, and abandoning the church, or the council the church had called into being, was a guaranteed recipe for spiritual suicide. Moreover, considering the insurgency that was taking place on the Catholic left, they said, the last thing the church needed was additional trouble from the Catholic right. As an association of lay Catholics dedicated to safeguarding transcendent truth, they insisted, CUF would be governed by strict loyalty to both the papacy and Vatican II.

Within just a year or so of declaring allegiance to the Second Vatican Council, CUF was confronted by another strategic decision of almost equal importance when Pope Paul VI, in April of 1969, authorized a new rite to replace the Tridentine Mass as the universal liturgy of the church. The Tridentine Mass was for centuries the keystone of Catholic worship worldwide, the church's monument to eternity, and many traditionally inclined Catholics bitterly resented the modernized and vernacular liturgy the pope installed in its place. Indeed, Gommar De Pauw spoke for more than just a few American Catholics when he decried the new Mass as "schismatic, sacrilegious, heretical, and possibly invalid" and warned that its implementation would potentially undermine "the whole basis of the Roman Catholic religion."[5] Once again, however, CUF's leadership wasted little time in distancing themselves from such extremist rhetoric. However disagreeable Catholics might personally find it, they insisted, the new Mass was authorized by Rome, and its authentic place in the liturgical life of the church was thereby assured. Denial of its validity would amount also to denial that God's will is made manifest through the Catholic hierarchy.[6]

In explicitly aligning itself right from the start with the Second Vatican Council and the new Mass, CUF was able to present itself as a moderate alternative to more extremist voices on the Catholic right for whom both the council and Mass were nothing short of liberal abominations. While Gommar De Pauw and others of his ilk were urging disaffected Catholics to withdraw from the institutional church in protest of the liberalizing effects of the council, CUF was inviting them to stay and fight liberalization from within. And more than just a few were only too happy to accept the invitation. Indeed, as the following remarks by a middle-aged woman from the New York City area suggest, CUF was regarded by at least some American Catholics as an outright godsend.

> You've got to realize the amazing confusion some of us felt after the council. Most everything we had held to be sacred was up for grabs, and simple cause-and-effect reasoning suggested that the council was to blame. The uproar over the new Mass just brought everything to a boil. My husband and I were being told by some people that the Church was now apostate, that the council was actually demonic. And it was tempting to believe this, but we just couldn't accept that God would desert the Church. This is where CUF came in. CUF was saying, "Yes, things are very bad with Catholicism, and we have to fight to restore its sanity. But we can do this while remaining in the Church, and without condemning the council." The point is, this is what many of us wanted to do anyways—to fight from within the Church, certainly not leave it. CUF gave us a sense of hope and unity, a sense of being part of something very important that was coming into existence in the Church.[7]

It was among Catholics such as this one, then—deeply conservative in both their piety and institutional loyalty, and yet just as deeply troubled by the liberalizing effects of the council—that CUF held its greatest appeal. With the founding of CUF, a major step was taken toward the creation of what may be termed a distinctly conservative subculture within American Catholicism. Over the years, this subculture has grown progressively larger and more complex, and today it encompasses an almost bewildering variety of groups and individuals. Despite this mounting complexity, however, the essential world view of Catholic conservatism has remained virtually unchanged since the late sixties, and it's to a brief discussion of this that I now turn.

THE CONSERVATIVE WORLD VIEW: AN OVERVIEW

Conservatives and the Council

It's rarely an easy matter for the conservative mind to reconcile itself with a revolutionary event that has disrupted an older and much cherished order. But this is precisely the predicament of Catholic conservatives in the United States. While deeply disturbed by its transformative consequences for American Catholicism, conservatives feel compelled nonetheless to defend the legitimacy of the Second Vatican Council. To do otherwise—to deny or even to call into question its legitimacy—would amount to conceding the fallibility of their church's supreme teaching authority. From the conservative perspective, it is simply inadmissible that God would permit an ecumenical council of the church to teach theological error. Thus, even though they sometimes confide regret that it occurred—or, at least, that it occcurred when it did—conservatives typically profess support for the council and absolve it of direct responsibility for the collapse of traditional Catholicism in the United States. Indeed, sober analysis of the conciliar documents, they contend, shows that Vatican II didn't have anything close to the revolutionary design claimed for it by Catholic liberals. The council fathers wanted at most to wipe clean the stained-glass windows of the church; they certainly never meant to smash them. Thus James Hitchcock, a leading conservative intellectual, concedes that Catholicism prior to the council was marred by legalism, formalism, and clericalism and was thus in need of renewal, but he rejects as wholly invalid the liberal view that the council was a Magna Carta of sorts for a transformed church. The tragedy for Hitchcock and conservatives generally, then, isn't that Vatican II transpired, but rather that so many Catholics have been taken in by the liberal interpretation of it.[8]

Conservatives favor a cautious, reconstructionist interpretation of Vatican II, one that emphasizes the council's continuity with the accumulated wisdom of the Catholic past. In calling the council, they claim, Pope John XXIII hoped to reinvigorate the life of faith and to rouse the church from complacency—it was clearly not his intention to consign centuries of Catholic tradition to the dustbin. And if its final documents are permitted to speak for themselves, conservatives contend, there can be little question that the council's paramount goals were to reinculcate among Catholics the traditional vocation to holiness, and to bring the laity more fully into the lifestream of the church, without in any way softening the radical antagonism between Catholicism and the secular world.

There's no point here, of course, in trying to decide what might be the "true meaning" of the Second Vatican Council; the exegetical issues are too complex, and what the council actually says on any particular matter is likely more ambiguous than either liberals or conservatives are prepared to admit. At the very least, however, it should be pointed out that the conservative reading of

Vatican II is no less selective than its liberal alternative. If the council says rather less than what is usually asserted by Catholic liberals, it almost certainly says much more than what conservatives would lead us to believe. In seeking to combat what they consider to be the interpretive excesses of liberals, conservatives frequently downplay, or ignore altogether, those components of the council's teaching that seem genuinely innovative. Thus, for example, there is very little appreciation expressed in conservative literature for the unprecedented dialogue that Vatican II promoted both between the church and other faiths and the church and the modern world. Nor is there much acknowledgment of the substantial opening created by the council for the employment of social-scientific and phenomenological tools in the task of theological reflection.[9]

Ironically, however, one of the most innovative teachings stemming from the council has been not only fully embraced by conservatives but, in the process, exploited to strategic advantage by them as well. In its Decree on the Apostolate of the Laity (and elsewhere in its documents), the council affirmed that lay Catholics, just as much as priests and nuns, are called to play a pivotal role in the church's life and mission. Now, it is certainly noteworthy that the church through Vatican II should finally realize the religious worth of the ordinary faithful; and liberal Catholics quite understandably heralded this development as the beginning of a new age of democratic freedom and spiritual equality for Catholicism. Emancipated at long last from clerical domination, lay Catholics were now in a position to hasten the course of reform upon which the council had set the church. The irony here is that conservatives, the great majority of whom are lay, have taken the council's teaching on the "apostolate of the laity" in a direction altogether unanticipated by Catholic liberals. Instead of seeking a greater liberalization of Catholic discipline and dogma, conservatives have declared it their right and responsibility—precisely as lay Catholics—to promote a decidedly traditional piety and morality. And rather than joining the liberal quest for a democratized church, they have dedicated themselves—again, precisely as lay Catholics—to defending the final teaching authority of the papacy.

Illustrative in this regard is the position of CUF, the flagship organization of Catholic conservatives in the United States. In this rebellious age, according to CUF, it is the special responsibility of faithful lay Catholics to uphold the hierarchical authority of their church. Or, in other words, lay Catholics today have been empowered by Vatican II and its teaching on the "apostolate of the laity" to perform a critical task for which most priests and nuns have demonstrated little inclination. These sentiments were succinctly expressed by CUF founder H. Lyman Stebbins in a letter addressed to the American Catholic bishops in October 1968. "[We] believe that in this period when there is so much contumacious defiance of God-given authority, the Church needs, and we owe, our unswerving support of her teaching and ruling authority."[10]

For the most part, however, Catholic conservatives find themselves in the peculiar position of claiming support for a council they secretly wish had never taken place. Even though the council itself isn't directly at fault, they contend, the years since its completion have resulted in an alarming breakdown of morality, theological identity, and authority within the American church.[11]

Crisis of Morality

It's like the sewer has backed up and flooded our homes with the excrement and filth of the entire neighborhood. And we're told by the mayor's office and the department of health: "There's no problem here. This shit's good for you. Wash in it, play with it, eat it. The stuff is liberating. You're too uptight always complaining about the shit floating into your kitchen and living room." Do you see the point? As an orthodox Catholic woman, I'm supposed to be thrilled with the garbage and pollution from the wider society streaming into my Church. And it's my own parish priests, the nuns who are supposed to be teaching my kids, my own bishop, my own so-called theologians who assure me that everything's fine and that there's something wrong with me for insisting that the Church take out the hoses and clean up the filth. They'd sooner we drowned in it than clean it up. But some of us—in CUF and in organizations like CUF—know shit when we see and smell it, and we're determined to wash it out of the Church. The value system of society isn't the value system of Catholicism. The two are completely opposed. And it's the value system of Catholicism that we want back.

These sentiments, confided to me several years ago by a New Jersey woman in her mid-thirties, capture almost perfectly the characteristic tone of conservative discourse. Indeed, one does not read far into virtually any conservative publication before encountering similar expressions of moral outrage. It isn't just the moral permissiveness of the broader culture that distresses conservatives, but, even more profoundly, the apparent ease with which it has infiltrated their church since the council. In sexual matters especially, they claim, most American Catholics over the past thirty years have abandoned traditional restraint for an ethic of indulgence. And perhaps nowhere, according to conservatives, has traditional morality taken a worse beating than in the American Catholic academy. Since the council, they contend, Catholic moral theologians have placed so great an emphasis upon the prerogatives of conscience in ethical decision-making that they have effectively turned sin into a matter of purely subjective interpretation. A benchmark for conservatives in this regard was the publication in 1977 of a study on human sexuality commissioned by the Catholic Theological Society of America, wherein it was asserted—to take but one noteworthy passage—that "A homosexual engaging in homosexual acts in good conscience has the same rights of conscience and the same rights to the sacraments as a married couple practicing birth control in good conscience."[12] Assertions of this sort, in the conservative view, constitute an assault not only upon objective moral norms but also upon the divinely appointed authority of the church to "bind and loose," to pronounce judgment on what is true and false about human experience.

It is significant in this connection that Catholics United for the Faith first arose in 1968 for the express purpose of battling dissent against the papal encyclical *Humanae Vitae*. Indeed, it would be difficult to overstate the immense symbolic importance for conservatives of *Humanae Vitae* and its teaching against artificial birth control. No other teaching of the church, in their view, is more discernibly at odds with the value system of the modern world, and yet no other teaching has been more widely disparaged by American Catholics. For Catholic conservatives, *Humanae Vitae* represents the touchstone of a contracultural piety, the dividing line between Catholics wholly committed to the faith and those only selectively or nominally committed. Adherence to the encyclical is regarded by them as a shibboleth of exemplary Catholic identity—a kind of badge of religious authenticity—at a time when the broader church has been almost entirely overtaken by moral permissiveness.

Crisis of Theological Identity

If traditional moral norms have fallen on hard times within the American church since the Second Vatican Council, the same is no less true of traditional theological norms. Over the past thirty years, as conservatives have protested helplessly from the sidelines, a new or progressive approach to Catholic theology has won almost complete ascendancy within the American church, and in the process everything from the Virgin Birth to the Resurrection has been debunked and deconstructed and demythologized practically into submission.[13]

In the most general sense, this new or progressive theology arose as an attempt by theologians after the Second Vatican Council to adjust Catholic thought to the complex cultural circumstances of the modern era. Taking their cue from Pope John XXIII's opening remarks at the council, progressive theologians in America and elsewhere argued that a radical updating of the language of faith was required if the very possibility of religious belief was to be salvaged in an increasingly secularized world. By the mid-sixties, according to progressives, the church's traditional understanding of faith, which stressed the conformity of the intellect to a deposit of revelation encoded in dogma, had become unworkably archaic; in draining faith of its experiential vitality, and in ignoring the role of the supernatural in the creation of personal and social life, it had succeeded mainly in reducing Catholicism to a skeleton of frigid concepts.[14] The new theology's task, then, was to reverse this intellectual rigor mortis and to reinterpret divine revelation as an immanent power, a dynamic symbolic discourse, that discloses the gracious presence and infinite possibilities hidden in human life. Rather than a passive submission to a deposit of dogmatic truth, faith in this new perspective is understood as a dynamic agency for transforming consciousness and transcending cultural limitations. And the historical facticity of central biblical narratives—such as the exodus-covenant experience of Israel and the Resurrection—is relegated within the new perspective to a position of almost negligible importance. Instead, what is crucial is the ongoing recasting of these stories and symbols for the sake of illuminating the meaning of sin and redemption in the historical present.

Although the ride hasn't always been smooth, this new theology—with its inductive approach to religious truth, its concern for cultural relevance, and, above all, its demythologizing approach to scripture and dogma—has risen over the past thirty years to a position of unquestioned preeminence within American Catholic intellectual life. It's been more than a decade now, in fact, since Thomas Sheehan, in the *New York Review of Books*, wrote of the almost total disappearance of traditional belief from Catholic higher education in the United States. By the early eighties, Sheehan observed, theology in American Catholic seminaries was commonly taught under the assumption "that Jesus of Nazareth did not assert any of the divine or messianic claims the Gospels attribute to him and that he died without believing he was Christ or the Son of God, not to mention the founder of a new religion." Indeed, from within the ranks of the "liberal consensus" that already then clearly dominated American Catholic theology, Sheehan contended, it would have been difficult to find a single scholar willing to stand behind traditional doctrines concerning, for example, the Resurrection, immortal life, or the Trinity.[15] The situation today is not much different from that described by Sheehan ten years ago. If anthing, the "liberal consensus," or progressive orthodoxy, of which he spoke is now so thoroughly ensconced within the American Catholic academy that more traditional theological approaches seem positively deviant in comparison.

From the point of view of Catholic conservatives, however, the dramatic successes of the new theology have been accomplished at great cost to the church's historic self-identity. A chief virtue of Catholicism prior to the council, they claim, was that it dared proclaim truths the world would rather not hear. This is the virtue credited by Chesterton (to whom conservatives feel close affinity) with making Catholicism "the only thing which saves a man from the degrading slavery of being a child of his own age."[16] But it is precisely such a slavery, according to conservatives, into which American Catholicism since the council has been sold. With the rise of the new theology, they claim, the scandalous truths of faith—the Virgin Birth, Resurrection, Heaven and Hell—have been reduced to the status of metaphor and conjecture. The very truths, in other words, that in a previous age compelled conversion and justified martyrdom have been made to appear almost inconsequential. In American Catholic education especially, conservatives claim, the new theology has succeeded mainly in fostering widespread doctrinal illiteracy and religious indifference. And in the church's ritual life, they also claim, its influence has resulted in a devastating loss of both mystery and supernatural drama.

Crisis of Authority

To Catholic conservatives, then, there seems no question that American Catholicism since the council has suffered subversion from within. Not only have intellectual elites within the church hastened the decline of traditional faith and morals, they contend, but these same elites have succeeded in establishing themselves as the new commissars of Catholic orthodoxy. For the most part today, according to conservatives, it is liberal theologians, liturgists, catechists, and diocesan bureaucrats—a self-annointed aristocracy of experts—who rule the American church, deciding which doctrines are worthy of belief and which rituals worthy of practice. And by all available evidence, they claim, these liberal elites are committed to the creation of a fully Americanized Catholicism, a Catholicism perhaps symbolically connected to Rome but otherwise autonomous and spiritually self-sufficient.

Although conservatives may be charged with a measure of hyperbole here, their claims are not entirely devoid of merit. For one thing, it is unquestionably true that the role of intellectuals within the American church has greatly expanded over the past several decades. Whereas Catholic theologians in the United States prior to the council served very much a middle-management function, ensuring smooth delivery of the church's official teaching, today they are far more likely to challenge that teaching and propose alternatives of their own. And they are far more likely to support the idea of a distinctly American Catholicism, suitably liberal in character and largely independent of Vatican control. Indeed, American Catholic intellectuals today, almost as a class, regard the current pope, with his conservative views on sexuality and church governance, as rather like a senile and overbearing uncle, worthy of occasional placation but best not taken too seriously.

While conservatives reserve their sharpest invective for the American Catholic intelligentsia, they are almost as equally displeased by the performance of other groups within the American church since the council. Parish priests have openly contested the legitimacy of *Humanae Vitae* and other papal teaching, and in many cases have gone so far as to disavow their own obligation to celibacy. Nuns, who previously served the American church as paradigms of piety, have increasingly abandoned traditional religious life and, in defiance of Rome, taken up the banner of feminism. And in the face of developments such as these, conservatives contend, most American Catholic bishops have remained strangely (and traitorously) silent.

———————

THESE, THEN, IN BROAD OUTLINE, are the areas of gravest concern to Catholic conservatives in the United States. In the space of just three decades, they contend, the church's moral discipline has been severely eroded, its theology and ritual have been secularized, and its traditional structures of authority radically subverted. Regardless of how things might appear on the outside, according to conservatives, the American church is in desperate shape, and the task of restoring it to proper health has fallen to the stalwart faithful. Just how this might be accomplished, however, is something about which even conservatives themselves are by no means fully agreed.

CATHOLICS UNITED FOR THE FAITH

Catholics United for the Faith prides itself on providing straight answers. On any given day at the organization's headquarters in Steubenville, Ohio, staff may be found taking calls from parents unhappy with the state of religious education in their diocese, parishioners distressed by the cancellation of yet another "outdated" devotional practice, or converts anxious for instruction in recent papal teaching.[17] That CUF, and not a local priest or bishop, should be consulted on these matters is quite clearly a sign of the times. In the view of at least some American Catholics, the institutional representatives of the faith in the United States can no longer be counted upon to stand firmly on the side of orthodoxy. As to where CUF stands, however, there would seem little room for doubt. According to its own statement of mission, the organization was founded for no less a purpose than "to support, defend and advance the efforts of the teaching Church."

In its self-appointed role as guardian of orthodoxy, CUF has cultivated a substantial following over the past three decades. Indeed, with a current membership of about twenty thousand, the organization may be described as the foremost voice of Catholic conservatism in the United States.[18] "CUF Catholics," as members sometimes refer to themselves, are ethnically diverse, though overwhelmingly white and more often than not of Irish descent. Although some are professionals of comparatively high social standing, the great majority have a high-school or college education and are best characterized as modestly middle-class. For the most part they are married with at least three children and thoroughly committed to "moral traditionalism" in the realms of family life and sexuality. And in this they share with their counterparts in the world of conservative Protestantism an abhorrence of sexual permissiveness, abortion, and cultural liberalism in general. In political disposition they are stubbornly patriotic, convinced of the essential goodness of America yet troubled by the decline of religious values in the national consciousness, overwhelmingly Republican in party affiliation, and staunchly supportive of free-enterprise capitalism.

For the most part also they are lifelong Catholics, middle-aged and older, and still very much attached to the authoritarian (or/) integralist piety that distinguished life in the Catholic ghetto of their childhood and early adulthood. A significant minority are younger adults or fairly recent converts who, despite only limited exposure to the older piety, feel disaffection nonetheless with the comparatively more anthropocentric thrust of contemporary Catholic ritual and theology. Moreover, and almost without exception, they regard themselves as loyal soldiers of the faith who have been deserted in this time of trial by the leadership of the American church. In an age of rampant secularism, it is they who have held fast to the tenets of sacred doctrine; and in the face of a pervasive cultural hedonism, it is they, again, who have bravely borne the weight of Catholic ethical strictures concerning sexual conduct and family life. As reward for this dedication, however, they have been branded as reactionaries and consigned to the margins of the institutional church, ignored by their bishops and frequently treated as personae non gratae in their local parishes.

Membership in CUF affords such Catholics a style of religious fellowship not otherwise available in the American church today. In small regional chapters they gather regularly for prayer, theological instruction, and for observance of such traditional (and, since the council, mostly neglected) devotional practices as group recitation of the rosary, Benediction of the Blessed Sacrament, and Perpetual Adoration. And through *Lay Witness*, a magazine published monthly by the CUF national office, they are kept abreast of current developments in the church and brought into contact with the writings of Aquinas, Newman, Chesterton, and other luminaries from the Catholic past. CUF doesn't exist for spiritual edification alone, however, and much of their energy is spent also in more explicitly activist pursuits: protesting sex education programs in Catholic schools, monitoring catechetical materials for "abuses against orthodoxy," and petitioning Rome for the appointment of more doctrinally conservative bishops.[19]

Even with such a highly dedicated membership, however, CUF has had difficulty gaining institutional acceptance within the American church. Since its inception, most American bishops have tended to view the organization as fractious and disruptive, and most have refused to accord it formal ecclesiastical support. As a result, contends current CUF president James Likoudis, the organization has been forced in its campaign on behalf of orthodoxy to cultivate an ethic of lay self-sufficiency. "It would be nice of course to receive more episcopal support, and we welcome the informal support of isolated bishops, such as New York's Cardinal O'Connor," Likoudis told me during a telephone interview several years ago. "But bishops usually don't want to hear from the laity; they're very uptight about safeguarding their own authority. In any event, as a private association of lay Catholics, CUF doesn't require the official sanction of the American hierarchy. We try to be deferential to the bishops, but we're not brown-nosers. We're not reluctant to tell them where they've gone wrong, and by now we're quite accustomed to carrying on the struggle without their help."[20]

Although the American bishops as a group have refused to line up on its side, CUF has managed over the past twenty years or so to find considerable support for its views in Rome. Since 1978 and the elevation of Karol Wojtyla (John Paul II) to the papal throne, the Vatican has been engaged in a vigorous campaign of its own against modernizing tendencies within the church. Theologians in the United States and elsewhere have been disciplined for promoting views at variance with traditional orthodoxy, seminary training has become more strictly regulated, and the pastoral policies of national episcopal conferences have been subjected to searching criticism. Next to John Paul II himself, the man most responsible for enforcing this hard line has been Cardinal Joseph Ratzinger, head of the Vatican's Sacred Congregation for the Doctrine of the Faith (formerly the Holy Office). Throughout his tenure in Rome, Ratzinger has won consistent applause from Catholic conservatives for his determined efforts to purge the contemporary church of theological dissent and ethical laxity. But the event that has brought the cardinal his greatest public notice—and also the highest praise of conservatives—was the publication in early 1985 of *The Ratzinger Report*, his withering appraisal of Catholicism twenty years after the council.

In *The Ratzinger Report*, the cardinal offered an assessment of the post-conciliar church which corresponded almost exactly to the thinking of CUF and other conservative organizations. After twenty years of exaggerated openness, he contended, Catholicism in the United States and elsewhere was in danger of becoming assimilated altogether into the dominant secular culture. What the church required in this situation of crisis, according to the cardinal, was not greater relevance but rather greater commitment to its own distinctive values and transcendent mission. In matters of doctrine, piety and, most critically, morals, he insisted, the church must not seek ratification from the secular culture but, rather, must risk appearing before it "like an anachronistic construct, a bothersome, alien body." In summary, said the cardinal, it must be made perfectly clear that "Catholicism calls for an attitude of faith which often conflicts radically with today's dominant view."

> After the phase of indiscriminate "openness" it is time that the Christian reacquire the consciousness of belonging to a minority and of being in opposition to what is obvious, plausible and natural for that mentality which the New Testament calls—and certainly not in a positive sense—the "spirit of the world." It is time to find again the courage of nonconformism, the capacity to oppose many of the trends of the surrounding culture, renouncing a certain euphoric post-conciliar solidarity.[21]

For Catholic conservatives in the United States, this was delicious vindication. Not only had the cardinal openly repudiated theological modernism, but the austere and newly retrenched Catholicism that he seemed to espouse coincided exactly with their own vision for the church. If there previously had been any doubt, *The Ratzinger Report* made vividly clear just how deeply within the Vatican conservative sentiment ran.

And certainly Catholics United for the Faith hasn't been at all hesitant in working this sentiment to strategic advantage. With only marginal institutional backing in the American church, the organization has made a practice over the past decade or so taking its concerns directly to Rome. And in Rome, according to James Likoudis, these concerns have almost always been accorded a sympathetic hearing. "Our people are activists, and we've encouraged them to write directly to the Vatican with their grievances. And on the whole, I think we're very much respected in the Vatican, for both our demonstrated loyalty to the pope and also our orthodoxy. So Rome is aware of our concerns, and takes us very seriously. So while we're getting the cold shoulder at home, the Vatican listens when we report on the unbelievable abuses that have taken place in dioceses like Seattle and Milwaukee. It's gratifying to know that we've established a presence in the only place that truly counts."[22]

It will take far more than support from Rome, however, to ensure CUF's future survival. As the twentieth century draws to a close, the organization finds itself with an aging membership and a severely limited capacity for recruitment. For American Catholics generally, and especially for those raised in the decidedly more permissive climate of the past thirty years, CUF is not much more than an exotic curiosity, admirable perhaps for its tenacity but almost wholly devoid of personal relevance. For the short term, CUF might be able to replenish its ranks with the offspring of current members, but with both time and cultural fashion aligned solidly in its disfavor, any prospects for sustained growth must be counted as doubtful at best.

James Hitchcock and Conservative Catholic Intellectuals

If CUF has led the way organizationally, no single individual has been more important to the conservative movement than James Hitchcock. Now in his mid-fifties and a professor of history at St. Louis University, Hitchcock has functioned for almost thirty years as the movement's foremost apologist and polemicist. Ironically, however, and in this he is by no means unique among conservative activists of his generation, Hitchcock began his intellectual career as a self-confessed theological liberal.[23]

Like many other American Catholics in the immediate aftermath of the Second Vatican Council, Hitchcock in 1966 was optimistic that his church had entered a new era of cultural relevance. Fresh from graduate studies at Princeton, he strongly supported the council's call for liturgical reform and ecumenical engagement, as well as its promotion of a greater intellectual openness in the Catholic academy. As it turns out, however, Hitchcock's optimism was exceedingly short-lived. In 1967 he came across a newly published book by an American priest named Jim Cavanaugh which convinced him that Catholicism in the United States was headed for crisis. More so than perhaps any other book of its day, *A Modern Priest Looks at His Outdated Church* exemplified the iconoclastic thinking to which many Catholic intellectuals in the United States were drawn in the wake of the council. Not only was the American church badly out of rhythm with the modern world, contended Cavanaugh, but its established structures of piety and authority had actually become impediments to authentic faith.

If relevance were truly to be achieved, and the council's promise fulfilled, he claimed, virtually every aspect of traditional Catholicism stood desperately in need of radical revision.

For James Hitchcock, reading Cavanaugh's book proved a rude awakening. For the first time, as he now recalls, it occurred to him that something was dramatically wrong with theological liberalism in the American church. Far from seeking renewal of the church along lines suggested by the council, liberal thinkers such as Jim Cavanaugh seemed dedicated instead to its radical transformation. That this in fact was the case, contends Hitchcock, became even more alarmingly clear the following year, when Catholic liberals in the United States publicly denounced the papal encyclical *Humanae Vitae* and its teaching against artificial contraception. Without question, says Hitchcock, much more was involved here than simply a dispute over birth control. In attacking *Humanae Vitae*, Catholic liberals were launching their first decisive strike on behalf of an American Catholicism fully emancipated from the claims of both tradition and papal authority.

It is significant in this connection that James Hitchcock was not initially himself a staunch supporter of *Humanae Vitae*. The encyclical's tough line on birth control was something even he had difficulty accepting. But in times of war, he felt, one is compelled to choose sides. And by late 1968, in what seemed clearly to him a time of escalating warfare in the American church, Hitchcock felt personally compelled—almost, as he now says, by a sense of sacred duty—to align himself with *Humanae Vitae* and the more traditional Catholic ethos that the encyclical exemplified.

Whatever else might be said of James Hitchcock today, he can hardly be charged with having taken this "sense of sacred duty" lightly. Over the twenty-five years or so since his embracement of *Humanae Vitae*, Hitchcock has been probably the most prolific (and easily the most articulate) critic of theological liberalism in the American church. If any one theme has consistently stood out in his writing over this period, it has been that of betrayal. In their frantic quest for cultural relevance, according to Hitchcock, liberal elites within the American church have betrayed not only Rome but also, increasingly, the very substance of Catholic faith itself.[24]

For conclusive evidence of such betrayal, says Hitchcock, one need look no further than the church's ritual life. In the 1950s, he notes, nothing so set American Catholics apart as a distinctive people than the manifold sights, sounds, and symbols of their common worship. At its best, he says, such worship was a wondrously transformative affair, capable of lifting its participants to new heights and to new spiritual purpose. This is not of course to say, concedes Hitchcock, that Catholic worship in the fifties and early sixties always succeeded in living up to this ideal. It was sometimes cheerless and perfunctory, all too often lacking in communal spirit, and as much therefore in need of renewal as any other aspect of American Catholic life on the eve of the Second Vatican Council.

Nevertheless, claims Hitchcock, what has actually happened to Catholic worship since the council hardly qualifies as renewal. In the course of just two or three decades, he says, ritual practices that had been centuries in the making have been routinely dismantled, plundered of symbolism, and, in some cases, targeted for outright extinction. And for the most part, he says, this ritual violence has been presided over by the very same men and women to whom the task of renewal was chiefly entrusted. Not content with merely reforming traditional worship, Hitchcock says, liberal intellectuals within the American church have subjected it instead to a torrent of radical changes.

And all of this change, says Hitchcock, has been undertaken, predictably enough, in the name of relevance. Cherished devotional practices—from Benedictions to Novenas—regarded by Catholic liberals as theologically backward, or as otherwise unsuited for contemporary consumption, have been stripped of significance and sometimes banished from parish life altogether. And the Mass itself, the symbolic font of Catholic worship, has been drained of dignity and drama and, in some cases, converted into a vehicle of expressly secular celebration. Indeed, liturgies in some parishes have been so drastically transformed, Hitchcock says, that faithful Catholics attending them are frequently made to feel like intruders in strange and hostile territory.

Although Hitchcock may be charged here with a certain polemical excess, his position is not entirely far-fetched. For one thing, there is no denying that Catholic worship in the United States has been dramatically transformed since the council. In taste, texture, and tone it no longer conveys the rampant supernaturalism of days past; it has been sanitized and streamlined and made more rational, more accessible, and, above all, more culturally respectable. And though in some ways this has been a positive development, something does in fact appear to have been lost in the process. To even the neutral observer, Catholic worship today seems more often than not a curiously bloodless and unimpassioned affair, as much a testament to middle-class decorum as to the trials and contradictions of faith. Indeed, in the typical suburban parish especially, worship today seems concerned not so much with challenging or inspiring its participants as with enveloping them in a haze of communal goodwill. And this, according to Hitchcock, is precisely the point. Since the council, he claims, liberal reformers have tried desperately to make the church a cozier and more comfortable place for its predominantly middle-class membership. Like most Americans, he says, Catholics today are preoccupied almost entirely with psychological well-being and the pursuit of material comfort. In their worship—as in virtually everything else—they are committed to winning freedom from traditional obligations, from self-sacrifice and ascetic demands, and from all institutional constraints. What they crave, Hitchcock says, is a church that will function as "a warm matrix within which and from out of which individuals have unlimited freedom of action, without the danger that membership in [it] will make inconvenient demands on them."[25]

35

And it is exactly such a church, Hitchcock claims, that liberal reformers in the United States have helped bring into being since the council. Not only is American Catholicism today blithely undemanding of its members, he says, but for the most part it seems to operate as little more than a sort of spiritual outlet for what the social critic Philip Rieff has termed the "therapeutic culture" of the contemporary West. Far from calling its members to a higher standard of belief and conduct, the church seems content instead with ratifying their present habits and assuaging their temporal anxieties. What has largely been lost, Hitchcock says, is "the perspective of eternity," the sense that Catholicism stands for something infinitely more important than merely the concerns of the moment. And without the perspective of eternity, he says, there seems no compelling reason for joining the church; and perhaps not much reason either for remaining in it.

> In seeking to make faith relevant and comfortable, within the confines of contemporary Western culture, many reformers have robbed it of even the possibility of grandeur. . . . The Catholic imagination is now thoroughly impoverished and expresses itself only in banalities. One of its greatest failures is precisely its inability to imagine the prospect of eternal life. Converts have been attracted to the Church not because they found there a warm human community (often they did not) but because they believed that what the Church taught was true, that it had the words of eternal life. Thus in making Catholicism more relevant on one level, these reformers succeeded in robbing it of its true relevance on a deeper level. The Church loses credibility not because it insists on teaching "outmoded" doctrines but because it lacks the courage to continue teaching what it knows to be true.[26]

SEVERAL YEARS AGO I MET WITH JAMES HITCHCOCK and his wife at their home in St. Louis. Since 1984, when she founded an antifeminist organization called Women for Faith and Family, Helen Hull Hitchcock had been a major player in her own right on the conservative stage, and the word I'd heard in conservative circles was that she was even tougher and more implacable than her husband. On the surface, at least, this in fact seemed to be the case. Whereas Hitchcock was relaxed and affable during the course of our interview, Helen Hull Hitchcock seemed grim-faced and suspicious, looking very much like someone who'd been burned too often in the past by outsiders to think of trusting one now.[27]

I asked Hitchcock whether he thought Catholic conservatives in the United States stood a realistic chance of reversing some of the gains made by theological liberalism since the council. "We're hopeful, but I don't know how realistic this is," he told me. "Right now we're certainly a minority voice within the American Church. The liberal activists are also smaller in number than most people realize, and this is some consolation to us, but they are infinitely more powerful than us in terms of money and institutional support. The liberal wing of American Catholicism is the establishment, and this is what we're up against. Nevertheless, I'm convinced that there's a great deal of vague and imprecise and unfocused discontent within the American Church over theological and ethical liberalism. Many laypeople have a sense that something is terribly amiss. They sense that the clergy is in horrible shape, and the liturgy also. We've got to find a way to tap into this discontent, to somehow galvanize all of those silently unhappy laypeople out there. So far we haven't been very successful at doing this."

Helen Hull Hitchcock suggested that there was mounting discontent with doctrinal and moral liberalism on the Catholic college campus. "There is a tendency among students to question received orthodoxies, and, ironically, this could actually work to our advantage," she said. "Liberalism has been the prevailing wisdom in Catholic higher education for over twenty-five years now, and recently there has been a stirring of young hearts on Catholic campuses, a questioning of this orthodoxy. At places like Boston College and Fordham University, students have been mobilizing against theological liberalism and pushing for a revival of authentic Catholic orthodoxy."

I suggested that these so-called orthodox students were still a fragile minority, and that there was absolutely no evidence their number was growing.

"Don't underestimate the power of truth, especially countercultural truth," she said. "These kids have been mugged by free sex and political correctness and do-your-own-thing Catholicism. All of this has been the obligatory orthodoxy, and some of these kids have already started to view orthodox Catholicism as an appealing, and countercultural, alternative. It clears away the cultural distortion."

Indeed, it was primarily in order to clear away some of this cultural distortion, Hull Hitchcock told me, that she had started Women for Faith and Family. In early 1984, the American Catholic bishops had announced their intention to write a pastoral letter on women's issues, and toward this end the bishops had invited Catholic women from around the country to engage in a process of consultation with them. From the very start, Hull Hitchcock said, it was obvious that this consultative process would be dominated by religious career women—nuns and ex-nuns, feminist theologians, and professional liturgists—and just about anybody could have submitted their script for them in advance: "The church was a patriarchal institution committed to perpetuating the historic subjugation of women. It was deaf and blind to the experiences of women, it denied women full and equal participation in its various ministries, its repressive teaching on abortion and sexuality was calculated to keep women in line, and its phallocentric theology divested women of any meaningful role in the drama of salvation," and so on and so forth. The bishops, in other words, were going to get hit hard with the feminist party line on Catholicism, a standard-issue litany of grievances and jeremiads, and anyone who dissented from it would be left out in the cold.

With the possible exceptions of homosexuality and abortion, nothing ranks higher in the demonology of Catholic conservatism than feminism, and Helen Hull Hitchcock was determined to show the bishops that more than just a few

Catholic women in the United States were still fully committed to traditional Catholicism. As its first major project, therefore, Women for Faith and Family prepared a petition statement, called "Affirmation for Catholic Women," asking women to pledge their allegiance to Pope John Paul II and to traditional Catholic teaching on such matters as marriage and family life, the sanctity of motherhood, and the priesthood. The petition was circulated widely within conservative Catholic circles across America, and in June 1985 ten thousand signatures were sent to John Paul II. Two months later a list of more than seventeen thousand signatures was given to the American bishops.[28]

While the "Affirmation" project was designed primarily as a public protest, Hull Hitchcock told me, working on it proved to be a turning point in her private life as well. Despite having raised her four children as Roman Catholics, she herself had come from a Protestant background, and she'd never felt an urgent need to undergo a personal conversion to the church. In the course of preparing the "Affirmation," however, Hull Hitchcock became convinced that only the Catholic church could speak with authority on matters of sex and salvation, sin and redemption, and almost immediately upon completing it, she too decided to become a Catholic.

Much like CUF and most other conservative Catholic organizations, Women for Faith and Family is run on a shoestring: its funding comes almost entirely from private membership donations, and its volunteer staff of seven or eight women work out of their own homes. The organization puts out a quarterly newsletter called *Voices*, and, in general, does its utmost to keep track of the feminist enemy within the church, which these days may include everything and everyone from altar girls to the Women's Ordination Conference to middle-aged nuns swaying bare-breasted to the incantations of goddess worship.[29] And in all of its endeavors, according to Hull Hitchcock, the organization is governed by a single motto: "Whatever the pope thinks, and whenever he thinks it."

———————————

CONSERVATIVE SCHOLARS SUCH AS JAMES HITCHCOCK are the displaced intellectuals of American Catholicism. They seldom publish in the more prestigious academic journals, they work for the most part on the fringes of their respective disciplines, and they are very rarely invited to serve on boards or committees of the institutional church. Moreover, in the Catholic academy they are widely regarded as yesterday's men, intellectual losers who remain stranded in the simpler and decidedly more authoritarian world of the 1950s. Mostly ignored by their bishops and disdained by their more liberal colleagues, one of the few places where they feel truly at home is an organization called the Fellowship of Catholic Scholars.

Founded in 1977 by Msgr. George A. Kelly, a onetime professor of sociology at St. John's University in New York City, the Fellowship functions as a sort of solidarity group for conservative Catholic intellectuals throughout the United States. Many of its approximately five hundred full-fledged members hold teaching positions in Catholic colleges or seminaries, about one-third are priests or nuns, and very few would dispute James Hitchcock's gloomy assessment of American Catholicism after the council. No less than CUF, the Fellowship is singularly (and insistently) Catholic in identity, and all newcomers to the organization are required to make an affirmation of personal faith and pledge allegiance to Rome. In addition to James Hitchcock and Msgr. Kelly, some of its more prominent members include Ralph McInery, a professor of philosophy at Notre Dame and co-founder of *Crisis*, a quasi-scholarly magazine generally hospitable to the views of conservative Catholics; Janet Smith, a professor of theology at the University of Dallas and probably the Fellowship's leading female light; and Joseph Fessio, S.J., director of the St. Ignatius Institute at the University of San Francisco and founder of Ignatius Press, the primary conservative Catholic publishing house in the United States.[30]

All things considered, the Fellowship is probably stronger today than it ever has been. Since the late eighties, the organization has managed to enlist almost a hundred new members, and its annual conference is generally a robust and well-attended affair. Nevertheless, it seems highly unlikely that the Fellowship will emerge anytime soon as a major force on the American Catholic intellectual scene. Despite its recent growth, the organization remains very much a preserve of white, male intellectuals, most of whom are middle-aged or older, and its capacity for attracting younger scholars—and especially women and Hispanics—must be counted as doubtful at best.

Moreover, much of the work that has been produced by James Hitchcock and other leading Fellowship scholars has an aura of unreality about it. What one encounters, on page after page of their books, is a litany of grievances, an almost endless recital of derelict bishops, rebellious theologians, and forsaken liturgies. So obsessed in fact are Hitchcock and his colleagues with recounting what has gone wrong with American Catholicism after the council that they rarely get around to discussing what might actually have gone right. Such unrelieved negativity might have had some strategic value in the turbulent aftermath of the council, but at this late stage of the game it only succeeds in making the Fellowship look isolated and unapproachable. At the moment, in fact, Hitchcock and his colleagues seem to be talking primarily to one another. Stuck as they are in a strictly defensive posture, and with only marginal support in the broader church, they are like a lost battalion fighting a war that hardly anyone else knows even exists.

E. MICHAEL JONES AND *FIDELITY* MAGAZINE

For all of its huffing and puffing, the Fellowship represents probably the most moderate and culturally respectable side of Catholic conservatism in the United

States. Very rarely does the organization go so far as to call for the blood of its enemies, and the writings of members such as James Hitchcock and Msgr. Kelly normally convey at least a semblance of civility and decorum. Civility and decorum, however, are qualities notably absent from the work of E. Michael Jones, the founding editor of a conservative monthly called *Fidelity*. Mid-fortyish, tall and angular, and palpably intense, Jones is the flamethrowing author of Catholic conservatism, a guerrilla journalist whose torrid exposés of wrongdoing in the American church practically blister on the page. In issue after issue of *Fidelity*, Jones employs a take-no-prisoners, slash-and-burn approach, attacking with abandon (and usually with obvious relish) anything and anyone that affronts his vision of Catholic orthodoxy. Next to E. Michael Jones, in fact, both the Fellowship and Catholics United for the Faith appear positively lethargic.

Like quite a few others of his generation, E. Michael Jones came to Catholic conservatism along a rather tangled path. Brought up in Philadelphia in a suburban Catholic household, Jones left the church at the age of twenty and, eager for new truths and new experiences, immersed himself in the bohemian counterculture of the 1960s. In 1969 he married Ruth Price, an Episcopalian, and their honeymoon was spent sitting in a massive traffic jam in upstate New York as they tried unsuccessfully to reach the Woodstock music festival. The couple's first child was born in 1971, and two years later they traveled to Germany, where Jones took a job teaching English at a private school. By this time, however, Jones was feeling increasingly miserable. Five years of exposure to the sex-and-drugs scene of the counterculture had left him emotionally unhinged, and he felt himself sliding into a kind of spiritual torpor, without any clear idea of who he was or where he might be headed. Clarity came to Jones unexpectedly one night, however, when he discovered a copy of Thomas Merton's *The Seven Story Mountain* in his school library. Merton's book was by far the most compelling testimony of faith he had ever encountered, Jones told me in a recent interview, and almost immediately upon finishing it he decided to return to the church. "The book completely changed my life. It impressed upon me my own creatureliness and the transcendence of God. And Merton impressed me as a literary man, as someone in touch with the entire range of octaves of human experience, and also in touch with the profound truths of faith. Reading it was like a conversion—I said, this guy's right and I'm wrong—and I went to confession for the first time in years. The whole experience was providential—God leading me along the path of true fulfillment."

Shortly after her husband's conversion, Ruth Jones also became a Catholic, and the couple cemented their newborn commitment of faith by having their two-year-old son baptized. They returned to the United States in 1976, after three years in Germany, and Jones enrolled in a doctoral program in English at Temple University. Three years later, with a dissertation on Hawthorne completed and a degree in hand, Jones joined the faculty of St. Mary's, a Catholic women's college located in South Bend, Indiana, not much more than a stone's throw from the University of Notre Dame. Here, however, things went badly almost from the very start. Before he had completed even his first semester, Jones became convinced that St. Mary's was the antithesis of what a Catholic college should be. Most of the students he met seemed almost entirely unversed in Catholic doctrine and morality, and most of the faculty seemed far more committed to feminism and other secular ideologies than to the supernatural truths of the church. Despite his untenured status, Jones made little effort to conceal his displeasure with this state of affairs, and by the end of his first year at St. Mary's many faculty had come to regard him as something of a nuisance. At the start of his second year, the chairwoman of the English department visited Jones with a warning to tone down his act. Most of his colleagues, she advised, were unhappy with him for openly supporting *Humanae Vitae* and other papal teaching in his lectures and writing, and unhappier still that he had posted a flyer for a pro-life rally on his office door. Jones pointed out in his defense that several other members of the department had been allowed to put pro-choice posters on their doors, and he questioned why *Humanae Vitae* (or any other papal document) should be censored at a college that advertised itself as Roman Catholic. His chairwoman visited Jones again six weeks later, and this time she told him that the department had concluded he was a religious absolutist and had decided against renewing his contract.

Jones stuck out the rest of the academic year at St. Mary's, and in his final semester he agreed to write a series of articles on his experiences at the college for a conservative Catholic newspaper called *The Wanderer*. Upon hearing of this, the president of St. Mary's met personally with Jones and requested—in the "interests of fairness and objectivity"—that he be permitted to review the articles prior to their publication. Jones replied that this would be unnecessary and indicated that he was simply interested in telling the truth, whereupon the president (in Jones's recounting of the incident) leapt to his feet and shouted: "Truth—Bullshit! Truth—Bullshit! Truth—Bullshit!"

Although Jones was now out of a job, St. Mary's had by no means seen (or heard) the last of him. Instead of looking for an academic position elsewhere, Jones decided to stay in South Bend and create a Catholic magazine that, in his words, "would be fully capable of telling the difference between truth and bullshit." "St. Mary's destroyed my academic career, but in a sense they did me a favor," Jones told me. "There's a passage in Genesis which says: 'The evil that you intended to do against me has been turned by God's power into good.' Well, getting fired from St. Mary's just made me that much more determined to speak out against the abuses that I saw happening in Catholic education and in the American Church more generally, and also to speak out on behalf of truth, and that's why I founded *Fidelity*."[31]

Since its publishing debut in December 1981, *Fidelity* has pursued these objectives with a vengeance. With Jones himself its featured writer—and ad hominem attack its primary stock in trade—the magazine has spent the past fifteen years serving up graphic exposés of wrongdoing in the American church. Indeed, hardly a month has gone by without some new scandal, chiefly of the sex-and-sin variety, finding its way onto *Fidelity*'s pages. When I met with Jones, I asked what purpose this scandal-of-the-month approach was intended to serve.

"It's absolutely true that sexual sin has been the preeminent focus of *Fidelity*, but there's a very good reason for this," he told me. "You've got to understand that the American Church has fallen into a state of apostasy since the council, and for the most part this has been a sexual apostasy. Most Catholics—just look at the situation in Catholic colleges today—have been completely taken over by what I call the blob, which is the modern world's consumerist and mechanistic attitude toward sex. And don't underestimate the significance of this: the sexual dimension is utterly important in human life, and the distortion or truncation of sexuality has a radical effect upon the total personality. The problem is that sexual sin never remains simply sexual; it spreads and eventually gets turned as well into intellectual sin. This is what corruption is, and this is what Peter Claver, a Jesuit who lived during the Restoration, meant when he claimed that the moral life is the source of heresy. And this is exactly the position of *Fidelity*. There is a kind of subversion going on that is only explainable by way of a sexual explanation. In all kinds of critical areas, the American Church has broken with the authority of Rome and also the authority of natural law; and sexual license is the most effective way to precipitate a break with authority. In order to justify their sexual sins, American Catholics and their liberal theologians have found it necessary to attack the very truth-structure of the Church."

Heresy, then, springs directly from the groin; and sexual sin is the root cause of virtually everything that has gone wrong with American Catholicism since the council. This, in sum, is the master thesis of *Fidelity* Magazine, and E. Michael Jones has wasted few opportunities in driving it home. In the January 1988 issue of *Fidelity*—to take just one conspicuous case in point—we meet up with Jones at a police station in South Bend, where he's trying to extract information from a certain Sergeant Trennery. A prominent liturgical theologian at the University of Notre Dame, the Rev. Niels Rasmussen, has recently committed suicide, Sergeant Trennery is investigating the case, and Jones smells a story. After considerable coaxing by Jones, the sergeant agrees to divulge certain details of the suicide, but not the more sordid ones that Jones is looking for.

He informed me, for example, that Father Rasmussen made a confession to a colleague about something.

"Was it about sex?" I wondered.

"No."

"Drugs?"

"No."

"Money?"

"No."

At that point my moral vocabulary was just about exhausted. What else was there to confess? Was he an habitual jaywalker? Did he have overdue books at the library?[32]

Of course—and just as Jones had suspected all along—the sordid details of the suicide turned out to involve sex. After obtaining a copy of the coroner's report, Jones learned that Fr. Rasmussen had shot himself in the basement of his house in South Bend, and that his body was found lying amidst "an array of guns, whips, other weapons, handcuffs and unusual paraphernalia." For some years, apparently, Rasmussen had lived a kind of double life, practicing Catholic theology by day and experimenting in homosexual sadomasochism by night. For E. Michael Jones, it just didn't get much sweeter than this. Here was an important Catholic theologian—and a tenured professor at Notre Dame, no less—whose final years were spent seeking out kinky sex rather than spiritual truth. And what's more, according to Jones, there was nothing in the least surprising in any of this. Notre Dame, after all, was simply a larger and more prestigious version of St. Mary's—a place where theological dissent ran rampant and only the trappings of authentic Catholicism still stood in place. And where there exists theological dissent, the Jonesian formula goes, sexual perversion can't be far out of sniffing distance. One is merely a rationalization of the other; and far from being anomalous, the tragic case of Fr. Rasmussen was merely a preview of the trouble that lay ahead for American Catholicism.

And so it goes—on page after steamy page Jones attempts to document the insidious connection that he's convinced exists between sexual and theological sin in the American church. Wherever there are horny nuns or philandering bishops or pederastic priests, Jones is certain to be on the scene, ready to cash in on yet another tale of fallen virtue and spiritual demise. To the uninitiated reader, understandably, all of this ideological riffing on sex-and-sleaze is bound to have something of a prurient (and voyeuristic) flavor about it. Jones, however, feels no need to apologize for his approach: in spiritual warfare, he claims, there is no point in sparing feelings or reputations, in passing over scandal, or in deferring to qualms of civility. The enemy, quite simply, must be exposed and brought to judgment.[33]

To the dismay of some of his readers, however, Jones has been remarkably democratic in deciding just who in fact should be brought to judgment. Although his sharpest invective has usually been reserved for the theological left, he has sometimes dealt just as harshly in his writings with what he considers to be some of the rather more unsavory elements of the Catholic right. "Liberal elites in the American Church have sold out to the hedonistic culture—there's no question about it—but that doesn't mean there's not also serious problems with some of the people who claim to be on our side," Jones told me. "The movement that CUF and the Fellowship and myself represent—call it conservative if you want—is dedicated to papal authority and to eternal Catholic truth. Unfortunately, however, there are a lot of so-called Catholic conservatives who are dedicated instead to phony apparitions and private revelations. And this is a major weakness of the movement. We have all of these people riding their hobby horses—trying to change the Church. Some of them would choose their phony crackpot apparitions over the pope. And in this they're no better than the liberals. We have to fight against anyone who tries to change the Church, regardless of whether they're coming from the left or the right."

In addition to terrorizing the liberal opposition, then, Jones has committed himself to policing the ranks of Catholic conservatism. And this second task has sometimes proven to be every bit as demanding as the first. For more than twenty-five years now, most of the intellectual leaders of conservatism—including James Hitchcock, Msgr. Kelly, and Jones himself—have advocated a tightly disciplined and intensely ultramontane kind of piety. Simply follow the pope in all things, and adhere strictly to the canons of traditional orthodoxy, they've repeatedly advised the conservative rank-and-file, and the battle against liberalism will eventually be won. By no means, however, has this advice always been taken completely to heart. As the American church has become increasingly more secularized since the council, more than just a few conservatives have lost confidence in the capacity of traditional orthodoxy and papal authority to sustain faith, and some have elected to turn elsewhere for some more immediate and more dramatic evidence of the supernatural. More often than not, this has meant turning to one of the various Marian cults that have cropped up throughout the Catholic world over the past thirty years or so. With their messages of apocalyptic forboding and their claims of miraculous intercession by the Virgin Mary, these cults have offered their participants precisely the sort of spiritual certitude and consolation that most of them have found lacking in the institutional church. For conservative intellectuals such as E. Michael Jones, however, this has mainly been a bogus certitude and a counterfeit consolation. Salvation simply doesn't come bottled in some favorite apparition, they've insisted time and again, and private revelation is no substitute for the tried-and-true authority of the papacy.

The Marian cult that seems to have bothered Jones the most happens also to be the fastest-growing one worldwide. In the late seventies, several young Croatians reported that the Virgin Mary was appearing regularly to them in the hitherto obscure Herzegovinian village of Medjugorje. Word spread rapidly, and before long Medjugorje was an international sensation, with pilgrims arriving by the planeload in quest of some personal brush with the supernatural. By the late eighties, in fact, Medjugorje had grown so popular that it threatened to eclipse even such long-standing cults as Fatima as the hottest property on the Marian scene. There were daily sightings of the Virgin Mary, reports of miraculous healings, and, of course, the usual accounts of spinning suns and rosaries transmuted into gold.

For his part, however, E. Michael Jones wasn't in the least impressed by any of this, and in late 1988 he wrote a two-part diatribe for *Fidelity* denouncing Medjugorje as a hoax and a fraud. There were no miraculous revelations taking place in Herzegovina, he insisted; the local bishop, Pavao Zanic of Mostar, had thoroughly investigated the claims of the young seers and found them to be preposterous. Like so many other cults, Jones claimed, Medjugorje owed its popular success to a combination of deception and gullibility—nothing else.[34]

As might be expected, not all of Jones's readers agreed with this assessment. In a letter that appeared in the June 1989 issue of *Fidelity*, James Woeber of Irving, Texas, told Jones, "On my next pilgrimage . . . I will be praying for you to have a MASSIVE HEART ATTACK for your attack against [Mary] and her apparitions. At the rate you're going you are certainly going to meet the Big Boys of history some day. I will also be begging Our Lady for the early demise of your rotten publication." Another reader, Toni Vercillo of Tacoma, seemed only slightly less agitated: "Question: Who from hell (literally!) is E. Michael Jones? Answer: Out on the desert plains there exists a creepy little nocturnal creature that hides during the day because he cannot tolerate the light of the Son. The only time this roach-like bug crawls out from under his rock is when he darts out to strike and bite the tender flesh of a passer-by. Then this cowardly insect quickly retreats into its hole. The name of this creepy creature is E. Michael Jones. . . . His two-part article on Medjugorje is the most incredibly vicious attack upon persons I have ever read. . . . I can't even verbalize (less much write) the rage in my mind and the pain in my heart." Keeping closely to the spirit of the occasion was Henry Buchanan of Bethesda, Maryland, who wrote: "Describing your article would be like describing the contents of a garbage truck. Many hours would be spent describing each piece of garbage. I don't think the effort would warrant the results. However, I feel strongly that I can present a factual account of Medjugorje which would refute your diabolical and misleading account in your recent issue of *Fidelity*."[35]

So much, then, for unity and goodwill on the Catholic right. Dozens of similar-sounding letters were sent to *Fidelity* in the months following publication of the Medjugorje diatribe, but Jones was too busy fighting other battles to take much notice. One of the more intriguing of these battles involved an organization called the Fatima Crusade, which was founded in the early eighties by a maverick priest named Nicholas Gruner. Operating out of Fort Erie, Ontario, Gruner offered his followers a message of tantalizing simplicity. During her miraculous appearances at Fatima earlier this century, he claimed, the Virgin Mary warned that a terrible chastisement would befall the church unless the Vatican consecrated Russia to her Immaculate Heart. Not only has this consecration yet to take place, Gruner insisted, but powerful officials in the Vatican and elsewhere have conspired to conceal the Virgin's warning from the ordinary Catholic faithful. But the ordinary faithful, Gruner claimed, simply can't wait any longer: as the hour of chastisement rapidly approaches, the full truth of Fatima must be told!

To E. Michael Jones, of course, all of this sounded like sheer lunacy; and in March 1988 he published an article by a *Fidelity* correspondent named James Donovan that attempted—in the best *Fidelity* tradition—to discredit Gruner's position by discrediting Gruner himself. When he wasn't busy fomenting apocalyptic fantasy in Fort Erie, Donovan claimed, Gruner toured North America with a metal casket that contained the remains of—what else?—a Marian statue! The so-called Fatima Pilgrim Virgin statue, which had been Gruner's prize possession, was smashed in a traffic accident in the mid-eighties, but Gruner, apparently, couldn't bear the thought of parting company with it. Fetishism aside, Donovan continued, it seemed quite likely that Gruner wasn't even a priest; there was no reliable proof of his ordination, and also no evidence that he had ever been incardinated in an American or Canadian diocese.[36]

Gruner certainly wasn't about to suffer indignities such as these quietly; and in the August 1988 issue of *his* bimonthly magazine, *The Fatima Crusader*, he had his right-hand man, a corpulent priest named Paul Leonard, launch a counterattack. Overdosing on invective, Leonard characterized Jones and Donovan as "hard core hypocrites" and "infamous scoundrels" who "have lost all sense of justice and decency in their blatant and utterly malicious display of calumny and slander." From here on, matters descended into outright farce. At an anti-abortion conference in Montreal later the same year, Jones was accosted, both physically and verbally, by Fr. Leonard and several other Gruner supporters, who demanded that *Fidelity* print an apology for its attacks against their leader. Unrepentant as usual, Jones refused to agree to this, and instead demanded that Fr. Leonard produce proof that his own priestly credentials were in order. Leonard wasn't willing (or able) to do so; and the parties went their separate ways only after considerable shouting and jostling. Finally, in the December 1988 issue of *Fidelity*, Jones offered a free subscription to any reader who could ascertain whether Paul Leonard was in fact a priest or, as Jones suspected, "an overweight version of Guido Sarducci sent to [the Fatima Crusade] from central casting."[37]

Medjugorje and the Fatima Crusade are just two of many cults on the Catholic right that Jones, at one time or another, has wound up lambasting in *Fidelity*. As we've seen, however, his efforts in this regard haven't always been fully appreciated. In 1987 *Fidelity*'s circulation reached a high-water mark of twenty thousand, but just three years later it had declined to somewhere in the vicinity of fifteen thousand—a severe blow, by any measure, for a magazine that's run almost entirely on subscriptions. Probably most of the readers who jumped ship were offended by Jones's derisive treatment of Medjugorje; or else by his equally rough handling of the Fatima Crusade, or Bayside, or Necedah, or TFP (Tradition, Family, and Property) . . . the hit list goes on and on. Many of the same readers, moreover, undoubtedly subscribed to some variant of the maxim "no enemies on the right," and they'd fully expected Jones to confine his literary raging to the wrongdoings of the theological left. As Jones took special pains to point out in his December 1988 issue, however, *Fidelity* wasn't set up to cater to the sins of special-interest groups on either end of Catholicism's ideological spectrum.

> Our intention is to tell the truth. This was why I founded *Fidelity* seven years ago this month. . . . The Church in this country has been torn into little pieces by sectarian ideologies. Those in power in the Church in this country espouse one or the other ideologies of the left. The gospel at the university, for example, is placed on the procrustean bed of feminism and everything which does not suit the feminist Zeitgeist is lopped off and thrown into the ash can of history. The antidote to this is not propagandizing for ideologies of the right. The antidote to the sectarian spirit is Catholic truth. I founded the magazine to give voice to this spirit. If anyone comes to it with expectation of anything else, he will, I fear, go away disappointed. So don't expect me to give preferential treatment to your hobby horse—whatever it is, your favorite apparition, your gold rosary beads—any more than I would give preferential treatment to the whining of the feminists.[38]

Truth and order. Truth and discipline. Truth and obedience. These are the marching orders of Catholic conservatism, and no one has been stricter about enforcing them than E. Michael Jones. In an age that values the individualistic and the experiential and the gnostic-mystical, Jones and most other self-appointed leaders of conservatism insist upon a controlled, ascetic, and Apollonian piety. The truths of salvation are already revealed, they've been placed under the protection of an infallible papacy, and there's nothing more that's needed and nothing more to be sought after. Private revelation, charismatic rapture, spiritual ecstasy: all of these are distractions at best, and quite possibly outright deviations from the straight path of orthodoxy. Authentic Catholicism today requires a regimentation not just of the sexual impulses but of the mind and the spirit as well.

———————

E. MICHAEL JONES PRODUCES FIDELITY MAGAZINE from the basement of his family home in South Bend, a large frame structure located on a tree-lined street just a short walking distance from the University of Notre Dame. When I visited him there several years ago, I asked why, in his estimation, the forces of the Catholic right had become so hopelessly divided in the years following the Second Vatican Council. "The biggest problem in the American Church since the council," he answered, "is that there's been a vacuum of authority. And as the maxim goes, Nature abhors a vacuum. The theologians, the priests and the nuns, the bishops—almost all of them have given themselves over to an uncritical embrace of the permissive, self-indulgent secular culture. The bishops are worst of all. I used to think that bishops were supposed to be like martyrs, but in the American context this is an oxymoron. With very few exceptions, the American bishops have thrown off their own authority in a futile quest for relevance and popularity. So I don't necessarily blame all of these proponents of wacky apparitions and phony revelations. Some of these prople are desperate for spiritual authority and direction, and they've been driven in their desperation into delusion and madness. Of course, legitimate spiritual authority still exists, but the only certain place to find it is in Rome. Catholics must align themselves with the papacy. It's as simple as that."

I asked Jones as well whether his unstated goal, in relentlessly prowling the precincts of both the Catholic left and the Catholic right for new evidence of sin and heresy, was to bring into being an American Catholicism of sectarian perfection. "I know it may appear like that, but nothing could be further from the truth," he said. "I'm not interested in creating some remnant Church, in excommunicating all sinners. This is the Donatist temptation, feeling the need to endlessly purify the Church, to boil it down to some holy remnant. Like Augustine, I acknowledge that the Church is composed of sinners, and it's ridiculous to think it should be otherwise. But to acknowledge this isn't to say we should compromise our truth or surrender our principles. The truths and the principles must stand, regardless of how alien or offensive they might appear to the modern mind. This is something that our bishops and theologians have not appreciated."

By this point, Jones's wife Ruth had also joined in the conversation, and she brought up the subject of artificial contraception. "This is the best illustration of how far the so-called leaders of the American Church have compromised Catholic truth," she said. "People today just don't understand the ramifications of the sexual life. I'm a convert to the Church, we have six children now, and I'd never consider using contraception. It trivializes sex, and, in the end, it trivializes life itself. Rome is absolutely right in condemning contraception, and this is one area where we absolutely must not sacrifice our principles. But how many homilies do you hear on the subject nowadays, and how many bishops and theologians are truly committed to *Humanae Vitae?*"

"What would you do," I asked, "if the Vatican changed its mind on contraception?"

"You mean if the Vatican were suddenly to say it's okay?" Ruth Jones said, looking momentarily nonplussed. "But this couldn't happen. Pope John Paul II has repeatedly come out in support of *Humanae Vitae.*"

"But what if his successor, some future pope, were to relax the church's teaching against contraception?"

"The teaching on contraception could never change. Never. This would be impossible. This wouldn't be the Church."

THE WANDERER AND THE POLITICS OF CATHOLIC CONSERVATISM

Fidelity might be the most widely detested publication on the American Catholic scene today, but it's also the most consistently entertaining. With its agitprop mentality and schoolyard posturing, it makes its competition on the theological left—including the trendsetting *National Catholic Reporter*—look positively stodgy in comparison. And on the theological right, the only publication that comes anywhere close to matching *Fidelity*'s polemical panache is a weekly newspaper called *The Wanderer.*

The Wanderer is actually much more than just a newspaper: it's a full-fledged publishing dynasty, owned and operated for almost a century and a half by the Matt family of St. Paul, Minnesota. Founded in 1867 as a journal of religious instruction for German immigrants to the midwest, it's one of the longest-running Catholic publications in the United States and, especially since the council, one of the most famously controversial as well.[39] In June 1992 I met with Alphonse Matt, Jr., the *Wanderer*'s current editor, over lunch and dinner at a restaurant in St. Paul. In his early sixties, tall, robust, and good-naturedly masculine, Matt, Jr., first joined the *Wanderer*'s editorial staff in 1965, just as the Second Vatican Council was drawing to a close in Rome. His father, Alphonse Matt, Sr., and uncle, Walter Matt, were still running the show at the time, and they (and virtually everyone else connected with the newspaper) were far from convinced that the council was a good deal for the church.

"You have to understand that the *Wanderer*, with my father and uncle at the helm, was theologically conservative in the first degree, and the council wasn't the easiest thing for us to swallow," Matt, Jr., told me. "The Church needed updating—this was the intention of John XXIII in calling Vatican II—but it certainly didn't need radical change, and it was obvious that Catholic liberals were using the council as a pretext for advancing their radical agenda. And at the *Wanderer*, understandably, we were very disturbed by this, and so for a while we weren't sure where we should stand."[40]

The *Wanderer*'s moment of decision came on April 3, 1969, when Pope Paul VI promulgated the Novus Ordo—the new and streamlined liturgy that the council had called into being to replace the centuries-old Tridentine Mass as the official rite of the church. For the Matt family, this posed an immediate dilemma: as much as they disliked the new Mass (and, at first, they disliked it considerably), they could hardly oppose it without also opposing the papal authority of Paul VI. But neither could they endorse it without also endorsing, if only implicitly, the legitimacy of the Second Vatican Council. After a great deal of soul-searching, Matt, Jr., and his father decided that the *Wanderer* should take the latter course, and in January 1970 the newspaper declared its reluctant allegiance to both the Novus Ordo and the council. "This was a very tough decision

49

for us," Matt, Jr., told me. "We didn't particularly like the new Mass—with its emphasis on the vernacular and communal participation, it struck us as flippant and secular, an embodiment of everything that worried us about the council. But there was no doubt that the pope intended it to be the official rite of the Church, and that it was suppressing the old Latin Mass. Like it or not, this was the mind of the pope, so we bit the bullet and accepted the Mass. And doing so helped to establish our legitimacy, and whatever hand we had to play was greatly strengthened. Henceforward, we could criticize abuses in the Church without people assuming we were supporters of Archbishop Lefebvre, and disobedient to the pope and council and so forth. It's funny, but now I actually find myself quite comfortable with the Novus Ordo Mass; the Latin Mass is a rite which has had its day. Looking back, I'm convinced that our support of the new Mass was the right decision."

Not everyone at the *Wanderer*, however, was quite so conciliatory. While Matt, Jr., and his father were negotiating their rapprochement with the new Mass, Walter Matt, who had been a mainstay at the newspaper for over twenty years, was digging in his heels. Neither pope nor council, he insisted, had any business altering the Tridentine Mass, which had stood unchanged as the principal repository of Catholic faith for four hundred years. Changing the Mass, in his view, was tantamount to changing Catholicism itself; and this was something that loyal Catholics were compelled to fight to the very end. When it became clear that his position was losing ground, Walter Matt left the *Wanderer* under a cloud of bitterness, and in late 1967 he started a rival newspaper called *The Remnant*, which immediately established itself as one of the most bellicose and uncompromising publications on the Catholic right.

Not that the *Wanderer*, for its part, was ever at serious risk of becoming mild-mannered. After making reluctant peace with the council and the new Mass, the newspaper turned its attention to the far more pressing business, as Matt, Jr., told me, "of fighting the liberal bastards who were running the American Church and doing their utmost to destroy it." And more often than not, this meant fighting the American Catholic bishops, whose ranks apparently included some of the worst liberal bastards of all. With very few exceptions, according to the *Wanderer*, it was the bishops themselves who were responsible for the rapid deterioration of traditional Catholicism in the United States after the council. It was the bishops who had stood aside and permitted feminism and liberalism to invade the American church, and the bishops as well who had turned a blind eye to theological dissent in the Catholic academy. Where courage and vigilance were required, the *Wanderer* insisted, the bishops as a group had demonstrated only a lukewarm commitment to protecting the faith—and sometimes not even that.

Although most Catholic conservatives in the United States shared this negative assessment of their bishops, some wished that the *Wanderer* wasn't quite so relentless in hammering it home. Indeed, Lyman Stebbins, the founding president of CUF, was on record as saying that conservatives should treat their bishops (at least outwardly) with deference and respect. There was no value in cultivating enemies, he reasoned, when the conservative movement needed all the friends it could get. Deference and respect were virtues that the *Wanderer* had little interest in mastering, however, and blasting the bishops rapidly became the newspaper's defining characteristic.[41]

And as time went on, some of the *Wanderer*'s best blasting was reserved for the bishops' political sins. In the years following the Second Vatican Council, and partly in consequence of it, the American bishops underwent a notable shift to the left in their political thinking. Taking their cue from the revolutionary theologies of liberation that were springing up across Latin America, and also from some of the left-leaning social teaching that was emanating from the Vatican, the bishops began a process of criticizing (and sometimes challenging) the dominant political and economic order of the United States.[42] For fifteen years or so their efforts in this regard attracted only slight publicity, but in May 1983 they hit pay dirt with a pastoral letter entitled *The Challenge of Peace* (TCOP). Released to a chorus of praise from liberals and peaceniks, TCOP unequivocally condemned the nuclear-arms race and the militaristic mindset that had helped sustain it. With the glow of this triumph still surrounding them, they came back, in November 1986, with an even more striking pastoral, this one entitled *Economic Justice for All*, that took direct and unforgiving aim at the inequities of American-style capitalism. "That so many people are poor in a nation as rich as ours," the bishops wrote, "is a social and moral scandal that we cannot ignore."[43]

From the *Wanderer*'s perspective, however, the bishops would have been far better off saying nothing at all. At virtually every turn, the newspaper charged, the pastorals on peace and the economy were animated by a woolly-minded and historically discredited socialism. Regardless of the social inequities it might produce, free-enterprise capitalism was the best economic system available—and the only one acceptable to Roman Catholics. In challenging capitalism and the military might that helped keep it ascendant, the bishops had shown themselves to be every bit as incompetent in affairs of state as in those of theology.

For the better part of the eighties, in fact, the *Wanderer* was so preoccupied with battling political and economic heresy that some of its more expressly religious concerns were pushed into the background. And this raises a critical question: with the *Wanderer* (and to some extent CUF and the Fellowship as well), it's sometimes hard to tell where religious conservatism ends and political conservatism begins. Although there is no necessary or inevitable connection between the two, they are constant bedmates on the *Wanderer*'s pages, bound together in an ideological monogamy of the strictest kind. But this wasn't always the case. In the 1890s and for several decades thereafter, the *Wanderer* was known for its liberal views on labor rights and social welfare. In fact, on the masthead of its first English edition, in 1931, the newspaper proclaimed itself American

Catholicism's "progressive" publication. With the onset of the Cold War in the late forties, however, the *Wanderer* took a dramatic, and apparently irrevocable, turn rightward. Adopting as its new epigraph Pope Pius XI's famous condemnation of socialism ("No one can be at the same time a sincere Catholic and a true Socialist"), the newspaper dedicated itself to attacking communism in all of its guises, and also to promoting capitalism as an economic system of ostensibly divine sanction. Throughout the fifties, the *Wanderer* managed to be more dogmatically right-wing than any other American Catholic newspaper; and in the presidential race of 1960 it went so far as to support Barry Goldwater, the ranking guru of the political right in the United States, over the man many American Catholics regarded as their chosen son—John F. Kennedy. And from there on it was mainly more of the same story: on every issue imaginable throughout the seventies and eighties—from the plight of the urban underclass in America to upheaval in Central America—the *Wanderer* came down consistently hard on the right-hand side of the political ledger.

Within the wider world of American Catholicism, of course, right-wing dogmatizing of this sort is by no means confined to the *Wanderer*. William F. Buckley, Jr., the founding editor of *The National Review*, and Patrick Buchanan, the syndicated columnist and political firebrand, are justly famous for their anticommunist gunslinging; and Michael Novak, Richard John Neuhaus, and George Weigel have spent much of the past decade defending the essential compatibility of Catholicism and capitalism. Indeed, political conservatives such as Buckley, Neuhaus, and Novak may be said to constitute a loosely bound intellectual subculture within American Catholicism: they appear in most of the same journals, they fight most of the same battles (against socialism primarily, but also against feminism, abortion, and other hallmarks of cultural liberalism), and, to a remarkable extent, they even employ the same syntax and vocabulary. Nevertheless, despite certain similarities, this is not the subculture of the *Wanderer*, of *Fidelity* or CUF, or, for the most part, of the Fellowship of Catholic Scholars. Whereas Buckley and Novak and company aim for mainstream respectability, as well as a certain measure of intellectual urbanity (there's no point, after all, in getting overheated), the *Wanderer* operates on the subversive fringes of American society, where respectability counts for nothing and intensity of commitment for almost everything. Moreover, while the writings of Buckley and Novak possess a distinctly Catholic sensibility, they convey very little of the *Wanderer*'s theological Sturm und Drang, or its overriding sense of spiritual desperation.

Consider, by way of illustration, the question of artificial contraception. Like CUF and *Fidelity* Magazine, the *Wanderer* regards opposition to contraception as the touchstone of authentic Catholic faith in the modern world. "There's no doubt that this is the issue upon which we stand or fall," Matt, Jr., told me. "When Pope Paul condemned contraception in *Humanae Vitae*, he was saying that man is a contingent being, that he isn't the master of his own destiny, even when it comes to sex. And this violates every conception of post-Enlightenment man, the sense that we're autonomous and fully in control and so forth. The fact that most American Catholics in practice reject the Church's teaching on birth control, and the fact that the American bishops were swept away so easily on the issue, is testimony to how badly the mainstream Church in the United States has been secularized. Defending *Humanae Vitae* is more important to us even than fighting socialism; it's proclaiming God's power and sovereignty."

Among mainstream conservatives like Buckley and Novak, however, *Humanae Vitae* is generally regarded with a mixture of indifference and annoyance rather than anything approaching reverence, and the *Wanderer*'s bleak depiction of American Catholicism after the council is thought to be greatly exaggerated.[44] As a group, the mainstreamers (as we might as well refer to them) find much that's positive with the contemporary American church: its suburban pews are mostly full, its intellectual credentials are vastly improved over what they were thirty years ago, and its public stature seems larger than ever. Of course, there are negatives as well—such as a moral carelessness that seems to have pervaded much of the laity and clergy—but nothing that could be counted as a full-fledged crisis. The church could be doing better, in other words, but it could also be doing considerably worse. In the *Wanderer*'s view, however, the church in the United States was doing about as badly as could be imagined, and there was something suspect about Buckley, Novak, and crew for failing to acknowledge as much. "It's true that although we share common political ground with the Novaks and so forth, there's a world of difference between us," Matt, Jr., told me. "We're convinced that there is a terrible spiritual crisis within the American Church, and, when all is said and done, this is the *Wanderer*'s primary concern, and the primary concern of CUF and people like Mike Jones also. We put our Catholicism first, and our right-wing political agenda afterward. With them, it sometimes seems the reverse."

Of itself, however, the *Wanderer*'s right-wing political agenda is by no means an easy thing to comprehend. Like CUF and *Fidelity*, the newspaper claims total and unswerving allegiance to Rome; and yet Rome, for its part, has hardly been unequivocally supportive throughout the years of free-enterprise capitalism. Over the past century, a steady succession of papal encyclicals has scolded capitalism for its win-at-all-costs competitiveness, its starkly individualistic orientation, and, above all, its social and moral corrosiveness. Indeed, the Vatican's social teaching—from Leo XIII's *Rerum Novarum* (1891) to John Paul II's *Laborem Exercens* (1981)—has been almost as tough on capitalism as it has on communism. But the *Wanderer*, for all its professions of loyalty to Rome, has operated for the past several decades as if this social teaching didn't even exist. "There's no question that we've got a problem here," Matt, Jr., admitted to me. "Before the Cold War, the *Wanderer* was hip-deep in papal social teaching, but for some time now we've mostly ignored it. Throughout the 1970s and eighties we were still fighting the Cold War when doing so had become unfashionable. We were so consumed by this that we gave short shrift to the papal encyclicals. This has put us in a very uncomfortable position, and it's something we definitely have to address."

Some of the *Wanderer*'s closest allies, in fact, have attempted to distance themselves somewhat from the newspaper's right-wing rhetoric. When I met with him in South Bend, E. Michael Jones insisted that Catholicism wasn't beholden to any political or economic creed, and in recent years *Fidelity* has published several articles critical of American-style capitalism.[45] Moreover, in 1991 Catholics United for the Faith published a book by Stephen Krason, a political scientist at Franciscan University of Steubenville, that pointed out the moral deficiencies of both political liberalism and political conservatism.[46] And James Sullivan, a former editor of *Lay Witness*, CUF's monthly magazine, assured me in an interview that "CUF Catholics," and conservative Catholics more generally, were by no means uniformly right-wing in political disposition. "The *Wanderer* doesn't speak for all of us," Sullivan said. "Conservative Catholics are at heart a mixed bag politically. Sure, most of us vote Republican and so forth, but this is often just a reaction to the unbelievable breakdown in national morality that we associate with the liberal policies of the Democratic Party. We tend to resemble Republican right-wingers not so much out of choice, in other words, but because we've been forced into it."[47]

All things considered, Sullivan isn't likely far off the mark here. To a large extent, the right-wing sympathies of Catholic conservatives seem much less a matter of ideological conviction than of existential anxiety. Since the 1950s, as they see it, American society as a whole has fallen into a state of moral anarchy: conventional sex roles have been smashed, violence and drugs have become nasty staples of urban life, pornography and sexual permissiveness have flourished while family solidarity has precipitously declined, and abortion—almost overnight—has reached epidemic proportions. And for the most part, in their view, this moral anarchy has been presided over by the denizens of political liberalism in the United States, including (most notably) the leadership of the Democratic Party. Opposing liberalism, then, is regarded by them as far more than an exercise in political partisanship: with the nation's very future hanging in the balance, it's a task of utmost moral urgency.

The *Wanderer* might not, as James Sullivan suggests, speak for all Catholic conservatives, but it manages nevertheless to speak for a sizable portion of them. Over the past several decades, the newspaper's circulation has hovered steadily around the forty-thousand mark, and it remains probably the most widely read conservative Catholic publication in the United States.[48] Much like "CUF Catholics," *Wanderer* readers, while mostly white, tend to be ethnically diverse, married with at least several children, and modestly middle-class in social standing. To the chagrin of the newspaper's publishers, however, they tend for the most part as well to be on the nether side of forty. Indeed, Alphonse Matt, Jr., told me that the *Wanderer*'s failure to attract a younger readership was one of his greatest worries. "We all—at the *Wanderer* and in the conservative movement as a whole—seem to be preaching to the choir. We're an aging breed, if not a dying one, and we're not successfully getting to the young kids. We haven't found the key to that. Modernist Catholics, ironically, are dying out, too. No young kids are buying into their feel-good religion. But this is small comfort to us; we have to do something to avert stagnation."[49]

————

DESPITE ITS AGING READERSHIP, the *Wanderer* has succeeded over the past several years in bringing a number of younger Catholic writers into its fold. Probably the most talented of these is William Doino, who lives with his parents in rural Connecticut. Doino recently turned thirty, and he's written for the *Wanderer* fairly regularly for almost a decade now, always with considerable aplomb and on topics as various as *Schindler's List* and liberation theology. Raised in the New York City area in a devout Catholic household, Doino was a self-described "ordinary kid" until the age of fifteen, when he began to suffer intensely from environmental allergies. His illness forced him to drop out of high school, and for three years he was extremely sick and at times almost on the verge of suicide. "For a while there I was utterly desperate," Doino told me during an interview several years ago at his family home in Connecticut. "I was emaciated, under a hundred pounds, and I considered killing myself several times. I went through the fires of hell."[50]

While still in the throes of illness, Doino began reading the works of Camus, Feuerbach, Sartre, and Russell, all of which impressed him enormously, and he came to regard himself as an "atheistic humanist." ("I couldn't believe in a God who would permit me to suffer so," he told me.) At the age of nineteen, however, Doino's mother gave him a copy of *Lives of the Saints* (as well as some other inspirational literature), and he describes reading it as the turning point of his life. "I said to myself that if people like these could be so holy and blessed, then God must exist, and I soon put away my Sartre and Camus and converted to Jesus Christ. I was leading a pagan lifestyle that over time probably would have resulted in promiscuity and drug abuse, but my conversion changed everything. I came back to the Church, and I came back expecting to find something of the same religious passion and commitment that I was feeling myself."

As might be expected, however, Doino's expectations were destined for disappointment; and within just several months of his conversion he found himself very much at odds with mainstream Catholicism in the United States. "Almost everywhere I looked, the situation seemed quite horrible," he told me. "The American Church as a whole seemed to have become part and parcel of the secular culture. There was very little talk of sin or salvation, heaven or hell, as if the very concepts were hopelessly out of date. But the truth is, they're as relevant now as ever, and they're central truths to our faith. There is a God, and a heaven and a hell, and we're all going to be judged. My personal salvation is absolutely the most important thing to me. Everything—sexual fulfillment, money—pales into insignificance compared to saving my soul. I'm not sure I'm saved now. You're never certain. You have to work out your salvation in fear and trembling. And this—contrary to what most of our bishops and theologians would seem to believe—is at the heart of our faith. . . . When I came back, I couldn't believe how much the Church had become an echo of the secular society."

In an earlier time, all of this earnestness and spiritual striving would have marked Doino as a prime candidate for the priesthood. As things stand today, however, the priesthood is one of the last places he and other similar-minded young men would want to wind up. "My feeling is that many young orthodox men are much like myself in holding no strong interest in entering religious life," Doino said. "Seminaries are in terrible shape, with their modernist climates, their rampant homosexuality, and their persecution of those with orthodox views. I doubt I'd even get past their initial psychological testing. Anyways, I've got healthy heterosexual drives, and despite my tremendous respect for celibacy, I don't feel a calling for religious life."

Doino, in fact, would like to get married, and preferably to someone who's open to the prospect of a large family. Like E. Michael Jones and Alphonse Matt, Jr., and so forth, he considers himself a strict disciple of *Humanae Vitae*, Pope Paul VI's 1968 anti-contraception encyclical, which he describes as "one of the most beautiful and distinctive teachings of the Church." Because he's still not fully recovered from his allergic condition, however, Doino very rarely dates, and his time is mainly taken up with writing. And in this, no one has been a bigger influence upon him than a longtime *Wanderer* veteran named John Mulloy.

Now in his late seventies and a resident of Fayetteville, Arkansas, John Mulloy began writing for the *Wanderer* a quarter of a century ago, "out of disgust," he told me during a telephone interview several years ago, "at the way the American Church was being run down by its religious leaders."[51] Shortly after returning to the church, Doino came across some of Mulloy's writings, was thoroughly impressed by their candor and polemical savvy, and in November 1986 phoned the older man in the hope of striking up an intellectual acquaintance. Mulloy was more than happy to oblige, and over the next several years he and Doino developed what has proven to be a strong and enduring literary friendship.

Within conservative Catholic circles, however, it's also been a friendship with a certain maverick streak to it. In both of their writings since the late eighties, Mulloy and Doino have openly criticized the one man—Pope John Paul II— whom most Catholic conservatives in the United States have tended to regard as absolutely beyond criticism. Despite the image of strength that he projects,

Mulloy told me, John Paul II has actually been a highly incompetent pope, and as much in need of prodding as the American Catholic bishops. "He simply hasn't done his job, and someone has to make this clear to him," Mulloy said. "He's had opportunities to discipline dissenting theologians, to really do something about the scandal of homosexuality in the clergy, but very seldom has he come through with tough and decisive action. He's an unbelievably weak pope, and certain people, of course, resent us for pointing this out. But look, we have to make a distinction between the pope's magisterial teaching, which is always infallible, and his prudential judgments, which are fallible and open to criticism. And with Pope John Paul II's prudential judgments, there's been much to criticize."

During a recent telephone interview, William Doino expressed almost exactly the same sentiments, but with even greater vigor. "In the popular media and so forth, John Paul has a reputation as a tough-minded conservative pope, but this is completely false," he told me. "He should be excommunicating dissenting theologians and heretical priests, he should be restoring order to the Church, but what he mainly does is put on a pious show. When I see the pope sitting in one of his typical poses, with his arms crossed, looking saintly and pious, it makes me absolutely sick. He's betrayed us in a sense by his inaction. Of course I'm still loyal to him, and of course I regard his teaching on faith and morals to be infallible—this is an obligation of faith—but Mr. Mulloy, who's been like an intellectual mentor to me, is perfectly correct: it's our right and responsibility to criticize the pope for not doing everything necessary to protect the faith."[52]

There's something charming about Doino's idealism and sincerity of purpose here, but also something terribly naive. It's been some time now since the Vatican had the power to intimidate dissenters into submission, or even the moral leverage to coax them into it. If Pope John Paul II were actually to launch a get-tough campaign against moral and theological dissent within American Catholicism today, it would likely only prove how little practical (as opposed to symbolic) authority he truly commands. By no means, moreover, is Doino the only Catholic conservative to expect more from Rome than Rome can realistically deliver. Living as they do in an insular, 1950s-style Catholicism largely of their own making, conservatives in general seem almost willfully out of touch with the complex political and cultural dynamics of the contemporary church.

———————

AND SO TOO, FOR THAT MATTER, DOES THE WANDERER. Since the close of the Second Vatican Council, the newspaper has made chronic complaint its journalistic way of life, and the restoration of a Catholic ghetto—safely shut off from the forces of liberalism—its defining mission. The problem with chronic complaint, however, is that it practically begs to be ignored, and this is especially the case when the complaining is unaccompanied by any sort of constructive engagement with the controversies of the day. The *Wanderer* might very well survive into the twenty-first century (and, at this point, there's little to suggest that it won't), but unless the newspaper learns something besides the language of reaction, its influence within the broader American church is almost certain to remain negligible.

CATHOLIC CONSERVATISM AND ANTI-ABORTION ACTIVISM

CHAPTER THREE

JOSEPH SCHEIDLER CAN PROBABLY BE ACCUSED of many things, but leading an insular life isn't one of them. Now in his late sixties and the founding director of the Chicago-based Pro-Life Action League, Scheidler has experienced enough public controversy over the past two decades to fill several lifetimes, and he shows little indication of slowing down. Born in 1927 in Hartford City, Indiana, where his father ran the town's two movie theaters, Scheidler was raised in a large German-American family that he describes as devoutly and thoroughgoingly Catholic. After serving in the Navy during the Second World War, he earned an undergraduate degree at Notre Dame, worked for a year at the *South Bend Tribune*, and, in 1951, entered a Benedictine seminary to study for the priesthood. Scheidler left the seminary after eight years, just before he was scheduled to take his solemn vows, and after teaching part-time for several years at Notre Dame and completing an M.A. in public speaking at Marquette, he eventually landed a job at a public-relations firm in Chicago, got married, and started a family.[1]

Scheidler spent the first half of the 1960s settling into his marriage and new career, but toward the close of the decade he began to feel a mounting sense of spiritual unease. Despite having left the seminary ten years earlier, he remained strongly committed to the church, and yet the church as he knew it seemed almost to be disappearing before his eyes. Many of the devotional practices that he had grown up with were being cast aside in the name of renewal, and the very idea of what it meant to be a Catholic seemed completely up for grabs. Like quite a few others of his generation, Scheidler found all of this change enormously disorienting, and by the early seventies he had fallen into a kind of spiritual lethargy, no longer certain if his faith had any purpose or significance in the helter-skelter world of American Catholicism after the council.

59

Scheidler was jolted out of his lethargy in January 1973, however, when the epochal Roe v. Wade decision of the American Supreme Court abolished state laws restricting abortion and effectively opened the door in the United States to abortion on demand.[2] Although he and his wife Anne had four (out of an eventual seven) children to support by this point, Scheidler quit his lucrative public-relations job within weeks of the Roe ruling and dedicated himself to full-time activism on behalf of the pro-life (or anti-abortion) movement, which was just then rising to prominence across the United States. If ever there was an issue which cried out for Catholics to take a stand, he reasoned, this was surely it. Liberalized abortion, in his view, was an evil of almost unparalleled magnitude, and joining battle against it in the pro-life movement was the most urgent requirement of faith confronting American Catholics after the Second Vatican Council.

It didn't take very long, however, for Scheidler to wear out his welcome with the pro-life movement. By the time of the Roe ruling, the movement's flagship organization was the National Right to Life Committee (which had been operating since 1970 under the auspices of the Catholic Family Life Bureau); and, almost without exception, the NRLC's top leaders favored what might be described as a pragmatic and reformist approach to the abortion issue.[3] Instead of shooting for some sudden and total victory on the anti-abortion front (and likely coming up empty in the process), they argued, pro-lifers should commit themselves to a long-term campaign of political lobbying and public education in the hope of gradually winning increased public support for their cause. Liberalized abortion, in their view, was a colossal mistake, a tragedy of ignorance. If Americans could only learn more of the fetus—if they could come to terms with its essential humanity—popular support for abortion would almost certainly evaporate. It was unnecessary (and quite likely counterproductive), they reasoned, to bring religion and morality into the equation. Simply advertise the relevant scientific facts, and invoke both the language and logic of civil rights, and Americans would eventually come to recognize the fetus as human and hence worthy of legal protection.

Although in most cases Roman Catholic themselves, the NRLC's top leaders were anxious to prove that a compelling case for the fetus could be made on strictly secular grounds, without reference to either confessional morality or religious dogma. As much as anything else, they wanted to dispel charges (which were rampant in the news media during the late sixties and early seventies) that pro-lifers were mere stooges of the Catholic hierarchy dedicated to imposing their own straitjacketed morality upon the entire nation. If the battle for public opinion was to be won, they reasoned, it was imperative that the pro-life movement jettison its Catholic stereotype and do everything possible to cultivate an image of strict religious neutrality. At its national conference in Detroit several months after the Roe ruling, accordingly, the NRLC severed all formal connections with the church and elected a non-Catholic woman named Marjorie Mecklenburg as its first president.[4]

Not all pro-lifers, to be sure, were happy with this pragmatic (and secularist) approach, and perhaps unhappiest of all was Joseph Scheidler. In January 1974 Scheidler was appointed executive director of Illinois Right to Life, one of the NRLC's largest state chapters, but within just a year or so of taking office he was fired for his insistence on playing by his own rules, which included organizing prayer rallies outside Chicago-area abortion clinics and distributing photographs of bloodied fetuses to the news media. Regardless of what the NRLC might claim, Scheidler argued, abortion was unquestionably a religious issue above all else, and it was foolish to pretend otherwise. The widespread extinction of unborn life in abortion clinics across America, in his view, was an ultimate blasphemy against the creator of all life, and overcoming it would require far more than a commitment simply to political lobbying and public education.

Despite losing this opening round to the NRLC, Joseph Scheidler was by no means alone in favoring a more explicitly religious response to the abortion issue. In the months immediately following the Roe ruling, the pro-life movement underwent considerable internal expansion, and many of its most ardent newcomers turned out to be conservative Catholics. Much like Scheidler himself, conservative Catholics as a group tended to define anti-abortionism in primarily religious terms. At a time when virtually all other criteria of Catholic belonging seemed cast into doubt, fighting abortion was seen by them as a hallmark of authentic Catholicism—a kind of last refuge of faith. If Catholics in the United States were unwilling to take an unequivocal stand on this, their thinking went, there seemed nothing whatsoever that they could take a stand on.

THE CONTRACEPTIVE-MENTALITY THESIS

Although religious sentiments of this sort held sway within conservative Catholic circles, the leadership of the NRLC succeeded for several years after Roe in keeping them underground—compartmentalized and safely hidden from public view. During the late seventies and early eighties, however, a combination of factors conspired to bring them dramatically to the surface. And the first of these factors, not surprisingly, turned out to involve artificial contraception. As America's abortion rate continued to escalate throughout the late seventies, Joseph Scheidler and other Catholic conservatives became increasingly more convinced that contraception (of all things) was significantly to blame. Far from serving as a preventative to abortion, they argued, widespread contraceptive usage in the United States had created a distinctive cultural mentality—the so-called contraceptive mentality—that made frequent recourse to abortion almost an inevitability. With the contraceptive mentality, a Canadian conservative named Donald DeMarco wrote in 1982, "the separation of intercourse from procreation is taken for granted and the contracepting partners feel that in employing contraception, they have severed themselves from all responsibility for a conception that might take place as a result of contraceptive failure. . . . At any rate, the 'contraceptive mentality' implies that a couple has not only the means to separate intercourse from procreation, but the right or *responsibility* as well." [emphasis in original] Or, as Fr. Paul Marx, the most famous American proponent of the "contraceptive mentality" thesis, expressed it, once sexual pleasure is divorced from procreation, the "resolve to prevent a child from coming to be is often sufficiently strong that one will eliminate the child whose conception was not prevented."[5] As might be expected, the contraceptive-mentality thesis encountered considerable resistance within the wider pro-life movement. Many pro-life activists, including quite a few Catholics, were unconvinced of the causal connection it implied between contraception and abortion, and some of these activists practiced artificial birth control themselves. Others who found the thesis persuasive in varying degrees were opposed to its public transmission on the ground that an attack against contraception would almost certainly nullify whatever credibility the movement possessed. A public seemingly reluctant to consider biological evidence for the humanity of the fetus could hardly be expected to swallow an argument of such decidedly Catholic flavor. The NRLC, for its part, did everything possible to distance itself from the thesis, and in the process made a special point of declaring itself completely neutral on the subject of birth control.

In the view of Scheidler and his conservative colleagues, however, neutrality on birth control was tantamount to outright surrender. Contraception was nothing less than the cultural gateway to abortion, they insisted, and condemning one without the other was an exercise in sheer futility. It wasn't accidental, of course, that the contraceptive-mentality thesis found its most receptive audience among precisely those Catholic pro-lifers who were already deeply committed to the anti-contraceptive teaching of *Humanae Vitae*. Many of these Catholics had never felt at home with the NRLC in the first place, and the contretemps over contraception gave them the incentive to establish alternative pro-life organizations of their own.

The first of these, the American Life League (ALL), was founded in Stafford, Virginia, in 1979 by a married couple named Judie and Paul Brown. For several years in the mid-seventies, Judie Brown had been a high-ranking administrator with the NRLC, but she wound up resigning her position in protest over the organization's official neutrality on birth control. "I had a number of problems with the NRLC—some personal and some political," she informed me in a recent interview, "but my main objection was their position on contraception. Their entire stance has been a monumental lie. Ninety-nine percent of the time, contraception results in abortion. How could the NRLC claim to be dealing with abortion when they refused to deal with this basic reality?" Significantly, Mrs. Brown wasn't in the least pleased either with the NRLC's scrupulously secular approach to the abortion issue. "Even before I left the organization," she told me, "I believed their nondenominational and nonreligious emphasis to be totally ineffective. The practice of religion belongs in the public arena. It is so wrong to suppress this. We should be able to say that abortion is a sin against God and God's law. The NRLC wouldn't stand for this."[6]

With the American Life League, then, the Browns attempted to place pro-life activism in the United States on an entirely new footing. Not only was their organization unabashedly religious in orientation, but it was also fully committed to taking a public stand against artificial contraception. And on this score, the Browns would receive invaluable support from an organization called Human Life International (HLI). Founded in 1981 by Fr. Paul Marx, a Benedictine monk and onetime sociology professor at St. John University in Minnesota, HLI advertises itself as "a non-profit organization devoted to educating people about the evils of abortion, sterilization, infanticide, euthanasia, contraception and other modern threats to life and family." With an annual budget of almost five million dollars, HLI publishes eight periodicals, sponsors pro-life educational conferences and seminars on Natural Family Planning, and maintains twenty-one chapters in the United States and forty-nine worldwide. Moreover, in its promotional literature, HLI boasts that its attacks against "anti-family and anti-life" policies throughout the world have caused Planned Parenthood to label it "Public Enemy No. 1."[7]

Despite its involvement with issues as wide-ranging as euthanasia and infanticide, HLI's major area of concern over the past fifteen years or so has been contraception and the associated ills to which it has allegedly given rise. "Contraception," an HLI position paper asserts, "poses numerous medical dangers to women. It introduces an artificial barrier between husband and wife. Acceptance of contraception has led to widespread sexual promiscuity and an ever-increasing explosion of crippling and deadly venereal diseases, including AIDS. Contraception does not prevent abortion; rather, contraception always leads to abortion, and to increased abortion rates." To Fr. Marx, in fact, it is simply mind-boggling that contraception hasn't been universally condemned by pro-lifers in the United States. "When I first started Human Life International," he told me during an interview several years ago at his organization's headquarters in Gaithersburg, Maryland, "there was great confusion within the pro-life movement over birth control. The NRLC seemed almost wilfully blind to the fact that contraception always—and I mean always—causes abortion. They wouldn't take a stand against it then, and they still won't. It's ridiculous to think we can stop abortion without first doing something about the contraceptive mentality that produces it."[8]

Although Fr. Paul Marx and Judie Brown are probably the best known proponents of the contraceptive-mentality thesis, they were actually preceded on the scene by a Catholic convert and onetime California hippie named Theo Stearns. Theo Stearns was born in 1940 in Asheville, North Carolina, and was raised by her fairly prosperous Presbyterian grandparents in a household that, in her words, "oozed anti-Catholicism." After graduating from Converse College in Spartanburg, South Carolina, where she majored in drama, Stearns got married, had a child, and moved to Seattle. Three years later, divorced and the mother of two children, she drifted down the coast and eventually helped found an urban commune in the San Francisco Bay area. Stearns spent several years cruising with the counterculture, but in 1973, while pregnant with her fourth and final child, she underwent a radical conversion to Catholicism. "This was the year of the Roe decision, and I was having terrible medical complications with my pregnancy," she told me in a recent interview. "A lot of very well-meaning people wanted me to have an abortion. I didn't. I immersed myself in Catholic theology, and in December 1973, just four months after Ruth was born and one month after Roe, I converted to the Church. I cherished the authority of the Church by this point. Everybody knew where the Church stood on abortion, and I became convinced that only the Church had the authority to speak on these matters. With my conversion, there was an awareness that I'd entered an entirely new world, and there was something wonderful and also something very safe for me in this."

Within several months of Stearns's conversion, the other members of her commune also became Catholics, and in 1974 they formed a pro-life organization called Catholics United for Life. "Much like myself, the community of hippies I was living with became convinced that Roman Catholicism offered objective, incarnational truth," Stearns told me. "And coming into the Church and becoming pro-life activists was all part of a single dynamic for us. With abortion clinics springing up everywhere after Roe, it was clear to us that we were called to pro-life ministry." Right from the start, however, CUL's relationship with the broader pro-life movement proved extremely rocky. To the chagrin of the NRLC and other moderate organizations, Stearns and her colleagues insisted upon linking contraception and abortion, and also upon broadcasting the distinctively Catholic motivation of their activism. "There was tremendous opposition to us from the mainstream pro-life movement," Stearns said. "The NRLC hated our name, Catholics United for Life, because it would make it too easy for people to write off pro-lifers as Roman Catholic. And they hated us because we went to abortion clinics and prayed the rosary. We were convinced that there should be a highly visible Catholic component within the movement, and for this we were opposed by almost all other pro-life groups. But what really infuriated the NRLC the most was our public stance against contraception. This was something that pro-lifers, according to the official line, weren't supposed to discuss. But we broke the taboo and discussed it loudly. We wanted to promote the full Catholic position on life, from both a natural and supernatural point of view. And we were absolutely convinced that there was a connection between contraception and abortion. The funny thing is, I'd been opposed to contraception even before my conversion. I associated it with materialism and the mechanization of sex. Why be a hippie and go live in the woods if you're going to bring diaphragms and condoms? As far as we were concerned, there was something artificial and plastic about contraception. And for publicizing our feelings, we were shunned—absolutely shunned—by the NRLC."

Despite its outsider status, Catholics United for Life wound up exerting considerable influence upon the broader pro-life movement. In 1978 the group moved to an abandoned mine near Coarsegold, California, and began demonstrating at an abortion clinic in Fresno. After just several weeks, however, they put away their placards and bullhorns and started a ministry that has since become known within pro-life circles as sidewalk counseling. "In the simplest terms, sidewalk counseling means talking one-on-one to women considering abortion," Stearns told me. "We decided that loud, in-your-face protesting was just turning people off, and that conversing with women in a gentle yet firm manner was far more effective. Over the years, we've saved many babies by doing this, and we've tried to base it all upon the constitutional right to free speech. Our method of sidewalk counseling was eventually discovered by the broader movement, and it's now used by a lot of different groups."

In 1983 Stearns and her group moved from California to a 110-acre site in New Hope, Kentucky, just a mile down the road from the Abbey of Gethsemani, the Trappist monastery which once housed Thomas Merton. When I dropped by for a brief visit in the summer of 1995, the place had a charmingly ramshackle, not-quite-finished, never-likely-to-be-finished feel about it. Buildings in various stages of construction were strewn about the property, and most of the dozen or so adults I met looked like they'd be perfectly at home at a Grateful Dead concert. These were aging hippies, but aging hippies who also happened to be fully committed to *Humanae Vitae* and the papacy of John Paul II. Stearns herself, rounded and funky in appearance, took me on a tour of the community's new chapel, its various residences, and its impressive printing facility. (Since moving to Kentucky, the community has supported itself and its anti-abortion ministry by printing a wide assortment of conservative Catholic material, including E. Michael Jones's *Fidelity* Magazine.)

I asked Stearns whether the members of her community were still as passionate today about opposing contraception as they were twenty years ago. "We're certainly older now, and we don't get out to the clinics as much as we used to do, but our position on birth control hasn't changed a whit," she said. "If anything, we're more convinced than ever that *Humanae Vitae* offers a solution to so many of the problems that plague our culture. We haven't been able to sell this to the broader pro-life movement though, and people like Fr. Marx and Joe Scheidler and ourselves are usually viewed as a crazy minority. But we're not about to back down, and the good news is we've succeeded in transmitting the beauty of *Humanae Vitae* to our kids."9

THE HATCH IMBROGLIO

Contraception was by no means the only source of contention within pro-life ranks during the early eighties. In December 1981—and in keeping with its generally pragmatic and reformist tendencies—the NRLC decided to lend its official support to a proposed constitutional amendment sponsored by Senator Orrin Hatch of Utah. Although the so-called Hatch Amendment wouldn't have actually banned abortion, its passage would have permitted individual states to legislate restrictions. While certainly not a perfect solution, according to the NRLC, the Hatch Amendment at least offered realistic promise of reducing the nation's abortion rate. Moreover, it stood a far better chance of surviving the ratification process than a more radical measure proposed by Senator Jesse Helms, which called for explicit constitutional acknowledgment that human life begins at conception. For the moment anyway, the NRLC believed, the Hatch Amendment was probably the most pro-lifers could reasonably hope for.[10]

In the view of many conservative Catholic pro-lifers, however, the NRLC couldn't have been more wrong. Endorsing something such as the Hatch Amendment, they claimed, was equivocation and compromise of the worst kind—a sort of bargaining with the lives of unborn children. If fetal life was truly sacred, pro-lifers were compelled to protect it absolutely and without exception, not settle for halfway measures whereby abortion, at the discretion of state legislatures, would be permitted in some cases and disallowed in others. If there had previously been any doubt, the dissenters claimed, it was now perfectly clear that the NRLC was not prepared to take an unqualified stand on behalf of unborn life.

Not surprisingly, some of the most vociferous opposition to the Hatch Amendment (and the NRLC's endorsement of it) came from militant Catholic groups such as the American Life League and Human Life International. What the NRLC utterly failed to appreciate, claims ALL president Judie Brown, was that abortion is an issue that transcends ordinary political solution. "With the Hatch Amendment and with contraception, the NRLC was always too anxious to compromise. But abortion isn't like other issues where compromise might make sense. We're talking life and death here. In accepting compromise, they've forgotten the baby in the womb, and they've forgotten that only God can finally stop abortion. With compromises like the Hatch Amendment, we limit God— God's out of the picture. We have to take the high moral road and count on God's power for victory." Fr. Paul Marx, of HLI, is no less emphatic on the question of political compromise. "The Hatch Amendment was totally disastrous," he says, "and it was shameful—but almost to be expected—that the NRLC supported it. Even if it had passed, the best we could have hoped for is that some states would have prohibited most abortions but allowed abortion for the so-called hard cases—rape, incest, some fetal deformity, and so forth. But this is totally unacceptable. The NRLC dislikes me because of my emphasis on contraception, and also because I refuse to support any measure that would eliminate even 99 percent of abortions. I'm an absolutist—and Catholics such as myself say, No Killing."

Perhaps the most deeply upsetting aspect of the Hatch affair for activists such as Fr. Marx and Mrs. Brown was the performance of the American Catholic hierarchy. After considerable internal debate, the National Conference of Catholic Bishops decided in late 1981 to throw its support behind the Hatch Amendment instead of the more radical measure sponsored by Senator Jesse Helms. From the perspective of Catholic conservatives, this was conclusive proof that the bishops as a group were governed more by considerations of political expediency than by genuine compassion for fetal life. It was bad enough that the NRLC was prepared to settle for a compromise solution, claims Fr. Marx, but the decision of the bishops to do likewise was nothing short of a national disgrace. "Of course the bishops should have known better," he says. "We already knew they were weak on contraception, and with their support of Hatch they proved they were weak on abortion too. Their actions were a scandal to the entire American Church. At least now we realized what we were up against—it was up to ordinary Catholics to fight the good fight in spite of their religious leaders."

THE RISE OF STREET PROTEST

In the end, both the Hatch and Helms measures failed to pass for lack of congressional support, but the controversy surrounding them succeeded in heightening tensions between moderates and Catholic militants in the pro-life movement. And in the meantime, Joseph Scheidler was doing his part to heighten them even further. After being banished from Illinois Right to Life in 1975, Scheidler spent several years in relative obscurity, picketing abortion clinics and helping out at crisis-pregnancy centers in the Chicago area. Toward the close of the seventies, however, Scheidler decided that the time had arrived to turn up the volume on anti-abortion protest. Conventional tactics such as picketing and cajoling simply weren't getting the job done, in his view, and pro-lifers truly serious about stopping abortion were left little choice but to pursue a far more radical (and confrontational) approach.

In the winter of 1980, accordingly, Scheidler founded an organization called the Pro-Life Action League, which signaled the start of a new era in anti-abortion protest across America. Breaking sharply with the decidedly more prosaic routine of the NRLC, the Action League was dedicated (in the words of one of its promotional brochures) to "the aim of saving babies' lives through non-violent direct action," which was meant to include everything from "sidewalk counseling to picketing to rescue missions at abortion clinics."[11] Above all else, it was the "rescue" component of direct action that propelled the Action League to rapid public prominence, and by the early eighties the organization was staging demonstrations, and conducting civil disobedience, at abortion clinics throughout the midwest.

This, however, was only the beginning. While Scheidler's Pro-Life Action League was cranking up the heat in the Chicago area, a number of similarly inclined organizations were emerging elsewhere across the country. Probably the most important of these was the Prolife Nonviolent Action Project, which was founded in 1983 by a Maryland native and Harvard graduate named John Cavanaugh-O'Keefe. Born in 1950 and raised as the fifth of nine children in a close-knit Catholic family, Cavanaugh-O'Keefe came to anti-abortion activism along a rather curious path. After one of his older brothers was killed in Vietnam, during the Tet Offensive of 1968, Cavanaugh-O'Keefe underwent what he describes as "a radical conversion to pacifism," and for several years afterward he was deeply involved with student anti-war protest at Harvard and elsewhere. As the war in Vietnam drew to a close, however, Cavanaugh-O'Keefe found himself increasingly drawn to the abortion issue. "As a pacifist and a Catholic, the connection between war and abortion seemed self-evident," he told me during a recent interview at his home in rural Maryland. "I remember vividly, in 1971, when a friend with whom I was working in Boston told me about the abortion she had had a year before. She was hungry for approval. I knew talking to her that something was terribly wrong; her child was dead, and there was no way she could grieve. She was in denial. I thought here was Vietnam come home, and I knew that, just like my brother's death, this was a wrong for all eternity. In the summer of 1972 I spent some time in New Mexico on a spiritual retreat, and while there I experienced a kind of awakening. I knew then that fighting abortion was the work I was called to do; and I also knew that the work should begin."[12]

After several years of such work, however, Cavanaugh-O'Keefe became convinced that the mainstream pro-life movement was merely spinning its wheels. And one of the biggest problems, in his view, was the movement's strategic silence on contraception. "It was wrong-headed of the NRLC not to denounce birth control," he told me. "Contraception is to abortion what greed is to war. You can't stop warfare without examining its economic underpinnings, and, similarly, you can't fight abortion without examining and critiquing the way people have come to view their bodies and their sexuality. Fr. Paul Marx is absolutely correct on this point. Contraception results in abortion. This is the truth, and we're responsible for telling the truth, not begrudging it or hiding it. The pro-life movement seemed deficient to me for failing to come to grips with this."

By the early eighties, the pro-life movement had come to seem deficient to Cavanaugh-O'Keefe in another respect as well. In campaigning for an eventual curtailment of abortion, in his view, the movement was discounting (if only implicitly) the value of unborn life that was already being lost in the present.

"From where I stood, it was really very simple," he told me. "The unborn were being killed, and the NRLC and the bishops were serenely working toward some future solution to the issue. But if the unborn truly are our sisters and brothers—if they truly are human life—we should do everything possible to protect them now, in the present. We should be prepared even to die for them. Otherwise, what does it mean to say they're our brothers and sisters? It's just a lot of overheated rhetoric. In the early eighties, I came to realize that the pro-life movement was missing a radical activist dimension, and this is what Joe Scheidler and myself and some other people committed ourselves to. . . . I'm convinced that the abortion issue doesn't lend itself to legislative or political solutions. The only solution is massive civil disobedience and street protest. We have to save as many unborn children as possible; and if this is done with enough intensity and conviction, it can hopefully bring about a transformation in our culture. The only appropriate response to abortion is direct action, and this has always been the primary purpose of the Nonviolent Action Project."[13]

Another organization that became involved with direct action during this period was Prolifers for Survival. Based in Chapel Hill, North Carolina, PLS was founded in 1971 by a onetime union activist named Juli Loesch for the purpose of combining opposition to abortion with opposition to capital punishment and the nuclear arms race. For the first decade or so of its existence, PLS kept a relatively low profile, concentrating mainly on educational efforts, but during the early eighties, Juli Loesch grew convinced that far more drastic measures were required. In the face of a steadily increasing abortion rate across America, in her view, legislative and educational initiatives were painfully inadequate, and so too were such largely symbolic gestures as picketing and leafleting outside abortion clinics. The whole point of direct action, she claimed, was to disrupt the operation of clinics and possibly shut them down altogether. "Symbolic action is very limited. . . . The analogy is if you had a fire and you called the fire department and they came and they picketed the fire and started chanting, 'No more fire, no more fire.' That's protesting fire. So we don't do [direct action] to express our inner feelings. . . . We do it to stop abortions in that clinic on that day."[14]

This call for direct action on the part of Scheidler, Cavanaugh-O'Keefe, and Loesch engaged the imagination of many pro-life activists who were already deeply disturbed by the conciliatory approach of the NRLC. Most of these activists were (at least, initially) conservative Catholics, most subscribed wholeheartedly to the contraceptive-mentality thesis, and practically all were adamantly opposed to any compromise on abortion. They were, by and large, the militant purists of the pro-life movement, and by late 1984 thousands of them across the country had committed themselves to veritable careers of civil disobedience—blocking access to abortion clinics, staging sit-ins and demonstrations, and sometimes vandalizing clinic property. Indeed, for many conservative Catholic activists, participation in civil disobedience carried with it an undeniable moral cachet: it was a badge of pro-life heroism, and they were more than willing to suffer arrest and even imprisonment in the bargain.[15]

The National Right to Life Committee, for its part, looked upon this latest development with considerable alarm. If progress was to be made, its leaders insisted, it was essential that pro-lifers limit themselves to legal and institutionalized avenues of protest. Public defiance of the law through civil disobedience, they claimed, would almost certainly cost the pro-life movement popular support and would likely as well damage its relations with the American political establishment.[16] For the most part, however, militant Catholic pro-lifers were unimpressed with this line of reasoning. Where unborn life was at stake, in their view, patience and prudence were virtues almost entirely without value, and most of them were prepared to demonstrate their commitment to the anti-abortion cause regardless of expense to themselves personally or to the movement's public reputation.

The NRLC's appeal for calm took on heightened urgency in early 1986 in the wake of a dozen or so bombings at abortion clinics across the country. Movement radicals such as Cavanaugh-O'Keefe were quick to disavow any connection with these bombings (claiming that they were the responsibility of individuals not formally associated with any pro-life group), but refused to condemn as immoral any action, if merely destructive of private property, that was intended to save unborn life. And Joseph Scheidler, adopting an ironic tone, told the news media that he "personally disapproved" of what the bombers had done but was hardly in a position "to impose [his] own morality upon them."[17] In the view of the NRLC leadership, comments such as these cast the entire movement in a negative light and further jeopardized its chances for cultural respectability.

The conflict within pro-life ranks between radicals (or purists) on the one hand, and moderates (or pragmatists) on the other, reached a climax of sorts in May 1986, at the NLRC's national convention in Denver. According to the NRLC's incumbent president John Willke and his staff, the Denver convention was an ideal opportunity for the anti-abortion movement to put on its best, most respectable face—to present itself as a paragon of middle-class rectitude. In an open letter published in *National Right to Life News* two weeks prior to the convention, accordingly, Willke called on all pro-lifers to abstain from acts of civil disobedience while in Denver and to limit themselves instead to peaceful picketing. Any illegal or particularly unruly acts of protest, he warned, would only play into the hands of a national news media eager to vilify the movement as a clearinghouse for social misfits and religious fanatics. And, lest anyone still not grasp the point, Willke stipulated in a convention handout that the distribution of radical or politically subversive literature at the convention site was strictly prohibited.[18] Not in the least deterred by such warnings, radical activists from around the country descended upon the convention site and immediately set up literature booths and began broadcasting plans for "rescues" (or campaigns of civil disobedience) that they intended to carry out at Denver abortion clinics. After about a day and a half of this, the NLRC leadership stepped in and had the radicals forcibly evicted from the site. Among those thrown out were Cavanaugh-O'Keefe and several other members of his Prolife Nonviolent Action Project, representatives from Human Life International and Prolifers for Survival, and about a dozen activists apiece from the St. Louis–based Pro-Life Direct Action League and Scheidler's Pro-Life Action League. If there had previously been any doubt, this episode made vividly clear just how deeply anti-abortionists were divided by the mid-eighties over questions of strategy, ideology, and—perhaps most important of all—spirituality.

The Evangelical Connection

By the mid-eighties, as well, Catholic militants were receiving, courtesy of evangelical Protestantism, a great deal of unexpected company on the direct-action front. Evangelicals (and conservative Protestants more generally) first began entering the anti-abortion movement in significant numbers during the late seventies, but for several years they limited themselves almost entirely to such relatively noncontroversial activities as operating crisis-pregnancy centers and organizing pro-life educational campaigns. During the early to mid-eighties, however, a growing number of them elected to join Catholic militants in street protest against abortion, and in the process one of the most unlikely (and abidingly controversial) ecumenical alliances on the American religious scene was brought into being. While demonstrating outside abortion clinics together, militant Catholics and evangelicals frequently discovered—sometimes to their mutual astonishment—that they inhabited strikingly similar worlds. Both regarded liberalized abortion as a sordid triumph of secular humanism, and both defined pro-life activism as primarily a religious (rather than a political) undertaking. Moreover, evangelicals were generally delighted to learn that most Catholic activists shared their commitment to traditional biblical teaching as well as their disdain for theological modernism. Although evangelicals sometimes cringed at the ardent Marian piety and anti-contraceptive views of their Catholic colleagues, they were willing to tolerate certain excesses when so much else seemed right. Militant Catholic activists, for their part, were greatly impressed both by the moral zeal of evangelicals and by the strength and apparent sincerity of their religious convictions.

During the latter stages of the eighties, in fact, conservative Protestants sometimes took a leading role themselves in establishing additional "direct action" organizations. The most influential of these by far turned out to be Operation Rescue, which was founded in 1986 by a Pentecostal minister named Randall Terry. Terry first got the idea for Operation Rescue in 1985 when he read *Closed: 99 Ways to Stop Abortion*, a newly published book by the ubiquitous Joseph Scheidler, and within just a few years he managed to maneuver his organization onto the very forefront of the direct-action scene. Indeed, by the late eighties Operation Rescue's protests had become celebrity media events, with conservative Catholics and evangelicals arriving by the busload in cities as various as Wichita and Buffalo for the purpose of shutting down, if only for a day or two, local abortion clinics.[19]

†HE AMERICAN CA†HOLIC BISHOPS

While conservative Protestants were solidifying their commitment to the anti-abortion cause, the American Catholic bishops seemed in the process of reappraising theirs. For the first decade or so following the Roe ruling, the bishops were more outspoken on abortion, and more actively engaged in fighting it, than the Catholic leadership of virtually any country in the Western world.[20] In addition to denouncing Roe in the media and testifying against it in Congress, they contributed their own specialized structures to the pro-life movement, including the National Committee for a Human Life Amendment, and throughout the seventies they lent moral, logistical, and (more rarely) financial support to the National Right to Life Committee.[21] By the early eighties, however, this close connection between movement and hierarchy was starting to show signs of strain. While some bishops remained staunchly loyal to the anti-abortion movement, others (I'll refer to them as the liberal camp) were looking to channel their energies in somewhat different directions. Many liberal bishops were disturbed by the right-wing alliance that the NRLC had fashioned with the Republican Party of then President Ronald Reagan; and some worried as well that the confrontational tactics employed by pro-life radicals might escalate into full-blown violence. Moreover, liberal bishops were concerned that the church had placed so great an emphasis on abortion since the Roe decision that it had neglected other issues of equal pastoral importance.

The leader, by all accounts, of the liberal camp was Cardinal Joseph Bernardin of Chicago. In 1983, during a speech at Fordham University in New York City, Bernardin unveiled what he called the "seamless garment" or "consistent ethic" approach to Catholic social action. It wasn't enough, he claimed, for Catholics to fight abortion without also fighting for a better economic deal for women and their children. And it was perilously shortsighted, he also claimed, to condemn abortion without also condemning militarism, racism, sexism, and poverty. All of these issues were interrelated, they all had bearing upon the "sanctity of life," and *together* they constituted a proper focus for Catholic social engagement.[22]

The seamless-garment ethic didn't wear at all well within most radical quarters of the pro-life movement. To many activists, it seemed that the cardinal was merely beating a strategic retreat from the anti-abortion position. To treat abortion as the moral equivalent of poverty or health care, in their view, was to dilute its significance. Moreover, they claimed, the seamless-garment or consistent-ethic approach gave Catholic politicians in the United States a convenient excuse to disregard abortion and focus instead on trendier concerns such as unemployment and economic justice.

As the seamless-garment ethic became increasingly popular within episcopal ranks during the late eighties and early nineties, many Catholic pro-lifers became increasingly convinced that the bishops as a group weren't seriously committed to stopping abortion. In June of 1993, for example, I met in Milwaukee with a prominent Catholic activist named Monica Migliorino Miller, just two weeks before she was scheduled to begin serving a nine-month jail sentence for acts of civil disobedience she had carried out in 1989. In her late thirties, an adjunct professor of theology at Marquette University, and the mother of two small children, Migliorino Miller has spent the past fifteen years battling abortion clinics in the midwest—and sometimes, in the process, her own bishops as well. "I love my Church, and I'm very hesitant to criticize it," she told me, "but the bishops simply haven't been doing their job. Four thousand human beings in the United States are butchered daily under the law, and the response of the American Catholic leadership has been weak-kneed and ineffectual and cowardly. Our bishop here in Milwaukee, Rembert Weakland, is a prime case in point. He talks about the seamless garment, but this just gives everyone, including himself, an easy out on abortion. I came to Milwaukee in 1985, after eight years of activism in Chicago, and I quickly asserted myself as a pro-life leader and organized the first rescue to take place here. And immediately my relationship with Weakland was full of tension and conflict. I'm convinced he hates pro-lifers, especially pro-lifers who are out protesting at the clinics. And this is the case with so many bishops today. The seamless-garment ethic has submerged and weakened the abortion issue. In the 1992 elections, the bishops were virtually silent on Bill Clinton's pro-abortion record. The bishops refuse to condemn the United States as a society of death; they've allowed the Gospel to be judged by secularism."[23]

Mary Anne Hackett and Richard O'Connor, both executive officers of Illinois Right to Life, couldn't agree more. "The seamless-garment ethic has done tremendous damage to the abortion issue," they informed me during a recent interview at their office in downtown Chicago. "It's allowed Catholic politicians to declare themselves pro-life for being against poverty and capital punishment, or whatever. And it's given most of our bishops something to hide behind while nothing is done about abortion."[24] Mary Anne Hackett has decided not to suffer such grievances in silence. In early February of 1993 she and five other Chicago-based activists formed an ad hoc group called the Committee of Pro-Life Catholics, and on February 17 they wrote their local bishop, Cardinal Bernardin himself, to complain about "the failure of the Church to respond to the defining moral issue of our time." Since 1973 and the Roe decision, they told the cardinal, "we [have] waited as the Bishops squandered years writing pastorals on peace, the economy, and women, but [have] heard no voice raised for the defenseless unborn." And at the parish level, they went on, "homilies on abortion are rare or non-existent. Many, if not most, parishioners have never heard one word on abortion from the pulpit in 20 years of legal abortion. Pro-lifers who have tried to educate the Catholic population . . . are driven away by the pastors, even vilified from the pulpit and in person and threatened with arrest."

In a personal letter of response dated March 4, Cardinal Bernardin defended his own position on abortion and reprimanded Mrs. Hackett and her committee for resorting to "divisive tactics [that] only serve to damage the credibility and effectiveness of all who represent the Pro-Life movement." In a rejoinder dated March 26, Mrs. Hackett and a colleague named Bonnie Quirke told the cardinal, "a more appropriate response from you would [have been] to tell us why daily prayer for the unborn and the end of abortion is such a radical suggestion that it cannot be implemented. . . . When we asked for bread, you gave us a stone." And Cardinal Bernardin, on May 12, replied once again that "I am saddened that at a critical time in the pro-life movement, when so much needs to be done to build unity among pro-lifers and increase credibility for our cause, you have chosen to focus your time and efforts on attacking me and the priests of the Archdiocese."[25]

This correspondence (and I've only quoted fragments of it here) conveys something of the contempt with which many (and especially radical) Catholic pro-lifers have come to regard their bishops over the past decade or so. Indeed, there are relatively few bishops today who command genuine respect from the anti-abortion movement as a whole. One of them is Austin Vaughan, Auxiliary Bishop of New York, who has actually been arrested for publicly protesting abortion. Another is Bishop René H. Gracida of Corpus Christi, Texas, who has gone so far as to excommunicate Catholic directors of abortion clinics. And perhaps most important of all, there is Cardinal John O'Connor, Archbishop of New York, who has won national notoriety for his public feuds with—among others—former New York Governor Mario Cuomo. Cuomo's position (and that of many other Catholic politicians as well) boils down to the proposition that in a pluralistic democracy such as the United States, one cannot enshrine the religious values of any particular group or groups into public law. And Cardinal O'Connor's position, which he has articulated time and again over the past several years, is that Catholic politicians behave neither as good Catholics nor as good politicians when they relegate their church's teaching on abortion to the domain of merely private moral preference.[26]

Anti-Abortion Protest and Conservative Catholic Identity

Throughout the 1980s and early nineties, then, anti-abortion protest in the United States assumed a progressively more militant (and desperate) tone. Religious passions that had previously been shielded—though never quite entirely—from public view were given full play, and efforts at persuasion were increasingly set aside for open confrontation. And nowhere at present is such passion and confrontation more clearly evident than on the doorsteps of abortion clinics across the country.[27]

As part of their ongoing campaign of public protest, radical Catholic activists (and quite a few Protestants as well) regularly participate today in what they often refer to as "public witness." Depending on the occasion, public witness may range from peaceful picketing outside abortion clinics to flagrant acts of civil disobedience; but in almost every case, it conveys an unmistakably religious flavor. Many Catholic activists pray the rosary almost incessantly, some carry statues or other devotional artifacts, and Catholics and Protestants alike join in chanting hymns and reciting scripture. To the outside observer, in fact, it sometimes seems that public witness is governed more by an expressive than an instrumental logic. When praying the rosary or singing Marian hymns on the picket line, activists seem primarily concerned with expressing their religious convictions and solidarity, sometimes without reference to anticipated results. Public witness, in other words, is arguably important as much for its spiritual gratifications and symbolic meaning as for its possible political effectiveness.[28]

Moderates within the pro-life movement continue to be deeply troubled by public witness. In their view, the dramatic and overtly religious activities with which it is chiefly associated have succeeded only in reaping for the larger movement public scorn and political impotency. With this in mind I recently asked a number of radical Catholic activists if they themselves had considered the possibility that public witness—and especially the intensive Marian piety that seems so central to it—might actually be damaging to the anti-abortion cause.[29]

John Cavanaugh-O'Keefe summed up the sentiments of most of those with whom I spoke on this topic when he described public witness as a spiritual calling that transcended any ordinary calculus of success or failure. "It's true that our public protests are potentially disastrous in terms of public image," he told me. "All of us have a very strong Marian piety which we bring to the streets with us, and of course this allows the enemy to label us as fanatical Catholics. But we can't worry about that. We're called to witness to the truth, and our Marian piety is the truth and the source of our strength. Mary's role in creation is immense, and she is a feminist model for today. After all, Mary said Yes at the Annunciation."

Julie and Steve McCreevy are a thirtyish couple who have been involved with public witness since the late eighties. At least twice a week they carry a life-sized, gold-framed image of Our Lady of Guadalupe to the picket line outside a busy abortion clinic in downtown Chicago. And like Cavanaugh-O'Keefe, they define anti-abortionism in manifestly supernatural terms. "For the first decade after Roe," Julie McCreevy told me in an interview several years ago, "pro-lifers attempted a strategy based on scientific evidence. They didn't realize the dimension of evil involved—that abortion couldn't be eradicated by appealing to people's good nature. This thing is straight out of hell, and you can't combat it without supernatural agency." I asked Steve McCreevy if he and his wife ever questioned the political value of their expressly religious style of protest. "Occasionally we do," he said, "but we believe that only God, through the intercession of Mary, can melt hearts and change people's minds on this issue. If we were to throw out our rosaries and statues, then we'd be playing by Satan's rules. We'd be throwing away our strength. This is exactly what our enemies would love us to do. Plus we suffer enormous abuse and ridicule at the abor, uary—the blasphemy against our faith is horrible—and we need Mary to sustain us through this. . . . What we are involved with here is a sacred crusade."[30]

Monica Migliorino Miller weighed in with almost exactly the same sentiments. "Ultimately abortion is a spiritual war, not a political one," she told me. "We're fighting an ethic, an entire philosophy of life, which places choice and convenience above the sacredness of created life. Our prayers and our rosaries are repugnant to the news media and repugnant to the secular world in general, but for us they're absolutely central. Through them we announce our belief in the sovereignty of creation, and we also announce that abortionists are blaspheming against God. And there's no question that we're also announcing who we are as Catholics. The media and the entire pro-choice establishment never tire of heaping invective upon Catholic pro-lifers. They hate Catholics and they hate everything we stand for. And there's absolutely no way we can allow ourselves to retreat in the face of this."

In June 1993 I met with Joseph Scheidler at the Pro-Life Action League's headquarters in Chicago. At the time of my visit, the League's offices were even more frantic than usual, as Scheidler and his wife Anne (who serves on the organization's executive board) were busy plotting legal strategies for an impending court battle. (Over the past several years the Action League and several other "direct action" organizations have been sued by pro-choice groups under the provisions of the federal RICO [Racketeer Influenced and Corrupt Organizations] law, and it remains to be seen how such litigation will affect the ongoing abortion wars.[31]) Scheidler himself was still recovering from recent cancer surgery, and his haggard, deeply lined face and impressive physical stature gave him a sort of end-of-the-line prophetic appearance.

When I asked him about the explicitly religious demeanor of most street protest against abortion, Scheidler was characteristically frank. "It's true that we put our religion on the line out there, and this might not be the best thing to do in terms of strategy," he said. "But pro-life activism is God's work, and our religion is the only thing that keeps us afloat on a day-to-day basis. Not many atheists become street activists, and even fewer stick with it. As for our Marian piety, look at it this way. Mary is our Patron. She had a crisis pregnancy and did everything possible to have her baby. Mary is the spiritual mother of all children, born and unborn, and we believe that she will sustain us in our work, regardless of the difficulties we face."[32]

One of the biggest difficulties currently facing the rescue movement is the specter of violence. In the early nineties several abortion clinic employees in Florida and Massachusetts were murdered by anti-abortion zealots, and the possibility of additional violence in the future should not be discounted.[33] Although the individuals responsible for these murders were freelancers without connection to any established pro-life organization, the reputation of virtually the entire rescue or direct-action movement has been severely tarnished as a result. Like every other Catholic activist I interviewed, Scheidler is personally committed to a strategy of nonviolence, but he professes to understand why someone might be driven to acts of terrorism against abortion clinics. "I think any violence is counterproductive, and I've tried desperately to close clinics peacefully," he told me. "The killing of abortionists in the name of life undermines all of our efforts, and I'll continue to repudiate such killings. But this doesn't mean that I'm a radical pacifist in the same way as someone like Cavanaugh-O'Keefe. I abhor murder, but I admit to holding some sympathy for some of the people who have bombed clinics in the knowledge no one would be hurt. At least this way the clinics are closed, and when they're closed they're not killing human life. Around the country there are about twelve convicted clinic bombers, and I'm on friendly terms with most of them and even correspond with some of them. I don't condone their actions—I even preach against them—but I can understand the frustration and anger that brought them to the brink."

Scheidler appears to have chosen a somewhat different outlet for his own frustration and anger. For the past decade or so, the Action League has operated a hot line that its supporters may call for the latest news on the abortion front. Several years ago I dialed the line and was treated to a two-minute taped harangue by Scheidler, the gist of which went something as follows: "Recent studies have shown that half of all American women have had premarital sexual intercourse, and that two-thirds have had intercourse outside of marriage. What does this tell us? Most of all, it tells us that two-thirds of American women are fornicating sluts." During my interview with him in Chicago, I asked Scheidler about this message (and several others of similar tenor that I happened also to listen in on over subsequent months). What purpose could such vituperation possibly serve? "I don't deny that I called women who have sex outside of marriage fornicating sluts," he said. "I still hold to this. What else are they if not sluts? I believe in calling a spade a spade. My people are sick of living in a world which has made good bad and bad good. They need a catharsis. They call my message and hear me calling sexually promiscuous women sluts, and they say: Damn it—someone is telling the truth."

Outright nastiness of this sort (which many Catholic activists themselves find disconcerting) might very well serve a cathartic function, but it hardly seems conducive to winning the Action League increased popular support. And increased support is something that the League and other direct-action organizations could sorely use. In addition to getting hammered in the media in the wake of the recent violence in Florida and Massachusetts, Catholic direct-actionists are currently having a difficult time simply paying the bills. Contrary to popular perception, they receive virtually no financial backing from the institutional church, and their day-to-day operations are financed almost entirely through private donations. "The Action League's probably better off than any other Catholic rescue organization, but we're still in pretty tough shape," Scheidler told me. "We're lucky to bring in $300,000 per year through mail solicitation—we've learned a great deal about this from the evangelicals—and the recent lawsuits have really drained our resources. We have twelve thousand supporters on our mailing list, and anywhere from six thousand to eight thousand people actually send us money. We survive off these individual donations. What many people don't realize is we don't receive a pittance from the Church. Individual priests and nuns will sporadically send donations, but rarely more than $100. If anything, most of the bishops have seemed anxious to distance themselves from us and our struggle."

Scheidler and other Catholic activists of his ilk would be perfectly willing to carry on the struggle, however, even if they were disowned altogether by the leadership of the American church. "When we're on the street, praying our rosaries and singing and getting arrested," Scheidler told me, "we're fighting abortion and we're also making a powerful religious statement. Most Catholics and even most bishops might have sold out, but there are still some of us who are fully prepared to pay the price for our religious convictions. If Catholics can't take a stand on the sanctity of life, we might as well just close up all the churches and send everybody home. This is where we draw the line. Those of us who are out on the street are believing Catholics, and I'm convinced most of us would actually sacrifice our lives for the cause. I've been arrested about twelve times, and if the situation arose I'd pray for the strength to die for my faith. . . . We are the Church Militant, not the Church Waiting Around or the Church Depressed."

Militant Catholic pro-lifers such as Joseph Scheidler may be regarded, in fact, as the activist wing of conservative Catholicism in the United States. Like James Hitchcock and E. Michael Jones and *The Wanderer*, they believe that the American church has been reduced since the Second Vatican Council to a mere shadow of its former self. As Catholicism in the United States has become progressively more attuned to the secular chorus of modern life, it has seemed to them at great risk of losing its transcendent purpose and salvific reach. For the great majority of American Catholics, in their view, the eternal truths of faith have become not much more than an afterthought, an occasional diversion; and the sort of intensive religious commitment that in previous ages inspired conversion, and sometimes even martyrdom, has been all but lost.[34]

In the view of such Catholics, there is only one place where exemplary religious commitment might still be demonstrated. And this is on the doorsteps of abortion clinics: protesting, praying, and engaging in public witness. Public witness, viewed in this light, may be understood as a protest against both abortion and the moral softness of mainstream Catholicism in the United States. At a time when virtually all other criteria of Catholic belonging have been cast into doubt, public witness affords the stalwart faithful an opportunity to testify to the enduring vitality of otherworldly faith. As Mary Anne Hackett of Illinois Right to Life told me: "Fighting abortion is the new arena of faith. . . . It's our responsibility to witness to the truth on contraception and abortion, regardless of public abuse and abuse from our own religious leaders. It's up to us to keep genuine faith alive, and, hopefully, to rejuvenate the American Church. We've been called to this struggle, and we won't back down."

Indeed, it seems highly unlikely that militant Catholic pro-lifers will in fact back down anytime soon. Unlike more moderate factions within the pro-life movement, they are implacably opposed to any compromise on abortion, and any attempt on the part of either the legal authorities or the Catholic bishops to curtail their street activism will almost certainly meet with failure. The fetus, for Catholic militants, is a reflection of transcendence, an unassailable symbol of divinity; and activism on its behalf is a vocational enterprise of the highest order. Through such activism, they aspire toward precisely the sort of religious virtuosity that most of them find almost entirely lacking in the post-conciliar American church.

CATHOLIC SEPARATISTS

CHAPTER FOUR

IT WAS ALMOST MIDNIGHT at the Holy Family Monastery in Berlin, New Jersey, but Fr. Nicholas Gruner was just hitting his stride. Slight and bespectacled, with just a hint of a paunch under his ankle-length soutane, Gruner stood on a makeshift stage in the monastery's main hall and addressed his audience in a lisping monotone.

It was both his right and his responsibility to challenge the pope and the Vatican, Gruner said. No less an authority than the eminent sixteenth-century theologian St. Robert Bellarmine taught that Catholics were entitled to use force against a pope or anyone else who threatened their faith. And the current pope, Gruner argued, by virtue of his repeated infidelity to the Virgin Mary and her Fatima messages, has put the faith of countless millions at grave risk. Indeed, Gruner continued, the Third Secret of Fatima warned that the Vatican would be overrun by communists, and this, in fact, is exactly the situation that exists today.

Several people in the audience gasped at this revelation, and about a dozen others nodded knowingly. But Gruner still had more conspiracy left to spin.

It wasn't surprising, he said, that the current pope was suppressing the Third Secret of Fatima and its warnings of a communist takeover of the Church. More than thirty years ago, Pope John XXIII signed a blasphemous accord with Moscow, and ever since then the Vatican has been strictly prohibited from speaking out against atheistic communism. Moreover, the Vatican-Moscow accord has been a critical factor behind John Paul II's failure to fulfill the Virgin Mary's most important request. During her miraculous appearances at Fatima seventy-five years ago, Gruner said, the Virgin promised that a great reign of peace would be given the world if the Holy Father, in synchrony with every single bishop of the Church, publicly consecrated Russia to her Immaculate Heart. Regardless of what powerful deceivers within the Church have tried to claim, Gruner said, this consecration has yet to take place according to the exact formula requested by the Virgin, and if it doesn't take place soon, the entire world faces a terrible, unthinkable chastisement. What's more, Gruner went on, St. John Bosco once prophesied that the day would come when the entire Church would be overcome with heresy, and also that a great cataclysm would strike the world during a month that has two moons. And March 1999 has two moons!

At this point, about twenty-five people in the audience gasped audibly, and four or five stood up and left the hall. Gruner decided to finish with a flourish.

Don't be fooled! he said. Communism still exists in Russia and elsewhere. A leopard doesn't simply change its spots overnight. Communism is alive and well, and more insidious than ever. And remember, Catholics have the right and obligation to defend their faith—with force if necessary. The faith is being undermined from within today—this is what the Third Secret of Fatima is all about—and loyal Catholics must rise to the occasion. Remember also that Jesus once told Peter, "Get behind me, Satan!" This tells Catholics that they should be loyal to the pope only as long as the pope is loyal to God and Mary.

Fr. Gruner stepped down from the stage to resounding applause, and within seconds he was engulfed by dozens of people looking for further news on the approaching chastisement. I slipped out of the main hall into a vestibule and introduced myself to a sixtyish woman named Mary who was standing behind a table stacked with back issues of Gruner's quarterly magazine, *The Fatima Crusader*. Mary had worked closely with Gruner for several years at his headquarters in Fort Erie, Ontario, and she was obviously star-struck.

"Did you know," she said, "that when Fr. Gruner was born his grandfather told the family that Fr. Gruner would be a prophet? And by saying this, the grandfather has also been proven to be a prophet."

I steered the conversation to the subject of E. Michael Jones, who has published several scathing articles about Gruner and his Fatima ministry in *Fidelity*.

"Fr. Gruner has filed suit against E. Michael Jones and his scummy magazine for defamation of character," Mary told me. "Jones is a worm. And he's one of them."

"One of them?"

"He's a Jew-boy."

"Jones?"

"Well, you know how they change their names. He's a Marrano."

———————

THE HOLY FAMILY MONASTERY, a rambling brick complex located on about ten acres of land in southeastern New Jersey, was built in the late sixties by a breakaway Benedictine monk named Brother Joseph Natale. For the past several years the monastery has hosted a three-day conference in early May on matters of interest to what may broadly be described as the extreme Catholic right. In addition to Fr. Gruner, the May 1994 conference featured as guest speakers Prince Henri de Bourbon-Parmé, who claims to be a direct descendent of Louis XIV and Philip V; Gary Potter, a longtime contributor to such right-wing Catholic publications as *The Remnant* and *Triumph* Magazine; Suzanne Rini, a journalist who has written extensively on fetal experimentation; and David Allen White, a professor of literature at the Annapolis Naval Academy and author of a book on the right-wing Brazilian prelate Antonio de Castro Mayer.

Altogether, about three hundred adults were in attendance at the 1994 conference, and almost as many children and teenagers. Some people had driven to New Jersey from as far as away as Cleveland and Chicago, and the monastery's parking lot was jam-packed with campers and trailers. For the most part, conference attendees were white and of working- or lower-middle-class social standing. Roughly one-third of the adults were over sixty years of age, and a sizable contingent looked to be in their mid- to late twenties. Over all, they were a scrubbed-down and clean-cut crew, and could easily have passed as participants in a 1950s church picnic.

The morning after Gruner's talk, I checked into a lecture by a certain Brother John, who was one of the monastery's resident monks. In his mid-thirties, brown-robed, and balding, Brother John had a long angular face with bulging eyes that seemed to grow larger for emphasis as he spoke.

Brother John's topic was the French Revolution, which he denounced (eye-bulgingly) as the most heinous event of the past three hundred years. It was the Freemasons, he said, in their quest for world domination, who plotted the Revolution of 1789, and nothing has ever been quite the same since. The Revolution dismantled the sacred order of Christendom, it forced the Church to its knees, and it paved the way for such modern-day scourges as liberalism, secularism, and homosexuality.

By Fr. Gruner's standards, this was pretty tame stuff, and the crowd began fidgeting. A middle-aged monk sitting across from me started to snore. Brother John picked up his pace.

The shame of it all, he said, is that the French Revolution could have been prevented. If the French monarchy had consecrated their country to the Sacred Heart of Jesus, they would have been spared the Revolution, and Christendom would have been preserved. Now it's up to us, he said, to dedicate ourselves to the Sacred Heart and build a new Christendom—a new Catholic kingdom. This can be done! We can defeat the evil surrounding us, but only through the Sacred Heart of Jesus. The Sacred Heart is the preeminent devotion of our time: it is our hope and our salvation.

Brother John's closing shots won generous applause, but Fr. Gruner sat at the back of the hall with several of his supporters, arms folded and grumbling. After several minutes I approached a blond-haired man named Tom, who was part of Gruner's retinue, and asked what he thought of Brother John's lecture. "It was pretty naive, don't you think?" he said. "Sure, the Sacred Heart devotion is important, but the only thing that can save us now is the secret Fatima messages. Shouldn't he know that by now?"

Breaking away from Tom, I managed to track down Brother John in a nearby hallway, and I asked for his assessment of conservative Catholics such as James Hitchcock and E. Michael Jones. "As far as I'm concerned, all of those people are completely off base," he said. "They're guilty of papolatry, a false worship of the pope. They have this ridiculous reverence for John Paul II, and they've been waiting for him to save the Church. If John Paul II really is a legitimate pope, he's also an unbelievably weak one. He's been contaminated by secularism and Freemasonry. And the *Wanderer* crowd doesn't think we should be criticizing him!"

LATER THE SAME DAY, after sitting through several more lectures, I had dinner at a local diner with a burly, baby-faced man in his late thirties whom I'll call Mark. Mark (who has asked that I conceal his real identity) is married, with four children, and works as a sales representative for a medium-sized firm in the midwest. For the past ten years or so, he's been a leading proponent of one of the Catholic right's most intriguing conspiracy theories.

"I was raised in a very devout Catholic home," Mark told me, "but after the Second Vatican Council I became very confused and very disturbed. As I saw it, the council had brought a completely new religion into being. The new post–Vatican II church—with its liberal theologies, its ecumenism, its secular liturgies, and its ethical pluralism—wasn't the Catholic Church any longer. It was a new and heretical creation. After graduating from college, I started attending a traditionalist Catholic chapel that had been founded by Fr. Francis Fenton of ORCM [the Orthodox Roman Catholic Movement].[1] I met my wife at the chapel, and by 1974 I was attending the Tridentine Mass exclusively. And in the meantime, I was trying desperately to figure out what had gone wrong. How did it happen that Pope Paul VI signed the council's document on religious liberty, which directly contradicted Pope Pius IX's Syllabus of Errors?[2] And how did it happen that Paul VI tossed out the Tridentine Mass and replaced it with a Mass that was obviously blasphemous? I wound up coming to the conclusion that Paul VI and John XXIII, who had called the council in the first place, weren't true popes. They were anti-popes, agents of destruction, who had been planted in the Vatican. But this was still only part of the puzzle. In 1988 I came in contact with a traditionalist Catholic named Gary Giuffre, and he told me he had some evidence that the real pope was a man named Cardinal Joseph Siri, and that Cardinal Siri was being held prisoner in a monastery in Rome. And ever since then, Giuffre and myself and a number of other people have been piecing together more and more of the puzzle. At this point in time, we believe we have a sustainable theory as to what has gone wrong with the Church."

The Cardinal Siri-as-real-pope-in-exile theory, which Mark laid out for me in breathless detail, runs something as follows:

After the death of Pope Pius XII in 1958, one of the leading contenders for the papal crown was Giuseppe Siri, a stiff-necked conservative from Genoa. Indeed, when white smoke began billowing out of the papal conclave at the Vatican on October 26, 1958, many people assumed that Siri had won the job. The white smoke was the traditional signal that the College of Cardinals had elected a new pope, and the Swiss Guards were dispatched to the conclave to greet him. But then something went wrong. After half an hour or so, the white smoke turned black, and the Swiss Guards were sent back to their quarters. The priest who had been announcing on Vatican Radio that a new pope was elected telephoned into the conclave and was told that the white smoke had been a mistake. Two days later, on October 28, Angelo Roncalli (John XXIII) was proclaimed pope, despite heavy rumors that he had been inducted into the Freemasons while serving as apostolic delegate to Turkey and Greece in 1934. When Roncalli himself then died, on June 3, 1963, another conclave was convoked, and the scenario that unfolded was eerily familiar. Once again Cardinal Siri opened as a strong favorite, once again white smoke emerged from the conclave only to turn black, and once again Siri was left out in the cold as Giovanni Battista Montini (Paul VI) was proclaimed pope.

It's at this point that the "Siri theory" really heats up. The white smoke that originally appeared at both the 1958 and 1963 conclaves, Mark told me, wasn't a mistake. In both cases the smoke signaled the election of a new pope, and in both cases the new pope was Cardinal Siri. But in both cases as well, Siri was forced to relinquish the papacy when secret messages that were somehow smuggled into the conclave warned that the Vatican would suffer some horrible punishment (possibly even nuclear bombardment) unless someone else was made pope. At the 1963 conclave, according to the testimony of a certain Paul Scortesco, who was professedly a cousin of one of the Swiss Guards charged with guarding the proceedings, the secret warnings were delivered by means of a dumbwaiter and handed directly to Siri upon his election. Moreover, the organization that Scortesco claimed was responsible for these warnings was B'nai B'rith, which was operating on behalf of a worldwide Judeo-Masonic conspiracy in an effort to dismantle traditional Catholicism. The Judeo-Masonic conspirators were determined to install their own agents on the papal throne, and Roncalli and Montini were precisely the men they wanted. Cardinal Siri, for his part, was sent to live in exile at a monastery in Rome after the 1963 conclave, where he remained incommunicado until his death in 1989. But not entirely incommunicado. Over the years, a number of people reported meeting secretly with Siri and asking about the true story behind the conclaves. His response was almost always the same: "I cannot speak with you about it. I am bound by the secret." Finally, during a private meeting with a Vietnamese priest named Father Khoat in 1988, Siri apparently broke down and admitted that he was in fact the true pope. When Khoat offered to take him away from the monastery to America, however, Siri refused, saying "I cannot leave here with you; they can kill me at any time."[3]

As mind-numbingly bizarre as the Siri theory might sound to the outsider, it offers Catholics like Mark a closed circle of explanation for the enormous changes that have taken place within the church over the past thirty-five years. The Second Vatican Council, the vernacular liturgy, the ecumenical movement, the new theology: all of this has come to pass under the watch of false popes bent on destroying the church while the real pope has been kept in exile. Moreover, conspiracy theories of this sort (and there are currently about half a dozen different ones making the rounds of the Catholic right) give their votaries the deep satisfaction of having the inside scoop, the real behind-the-scenes story, while the rest of the world grasps at appearances. James Hitchcock and E. Michael Jones and the *Wanderer* crowd might think they know what's going on with the church, but we happen to know otherwise. Whereas others, out of fear or misplaced piety, seem content merely with scratching the surface, we get bravely to the bottom of events for their true meanings and hidden purposes.

The conspiracy culture of the extreme Catholic right seems governed, in fact, by a perverse economy of scale: the more outlandish or fantastic the theory, the more it defies common sense, the greater the prestige it seems to carry. (While the entire world assumes that communism has fallen on hard times, in reality it has never been stronger. And while almost everyone under the sun looks upon John XXIII and Paul VI as authentic popes, nothing could be further from the truth.) All of this, of course, is partly an exercise in titillation, and the conspiracy-spinning of people like Mark and Fr. Gruner sometimes seems like a parlor game for severely disaffected Catholics, a sort of intellectual recreation for the religiously forlorn. When standing outside of ordinary historical time, after all, one needs some way to occupy the mind.

Mark insisted that we take time out to play Faith Hill's cover version of the Janis Joplin song *Piece of My Heart* on the diner jukebox, and then we headed back to the monastery for a late-night meeting with Fr. Gruner. After Mark and Gruner swapped conspiracy tales, the talk turned to conservative Catholics such as E. Michael Jones and James Hitchcock. Mark argued that leading conservatives were engaged, in some cases inadvertently, in a cover-up of what was really happening in the church. Gruner told me that publications such as the *Wanderer* and *Fidelity* Magazine and organizations like CUF were secretly funded by the Vatican in an effort to subvert the Fatima prophecies. He also told me that E. Michael Jones was simply masquerading as a Catholic.

"You know, of course, that Jones is secretly a Jew. He's a Marrano, planted in the American Church to confuse Catholics and sow hatred against people like myself. I think most of us have figured that out by now."

The Separatist (Or Traditionalist) Option

Brother John, Mark, and most of the other participants at the annual conference in Berlin, New Jersey, belong to the theological demimonde of American Catholicism. Their world is a complex shadowlands of steamy prophecy, exotic conspiracy, and sectarian intrigue. Having given up for the most part on the institutional church, which they regard as either hopelessly benighted or hopelessly corrupt, they seek solace in enclaves of the like-minded, and await their day of final vindication. The crisis currently confronting Roman Catholicism, they claim, runs far deeper than incompetent bishops, self-aggrandizing theologians, and philandering clergy. Infidelity and heresy, in their view, have invaded the highest reaches of the church's authority structure, including the papacy itself, and only in small bands of the truly faithful is authentic Catholicism still kept alive. Most of these Catholics reject both the Second Vatican Council and the new Mass, and most regard the conservative Catholics who were the subject of the previous two chapters as not much better (and in some respects as far more dangerous) than theological liberals. They generally refer to themselves as Catholic traditionalists, and they attempt to replicate in their own communities the same patterns of doctrine, ritual, and authority that were the defining features of Catholicism prior to the council.[4] Most of them have separated from both Rome and the American Catholic hierarchy, and they frequently maintain their own chapels, their own schools and seminaries, and sometimes even their own bishops. Beyond their shared conviction that something has gone unspeakably wrong with the institutional church, however, they are bitterly divided themselves over fundamental questions of strategy and theology, and much of their time is spent in rancorous internal dispute.

The Holy Family Monastery is just one of more than three hundred centers of traditionalist (or separatist) Catholicism currently in operation across the United States.[5] The monastery was founded in 1967 by a self-proclaimed Benedictine monk named Brother Joseph Natale as a community for handicapped men, but it rapidly evolved instead into a beachhead of right-wing radicalism. Throughout the late sixties and early seventies, Brother Joseph fervently denounced both the Second Vatican Council and the new Mass, and by the mid-seventies his community had broken off entirely from the institutional church to become probably the first independent traditionalist monastery in America. Over the years, a number of church officials, including the current bishop of the Camden, New Jersey, diocese, James T. McHugh, have attempted to approach the monastery to discuss the possibility of working out some sort of rapprochement, but Brother

Joseph has consistently refused to answer their calls. In the mid-eighties, there were a total of ten monks in residence at the monastery, but since then the number has shrunk to just three. (The most recent defection occurred shortly after the May 1994 conference, when Brother John, the aforementioned Sacred Heart lecturer, fled to Fort Erie to work with Fr. Gruner.) In addition to its annual conference, the monastery sponsors monthly retreats and a Tridentine Mass on Sundays that draws between two and three hundred people.

Several months after the 1994 conference, I visited the monastery again, this time to meet personally with Brother Joseph. Upon arriving, I was ushered into a paneled waiting room by a rotund monk in his mid-fifties who identified himself as Brother Thomas. On one wall there were framed photographs of Popes John Paul I and John Paul II, and on another there was a larger photograph of Brother Joseph and Brother Thomas, both beaming and wearing suits, with a beaming Jimmy Durante standing between them. After finishing his lunch, Brother Joseph came into the room on crutches, greeted me warmly, and took a seat behind a large wooden desk.

He told me that he had been born into a working-class family in Philadelphia in 1933, but had contracted tuberculosis of the bone at the age of four and had been forced to spend most of the next seventeen years shuttling in and out of hospital. After a stint in the private import business, he entered the Benedictine Archabbey in Latrobe, Pennsylvania, in 1960 as a lay postulant, but left less than a year later to lay the groundwork for the Holy Family Monastery. (I was later informed by the archivist of the Saint Vincent Archabbey in Latrobe that Brother Joseph left before taking final vows and thus never actually did become a Benedictine monk.[6])

Brother Joseph suggested to me that he had been infused as a young man with a gift of prophecy ("a special, mysterious, divine knowledge," is how he referred to it), and it was this that had afforded him special insight into the travails of contemporary Catholicism. "I know this is hard for you to understand, so I'll just give you a couple of illustrations," he said. "Even before Vatican II was finished, I knew, and knew absolutely, that it was part of a communist conspiracy to destroy the Church. The bishops at the council wanted to democratize Catholicism, they wanted an egalitarian theology, and most of them were secret communists and Masons. They knew exactly what they were doing. My community here was the first one in the United States to see the council for what it really was, and we rejected it completely." Brother Joseph's second illustration of his prophetic powers concerned Pope John Paul I, who was found dead in his quarters of an apparent heart attack on September 28, 1978, just one month after his election to the papacy. "Regardless of what you have been told," he said, "John Paul I did not die of natural causes. He was murdered. Shortly after his election I went into a kind of trance and was told that John Paul I would be murdered because he wanted to return the Church to its traditions. He was murdered by his own. The communist infiltrators in the Vatican and the College of Cardinals, working together with the Masons, killed John Paul I. At the same time I also had a vision of John Paul II, and I was told that he would be the next pope and also that he would be an authentic pope, even though most of his actions would be controlled by communist advisers and manipulators in the Vatican."

His prophetic credentials now established, Brother Joseph next showed me a copy of a grade-six catechism, *Christ With Us,* published in 1967 by William Sadlier, Inc. On the first page was an excerpt of a prayer delivered by Pope Paul VI to the United Nations that the publisher had decorated with what seemed to be a random sprinkling of brown dots. With a sheet of tracing paper Brother Joseph connected the dots and, in the process, produced an image that crudely resembled a hammer and sickle.

"Do you know what this is?" he asked, triumphantly. "It's the emblem of communism, and it was secretly put on these catechisms for Catholic school-children. Do you see the point? The Second Vatican Council was an ingenious plot devised by communists to take over the Church, and after the council was finished, communism infected every aspect of the Church. Communism isn't dead; it's stronger than ever. Satan has overseen the communistic takeover of the Church. The United States is next, and then the entire world!"

At this point we were briefly interrupted when Brother Thomas entered the room and asked permission to go into town for a haircut. Brother Joseph handed him a ten-dollar bill and reminded him to bring back the change.

I asked Brother Joseph where the operating funds for the monastery came from. "Almost all of our money comes from private donations, which almost never exceed $100," he said, "and the rest comes from sales of our books and videos." (The monastery operates a small gift shop that is heavily stocked with "traditionalist" Catholic literature.) "We have a mailing list of one hundred thousand homes across the country, and we send out begging letters to every one of them. We also send our newsletter, *Cry in the Wilderness,* to traditionalist Catholics in twenty countries, and this brings us some donations. But we don't have any big financial backers. In twenty-eight years, the biggest donation we've ever received was $10,000, and that was only once."

As I prepared to leave, Brother Joseph broke into an apocalyptic tirade that was clearly intended to prolong our conversation. "Five years is about all the time the world has left," he declared. "Canada and the United States today are completely atheistic.... Doomsday is on the way.... What's the United Nations? It's a communistic house of subversion designed to bring about a one-world government.... What's gun control? It's an effort to disarm the American people so they won't be able to resist the communistic takeover.... Why isn't Bill Clinton impeached? He's totally immoral; his wife's a homosexual.... Who puts drugs out on the street? Who? Government agents, that's who. Doping the people makes them helpless...."

THE RISE OF CATHOLIC SEPARATISM
IN THE UNITED STATES

Although Brother Joseph would undoubtedly like to claim the honor for himself, the first Catholic traditionalist/separatist of any prominence in the United States was a Belgian-born priest and professor of theology named Gommar De Pauw.[7] In March 1965, while he was still serving as academic dean at St. Mary's Major Seminary in Emmitsburg, Maryland, De Pauw formed an organization called the Catholic Traditionalist Movement (CTM), which was dedicated to slowing down (and possibly reversing) some of the more radical changes in liturgy and theology that were taking place within the American church at the tail end of the council. Within just a month of its founding, however, Archbishop Lawrence Shehan of Baltimore accused the CTM of being at odds with the teachings of Vatican II and ordered De Pauw to dissociate himself completely from it.[8] De Pauw responded by shifting his base of operations to New York City, and when he refused to return to Maryland, Shehan suspended him from his priestly functions and denounced the CTM as a renegade organization. Still undeterred, De Pauw took his show on the road, lecturing to groups of concerned Catholics across the country and regaling the news media with tales of theological woe. By the end of 1966, he had become branded in the media as "the rebel priest" and written off in chancery offices throughout America as an incorrigible reactionary.

In his writings of the mid-sixties, De Pauw tried hard to depict himself as an enlightened moderate, a true theological democrat, concerned with protecting the rights of ordinary Catholics against the tradition-bashing of professional liturgists. The CTM's real complaint, he insisted, wasn't with the Second Vatican Council or its Constitution on the Liturgy, but rather with "the almost pathological fanaticism displayed by our Litnicks (liturgical beatniks) in their fight against Latin in the liturgy." Whereas the professional liturgists (or "glorified altar boys," as De Pauw liked to call them) were committed to imposing their iconoclastic will upon the entire church, the CTM was in favor of "full and complete freedom of choice" in matters of worship. Instead of force-feeding the new Mass to everyone, he asked, why not provide "every Catholic with the liturgy best suited to his or her spiritual needs?" In any given parish, he said, the traditional Latin Mass could be offered alongside the new vernacular one, and no one would have cause to feel liturgically put upon.[9]

As the liturgical revolution within the church became an accomplished reality during the late sixties and early seventies, however, De Pauw's reasonableness of tone rapidly gave way to stridency and panic. In April 1969 the new vernacular Mass (or Novus Ordo liturgy) officially replaced the Tridentine Mass as the universal rite of the church, and in November 1971 Pope Paul VI effectively banned the Tridentine Mass altogether. De Pauw responded to these developments by condemning the new Mass as "schismatic, sacrilegious, heretical, and possibly invalid" and by pledging his own unswerving allegiance to the Tridentine liturgy.[10] (One of De Pauw's chief grievances with the English version of the new Mass was that the Latin words "Pro Vobis et Pro Multis" in the formula of consecration were erroneously translated as "For You and For All Men." This, he argued, implied the heretical idea that all men would necessarily be saved.[11]) Now cut off almost entirely from the institutional church, De Pauw retreated to a chapel in Westbury, Long Island, which was housed in a former Ukrainian Orthodox Church that his supporters had purchased in 1968, and dedicated himself to keeping the Tridentine Mass alive and maintaining the CTM as a "little oasis of true Roman Catholicism" in an age of widespread spiritual and liturgical apostasy.[12]

While De Pauw was keeping the Tridentine Mass alive in the New York City area in the early seventies, additional traditionalist chapels were cropping up by the dozen elsewhere across the country. Some of these chapels, such as the one presided over by Brother Joseph at the Holy Family Monastery, enjoyed the luxury of a permanent address, but most led a considerably more transitory existence. Disaffected Catholics from a particular region, aggrieved by the sudden loss of the Tridentine Mass in their local parishes, would align themselves with a similarly disaffected priest and set up liturgical shop in a private home, a hotel room, or sometimes even a restaurant. In the years immediately following the mandatory implementation of the Novus Ordo Mass in 1971, these fugitive chapels developed their own informal networks and sense of collective identity, and by the mid-seventies they constituted a significant underground economy of ritual and sacrament within the broader world of American Catholicism.

As important as these local initiatives undoubtedly were, the Catholic traditionalist (or separatist) movement in the United States received probably its greatest burst of momentum during the mid-seventies from a dissident French prelate named Marcel Lefebvre. Born in northern France in 1905, and consecrated a bishop in 1947, Lefebvre first gained international attention at the end of Vatican II when he refused to sign the council's documents on Religious Liberty and the Church in the Modern World. Convinced that the church after the council had capitulated to modernism and secularism, he established the traditionalist Ecône seminary in Switzerland in 1970, and later the same year he also established a priestly fraternity called the Society of St. Pius X (SSPX). In 1973 and 1974 the first American priests to be ordained by Lefebvre at Ecône returned home to set up traditionalist chapels in California, New York, and Texas, and over the next several years the SSPX rapidly evolved into the leading traditionalist organization in America.

As time went on, moreover, Lefebvre himself became an increasingly more prominent player on the traditionalist stage. In November 1974 he publicly denounced both the council and the new Mass as heretical, and when Pope Paul VI subsequently ordered him to shut down the Ecône seminary, he responded by expanding its operations and increasing its rate of ordination. As punishment for this insubordination, Lefebvre was suspended from his priestly faculties in July 1976, but this only enhanced his prestige among rank-and-file traditionalists in America and elsewhere. Over the next several years Lefebvre maintained a steady stream of invective against the council and its reforms, and in October 1983 he once again forced the Vatican's hand by threatening to consecrate, without papal approval, an episcopal successor for his priestly fraternity. At this point the Vatican decided to pursue a more conciliatory approach, and in October 1984 Pope John Paul II promulgated an indult granting Catholics permission to attend the Tridentine Mass under carefully regulated conditions. In Lefebvre's view, however, the indult was nothing more than a diversionary tactic, and he advised traditionalist Catholics not to be taken in by the duplicities of Rome. Three years later Lefebvre again threatened to consecrate a successor without papal mandate, and this time the Vatican entered into frantic conversation with him in the hope of negotiating some sort of rapprochement. A rapprochement seemed in fact to have been reached when Lefebvre, on May 5, 1988, signed a protocol with the Vatican that required him to profess loyalty to the papacy and to affirm the validity of the new Mass in return for official recognition of his priestly fraternity and the right of SSPX chapels to continue their exclusive use of the Tridentine liturgy. Just one day later, however, Lefebvre backed out of the protocol, and on June 30, 1988, while proclaiming the need to keep the SSPX completely independent of "modernist Rome," he consecrated four of his priest-followers to the Catholic episcopacy. Shortly afterward, Lefebvre and his new bishops and all members of his priestly fraternity were excommunicated, and the SSPX passed into a state of formal schism.[13]

By the time of his death in March 1991, Lefebvre was widely regarded by Catholic traditionalists in America and elsewhere as a sort of martyr-saint of authentic orthodoxy, and the SSPX was firmly established as the largest and most conspicuous traditionalist organization in the world. In the United States alone today, the Society operates approximately one hundred chapels and twenty elementary or secondary schools, and since 1979 it has also operated its own college in St. Mary's, Kansas. In 1994 the Society claimed to have forty fully active priests in the United States, and another dozen or so priests-in-training at its seminary in Winona, Minnesota. After stints in Oyster Bay, Long Island, and Winona, its national headquarters is currently located in Kansas City, which is also home to the SSPX-run Angelus Press, by far the largest traditionalist publishing house in America.[14]

Although precise figures are difficult to come by, the SSPX currently has somewhere between twenty and thirty thousand lay adherents in the United States. Moreover, the level of lay support for the Society seems not to have been adversely affected by its excommunicate status. According to Fr. Peter Scott, the District

Superior for the United States, weekly attendance at SSPX chapels has increased annually by 10 percent since the late eighties.[15] Like most other traditionalist organizations, the SSPX depends heavily on private donations for economic survival, and its primarily lower-middle- and middle-class congregations have thus far been quite willing to shoulder the burden. Compared to more mainstream religious bodies, in fact, the SSPX seems to call forth an extraordinary degree of dedication, and entire families have frequently transplanted themselves to different parts of the country in order to be closer to one of the Society's centers.

When the first SSPX chapels were established in the United States during the mid-seventies, they attracted Catholics who were acutely, and implacably, disturbed by the changes that had been set in motion within the church by the Second Vatican Council. Unlike the conservative Catholics profiled in earlier chapters, these Catholics found it impossible to make peace with the new Mass, or with the new spirit of ecumenism that followed the council, and many of them became convinced that the mainstream institutional church was no longer truly Catholic. The SSPX was attractive to them not only because it represented a link with the Catholic past but also because the leadership of Archbishop Lefebvre seemed to accord it a legitimacy that was absent from most other traditionalist organizations. As a validly consecrated bishop of the church, Lefebvre was endowed with the sacramental power to perform ordinations and confirmations, and also with the sort of public prestige that guaranteed that his actions would not go unnoticed.

Like other traditionalist organizations, the SSPX has never actively solicited new members, and newcomers have been drawn to it mainly through word of mouth and the informal networks of family and friends. This has placed a premium on the organization's ability to retain the allegiance of younger generations, and judging from the numerous families with children in regular attendance at SSPX chapels throughout the country, its prospects for long-term survival seem impressively strong.[16] Quite in contrast to the now-and-then sort of involvement that characterizes life in most mainstream Catholic parishes, the SSPX demands of its members nothing less than a total and all-embracing commitment. They are expected to adhere rigorously to traditional doctrinal and moral precepts, to participate faithfully in the Society's expansive ritual life, and to support its various ministries. This is religion with a price, but a price that thousands of Catholics in the United States seem eager to pay.

SOCIETY OF ST. PIUS V

As unlikely as it may sound, the SSPX actually occupies a moderate position within the broader world of Catholic traditionalism. While bitterly opposed to the new Mass, and to the new spirit of religious tolerance that was endorsed by the council, the Society hasn't gone so far as to reject the so-called Vatican II popes, nor has it fully closed the door on a future reconciliation with Rome. In February 1992, for example, Archbishop Lefebvre's successor as head of the Society, a German priest named Franz Schmidberger, told the *Catholic World Report*: "We are ready to engage in dialogue. We pray continually for the Pope."[17]

Throughout his own traditionalist career, in fact, Archbishop Lefebvre was famous for sending out mixed signals. At points, his anger seemed almost boundless: the new Mass was a bastard rite and the Second Vatican Council a farrago of heresy; the council's teaching on religious liberty and ecumenism was a diabolical betrayal; and the Vatican itself was a hotbed of deceit and unbelief. But Lefebvre also had his more conciliatory moments, where he fudged his opposition to the council and softened his rhetoric against Rome. While standing angrily outside the institutional church, in other words, he was also looking furtively over one shoulder in the hope of being asked back in.

Over the years, this rather more conciliatory side of Lefebvre's sometimes proved to be a source of contention within the Society of St. Pius X itself. During the early eighties, a group of nine American priests, all of whom belonged to the Eastern District of the SSPX in the United States, became convinced that the grandfather of Catholic traditionalism wasn't sufficiently committed to his own cause. In attempting to keep his options open with Rome, in their view, Lefebvre was too often guilty of sacrificing principle to expediency. He was far too lenient, they claimed, in accepting marriage annulments that had been issued by the Vatican; he seemed reluctant to deliver an unequivocal, once-and-for-all condemnation of the new Mass; and he sometimes accepted into the SSPX priests who had been ordained in the post-conciliar church. And then there was the critical matter of the papacy. As much as he deplored their role in implementing the reforms of the council, Lefebvre not only accepted the legitimacy of the so-called conciliar popes but also insisted that all members of his Society pray for them. To the American malcontents, this was particularly galling: considering everything that had gone wrong with the institutional church under their tenure, why on earth should it be assumed that men such as Paul VI and John Paul II were valid popes?

After signaling their refusal to pray for John Paul II, the dissident American priests were expelled from the SSPX in April 1983, and the following month they started a rival organization called the Society of St. Pius V (SSPV). Over the next several years, the two organizations battled fiercely in the courts for control of parish property and other assets, and the Society of St. Pius V eventually succeeded in winning title to the Oyster Bay, Long Island, estate that had previously served as the SSPX's American headquarters. Although severely handicapped by the lack of a bishop of its own to perform confirmations and ordinations, the SSPV managed to carve out a fairly secure niche for itself on the extreme Catholic right, and for a time in the late eighties it threatened to supplant the Society of

St. Pius X as the preeminent traditionalist organization in the United States. (At present the SSPV operates approximately forty chapels nationwide with a combined lay membership of more than four thousand, as well as a convent in upstate New York and four elementary schools.)

On a Sunday morning in February several years ago, I traveled from New York City to the village of Oyster Bay in the hopes of tracking down Fr. Clarence Kelly, who had been the ringleader of the Gang of Nine's revolt against Lefebvre. Even within the relatively hermetic world of Catholic traditionalism, Fr. Kelly has a reputation for secretiveness and elusiveness, and I'd been consistently thwarted in my efforts to reach him by telephone. After passing through a wrought-iron gate at the edge of the village and following a curved driveway for a hundred yards or so, I came to a large, cement-block building that housed a parish hall, a small cloister, and the St. Pius V Chapel. Outside the main door of the chapel, atop a seven-foot pedestal in a sunken quadrangle, was an impressive bronze statue of Pope Pius IX holdings keys and a scroll.

Stepping inside, where the congregation was assembling for Mass, I picked up a parish bulletin that contained the following manifesto:

A WORD OF WELCOME AND EXPLANATION
TO NEWCOMERS

Since the close of the Second Vatican Council in 1965, a revolution has taken place in the Catholic Church. The Mass has been changed. The Sacraments have been changed. And in so many places the doctrine, as well as the moral teaching, of the Church has been changed.

We believe these changes are irreconcilable with what the popes have taught, especially the pre-Vatican II popes of the last 200 years. And so we do not go along with the changes.

Until such time as Our Lord restores order and normalcy as regards the situation in the Church, we hold fast, as St. Paul said, to the TRADITIONS.

In this chapel, only the traditional Latin Mass is celebrated. And we adhere without reservation or qualification to the traditional Catholic Faith and the unchangeable moral teaching of the Church.

We believe that as Catholics we have a right and a solemn duty to hold fast to the traditions as we have received them from the Church.

The bulletin also spelled out a dress code ("Women should have their hair covered. Slacks, short skirts, sleeveless or revealing clothing are forbidden.") and stipulated certain conditions for the reception of Holy Communion.

One must accept and profess all the teachings of the Catholic Church. One must believe and abide by the traditional Catholic moral teaching, especially in regard to purity and marriage. . . .

One must, of course, be in the state of sanctifying grace to receive Holy Communion, having made a good confession to a Catholic priest ordained in the traditional rite, which rite was used before 1968.

Young people must be trained in the traditional Catechism, such as the Baltimore Catechism, and they must be tested in the traditional Catechism by a traditional priest. . . .

Not for the Society of St. Pius V, then, the casual, happenstance community of the typical American Catholic parish; attending Mass here was a deadly serious business, implying close (and purposive) commitment to an explicit code of belief and conduct. Altogether, about 150 people were in attendance for the 10 A.M. Mass (roughly the same number had attended an earlier service the same morning), and the small chapel was filled to capacity. There were numerous families with young children, and at least half a dozen of the mothers looked to be under twenty years of age. With the exception of two people, a young man and a middle-aged woman, the congregation was entirely white; and, as I would learn later, it ran the gamut from working- to upper-middle-class. The service proceeded according to the slow and solemn Latin rhythms I recalled from my earliest childhood, and many of the congregation followed it in small, black Mass books. Fr. Kelly, gray-haired, bespectacled, and mid-fortyish, delivered a homily on the perils of theological modernism and the urgent importance of keeping faith with Catholic tradition. After Mass, dozens of people lingered in the parish hall, where there was a breakfast bar with coffee and bacon-and-egg sandwiches for sale.

I caught up with Fr. Kelly in a makeshift sacristy at the back of the chapel, and he greeted me with a sort of polite wariness. He had been born and raised in Brooklyn, Kelly told me, and had attended Immaculate Heart Seminary on Long Island and Catholic University in Washington, D.C., before hooking up with Archbishop Lefebvre in Ecône, Switzerland, in the early seventies. Upon returning to the United States, he wrote a book on Freemasonry entitled *Conspiracy Against God and Man*, undertook some speaking engagements for the John Birch Society, and eventually settled in as pastor at the chapel in Oyster Bay. By the late seventies, however, he and his fellow dissenters in the Society of St. Pius X had become convinced that Lefebvre was more interested in kowtowing to Rome than in preserving Catholic tradition, and from that point on their relationship with the Society rapidly deteriorated. I asked Fr. Kelly if the Society of St. Pius V went so far as to reject the papacy of John Paul II. "We don't have an official position on this," he said, evasively. "We don't have any authority to settle the question of whether the person now claiming the papacy is actually the pope. We think it's perfectly legitimate to raise the question, but we're not imposing our view as dogma."[18]

After ten minutes or so Fr. Kelly broke off our conversation, saying he was in a rush to make afternoon Mass at the SSPV's chapel at the Warwick Hotel in midtown Manhattan. He told me that we could meet again sometime in the near future for a longer talk.

After trying unsuccessfully over the next several months to contact Fr. Kelly,

I decided to visit the St. Joseph's Novitiate, a convent run by the Society of St. Pius V in upstate New York. Located in a down-on-its-luck rural community called Round Top, about thirty miles south of Albany, the St. Joseph's Novitiate was the focus of a short-lived controversy in the late eighties when one of its novices, a twenty-two-year-old woman named Marisue Greve, was forcibly abducted from the road outside its front gate by her parents and three brothers. The Greve family claimed that Marisue had been subjected to mind control, nocturnal abuses, and a more general program of zombification by Fr. Kelly and his crew, and they whisked her away to a remote cabin for a session of deprogramming. Although I didn't place much credence in these accusations, I was curious to learn more about the convent and the twenty-two women, the Daughters of Mary, who resided behind its semi-cloistered walls.[19]

On a sweltering afternoon in June 1995, I pulled onto the convent's grounds and parked behind a rambling frame house, white-shingled and blue-trimmed, that served as the primary residence for the Daughters of Mary. Outside of an occasional nun, in full black habit, returning to the residence from a nearby chapel, the grounds were absolutely still. After about fifteen minutes, Fr. Paul Baumberger, a young priest whom I'd previously met on one of my visits to Oyster Bay, passed behind me and disappeared into a ramshackle frame house at the edge of the property. A little later I wandered over and found Fr. Baumberger on the back porch smoking a cigar and reading a breviary.

"Dr. Cuneo, what a surprise!"
"Father Baumberger, I know I'm here uninvited and unannounced."
"Yes. You are."
"Feel free to get the shotgun and throw me off the property."
"I don't think I've got a shotgun nearby."
"Can we talk then?"
"I'm getting ready to give a retreat to the sisters now."
"What about sometime this evening or tomorrow?"
He agreed to give me forty-five minutes the following morning.

While I was driving to my appointment with Fr. Baumberger the next day, a deer walked in front of my car, stopped, and stood gazing at me with a trapped and troubled expression. This was very much the same expression worn by Fr. Baumberger during our subsequent interview. Tight-lipped and timid and determinedly circumspect, he looked like a man trapped into a momentary confrontation with a vaguely hostile intruder. The interview was clearly a nasty bit of business for him, and he seemed greatly relieved when our forty-five minutes had expired.

Born in Minnesota in 1958 and raised as the youngest of four children in a comfortably middle-class and fervently traditionalist household, Fr. Baumberger

THE SMOKE OF SATAN

claims that even as a young boy he felt a deep calling to the priesthood. At the age of twenty-two he enrolled in the Society of St. Pius X seminary in Richfield, Connecticut, and ten years later, after having shifted his allegiance from the SSPX to the Society of St. Pius V, he was ordained to the priesthood by a retired Roman Catholic bishop, Alfred F. Mendez, who was sympathetic to the traditionalist cause. Fr. Baumberger claims that the "Novus Ordo" or "modernist" church has betrayed the "immutable truths" of Catholicism, and he looks upon John Paul II as an impossibly weak, and quite probably apostate, pope. "It's not an article of faith for us that John Paul II is a heretic," he said. "This is a matter of opinion, and my mind's open on this question. Still, we have to consider the evidence. John Paul II has supported the innovations of Vatican II, he's been openly supportive of ecumenism, and he's helped put millions of souls at peril of damnation. This wouldn't seem to be the work of a valid pope."

Fr. Baumberger told me that I wouldn't be permitted to interview any of the Daughters of Mary without the explicit approval of their Mother Superior. (The Mother Superior had already turned me down by phone the previous evening.) Nevertheless, he said, the convent was probably in better shape than ever before, and so too was the Society of St. Pius V as a whole. "We have gone through a period of troubles, but the worst of them are hopefully behind us," he said. "The commitment and morale of our sisters is very high, we're continuing to open up new chapels, and we're also planning on starting up our own seminary. Our patience and perseverance and suffering have been rewarded, and we have great hope and expectations for the future."[20]

———

THE "PERIOD OF TROUBLES" referred to by Fr. Baumberger in his tightly scripted comments stemmed in large measure from the SSPV's lack of a bishop of its own following its breakup with the Society of St. Pius X. Within the broader world of Catholic traditionalism, there are few things more valuable than being able to lay claim to a bishop. In addition to wanting to perpetuate themselves, groups such as the Society of St. Pius V are strongly committed to a theory of apostolic succession. They want to be seen as standing in sacred, unbroken continuity with the primitive church, a living link with the apostolic past; and for this, a duly consecrated bishop of one's own is an absolute necessity.

The problem, of course, is that according to the laws and traditions of Catholicism, only a bishop in good standing with the church has the authority to confer episcopal consecration, and only after having received an explicit mandate to do so from the pope. Traditionalist groups such as the SSPX and SSPV have thus far dispensed with the first of these requirements—the papal mandate—by invoking a kind of theological defense of necessity. In these times of unprecedented crisis within the church, when even the Vatican gives every appearance of having succumbed to heresy, they've argued, there seems little point in seeking papal approval for episcopal consecrations.[21] This still, however, leaves the difficult trick of finding bishops willing to perform consecrations without papal approval, and toward this end Catholic traditionalists in the United States have forged some strange alliances.

Consider, for example, the case of Pierre Martin Ngo-Dinh-Thuc, onetime archbishop of the Hué diocese in Vietnam and older brother of former South Vietnamese President Ngo Dinh Diem. Born in 1897, Thuc was ordained a priest in 1925 and consecrated a bishop in 1938. After attending the Second Vatican Council, Thuc was prevented by the mounting political turbulence in his homeland from returning to his see, and in the late sixties he took a job as assistant pastor at a parish in the Italian village of Arpino. Several years later, however, his career took a decidedly more exotic turn. In late 1975 Thuc traveled to Palmar de Troya, a Spanish village located twenty-five miles south of Seville, to meet with a self-styled prophet named Clemente Dominguez Gomez. Since the late sixties Dominguez had built up a cult following in the area by claiming to be the recipient of private revelations from the Virgin Mary, and in one of her more recent communications the Virgin had informed him that Pope Paul VI was being held prisoner in the Vatican while an imposter (an "exact double") ruled in his place on the papal throne. The Virgin had also told Dominguez that she wanted Archbishop Thuc to ordain him and several of his cult followers to the priesthood, and Pope Paul VI, appearing to the prophet by means of "bilocation," had seconded the request. Thuc carried out the ordinations on December 31, 1975, and two weeks later he consecrated Dominguez and four of his followers to the episcopate.[22] (When Pope Paul VI, or at least the imposter claiming to be Paul VI, died two years later, Dominguez declared himself leader of the church and took Pope Gregory XVII as his new name.)

For Archbishop Thuc, the Palmar de Troya affair was just a warmup. Over the next seven or eight years he carried out unauthorized consecrations on several continents, usually without the imprimatur of even a bilocating pope. And in many cases, these "first-generation" Thuc bishops subsequently carried out consecrations of their own, creating in the process a far-flung episcopal dynasty that was entirely independent of Rome. On May 7, 1981, for example, Archbishop Thuc consecrated a breakaway French priest named Guérard des Lauriers to the episcopate, and several years later des Lauriers did the same for an American traditionalist named Fr. Robert McKenna.[23] And while McKenna was busy peddling his episcopal wares to a variety of traditionalist groups in the United States, another Thuc bishop, a Mexican named Moises Carmona Rivera, was conferring consecration upon a Lithuanian-American named Mark Pivarunas, one of the leaders of the militantly traditionalist Mount St. Michael's community located in Spokane, Washington.[24]

Besides turning to one of the wayward Thuc bishops for consecrations, Catholic traditionalists in the United States have sometimes hooked up with an older sectarian movement usually referred to as the Old Catholics. The Old Catholics first arose in 1724 when a small group of Dutch Jansenists, including three bishops, broke away from Rome to form the Church of Utrecht. In 1889 this original group was joined by a group of schismatic Catholics from Germany and Switzerland who had broken with Rome in 1870 over the issue of papal infallibility, and in subsequent decades the movement took on schismatic groups from several additional countries, including the Polish National Catholic Church of America and the North American Old Roman Catholic Church. Today all of these groups maintain a loose association with one another; and taken together they practice a theology that's not much different from what would be found in a typical liberal Protestant denomination. Despite retaining many of the liturgical trappings of Roman Catholicism, they reject the Catholic church's teachings concerning, among other things, papal infallibility, the veneration of saints, clerical celibacy, and the necessity of auricular confession.[25]

Although Catholic traditionalists are worlds apart theologically from the Old Catholics, the Old Catholics possess precisely the commodity that many traditionalists most desperately want: a line of bishops presumably extending back to the founding of the Church of Utrecht in 1724, and before that to the apostolic era itself. And the Old Catholics have sometimes been more than willing to share this commodity with those less fortunate than themselves. During a three-week span in the autumn of 1971, for example, Francis Schuckardt, the founder of the Tridentine Latin Rite Church, a radical traditionalist community then based in Coeur d'Alene, Idaho (the TRLC would later move to Spokane and become more popularly known as the Mount St. Michael's community), was both ordained a priest and consecrated a bishop by a bishop of the North American Old Roman Catholic Church named Daniel Q. Brown. On the strength of this episcopal windfall, Schuckardt immediately set about ordaining priests of his own, and in the process the TRLC was rapidly elevated from a position of relative marginality on the traditionalist scene to one of considerable prominence.

ALTHOUGH THE SOCIETY OF ST. PIUS V, following its break with Lefebvre, could easily have taken one of these routes toward securing a bishop, the organization was committed to playing it as straight as possible. According to Fr. Clarence Kelly and other leading lights of the Society, it was absolutely perverse to think that consecrations conferred by the schismatic (and theologically liberal) Old Catholics were in any sense valid. And the consecration-on-demand policy of Archbishop Thuc was regarded by them as the outcome of either senility or insanity. Playing it straight, however, sometimes proved exceedingly difficult. As time went on, and the SSPV continued to go without a bishop, some of its lay members defected to groups such as the Society of St. Pius X or Mount St. Michael's where they could get their children confirmed and, in some cases, their sons ordained. And even more demoralizing, several of the Society's core group of priests eventually wound up jumping ship as well.

The most serious of these priestly defections involved Fr. Daniel Dolan, who is currently one of the four or five most influential traditionalists operating in America. Dolan was born in Detroit in 1951, and in 1973 he entered Lefebvre's seminary in Ecône to study for the priesthood. After his ordination and a brief stint in England, Dolan returned to the United States and rapidly won a reputation as a kind of latter-day St. Paul, traveling extensively throughout the country and establishing more than thirty-five traditionalist Mass centers in states as various as Montana and Ohio. During the early eighties he served as Fr. Clarence Kelly's second-in-command in the revolt against Lefebvre, and for several years afterward he worked closely with Kelly at building the Society of St. Pius V into a force to be reckoned with on the traditionalist scene. After a while, however, working at close quarters with the imperious Kelly (with still no bishop in sight) proved too much for Dolan, and on July 4, 1989, he and a close colleague named Fr. Anthony Cekada left the SSPV and took upwards of five hundred lay supporters with them.

This was bad enough for the Society of St. Pius V, but worse was still to come. After working for several years as independent traditionalists, ministering to various Mass centers on a circuit that covered five states, Dolan and Cekada eventually joined forces with the radical Mount St. Michael's community of Spokane, and in the summer of 1993 Dolan agreed to be consecrated a bishop by Mark Pivarunas. This was the same Mark Pivarunas who himself had been consecrated by the Thuc bishop Moises Carmona Rivera and trained for the priesthood by Francis Schuckardt, who had derived his own priestly and episcopal credentials from the Old Catholic bishop Daniel Q. Brown. The consecration took place on November 30, 1993, and Fr. Dolan, who had done as much as anyone else to secure a place for the Society of St. Pius V on the traditionalist map, was now a major player for the principal competition.

In the autumn of 1994 I met with Dolan in Spokane and asked why he had accepted episcopal consecration under such dubious circumstances. Smooth-faced, slightly chubby, and almost cherubic in appearance, Dolan didn't betray so much as a tinge of regret. "Some of my opponents like to claim I left the Society of St. Pius V simply because I wanted to become a bishop at any price, but this is preposterous," he said. "The main reason I left was because of personal conflicts with Fr. Kelly. He exercised a strong, cult-like leadership. He was a bit of a Francis Schuckardt type—very charismatic and manipulative. And not having a bishop in the Society made the situation especially taxing. But I certainly wasn't looking to better myself by becoming a bishop. Bishop Pivarunas approached me first with the idea, and at first I had serious reservations about the Archbishop

Thuc and Old Catholic background of the Mount St. Michael's community. I don't deny that there have been problems here, but we're not living today under normal circumstances. We're faced with a vacuum of authority; the papacy has been vacant for more than twenty years now, and desperate times call for desperate measures. Our people need to receive the sacraments, and for this they need priests, and it takes bishops to make priests. And this is precisely the role that Bishop Pivarunas and myself play. We don't claim to possess ordinary jurisdiction, or the power of excommunication. We have moral authority, but we don't boss people around. We're sacramental bishops, and traditionalist communities simply can't survive for very long without sacramental bishops."[26]

When the news of Dolan's impending consecration broke within traditionalist circles during the summer of 1993, Fr. Clarence Kelly apparently became convinced that his own community couldn't survive much longer unless it too came up with a bishop. On September 7, 1993, accordingly, Kelly and Fr. William Jenkins, a longtime Kelly loyalist in the Society of St. Pius V, traveled to California to meet with an eighty-six-year-old bishop named Alfred Mendez. Mendez had served as the bishop of the Diocese of Arecibo in Puerto Rico from 1960 until his retirement from active ministry in 1974, and since the late eighties he had extended an occasional helping hand to the SSPV. (It was Mendez, in September 1990, who ordained Paul Baumberger and another young traditionalist named Joseph Greenwell to the priesthood.) After Kelly and Jenkins made their pitch, Mendez agreed to consecrate Kelly a bishop, and the ceremony was fast-tracked to October 19, which meant that Kelly actually wound up beating Dolan to the episcopal punch by several weeks.[27]

As Fr. Baumberger suggested to me in Round Top, things have gone quite a bit better for the Society of St. Pius V since 1993 and Fr. Kelly's elevation to the episcopacy. The flight of lay members has been halted, the morale of the Society's six remaining priests seems considerably improved, and there are plans afoot for starting up a new elementary school and a seminary. Despite this recent upswing in its fortunes, however, the SSPV remains intensely bitter over some of the rather more questionable deals that some of its competitors seem to have cut in procuring bishops for themselves. Indeed, the SSPV has probably expended more energy over the past several years attacking other traditionalists than it has attacking Rome. And the principal target of its invective has been the very same traditionalist community that, in theological terms, the Society of St. Pius V most closely resembles.[28]

MOUNT ST. MICHAEL'S

Francis Schuckardt is the rock-and-roll outlaw of Catholic traditionalism—the bad influence that people somehow can't bring themselves to stop talking about. During the late sixties and early seventies, Schuckardt almost single-handedly

founded an influential community in the Pacific northwest that was characterized by a peculiar blend of Catholic survivalism, paranoia, and lockstep dogmatism. Although he's spent much of the past decade either on the run or in hiding,
Schuckardt remains a figure of immense symbolic importance for the extreme
Catholic right in the United States.

Schuckardt was born in 1937 in Seattle, and he graduated with a double major
in education and linguistics from the Jesuit-run Seattle University in 1959. After
brief stints as a seminarian and a high-school teacher, he joined the Blue Army, a
fairly mainstream Catholic Marian organization, and rapidly rose through its
ranks to a top administrative position. He was dismissed by the Blue Army in
1967 for publicly condemning the Second Vatican Council, and the following
year he founded a militantly traditionalist community in Coeur d'Alene, Idaho,
called the Fatima Crusade. In the autumn of 1971 Schuckardt was both ordained
a priest and consecrated a bishop by Daniel Q. Brown, one of the numerous bishops connected with the North American Old Roman Catholic Church, and
immediately afterward he changed the name of his community to the Tridentine
Latin Rite Church (TLRC). Over the next several years, Schuckardt traveled
extensively throughout the American west and midwest lecturing to groups of
disaffected Catholics on the evils of the council and new Mass. By all accounts, he
was a powerful and compelling speaker, and throughout the seventies dozens of
families from as far away as Illinois and Southern California transplanted themselves to Idaho in order to become full-fledged members of the TLRC. Some of
these people settled in Coeur d'Alene, and others started up a satellite community—the so-called City of Mary—in the neighboring town of Rathdrum.

In these formative years of the TLRC (and consistently thereafter), Schuckardt
preached a message of apocalyptic extremism. From beginning to end, he
insisted, the Second Vatican Council was a demonic conspiracy aimed at sub-
verting the traditions of the church and thereby preparing the way for an atheistic world order. And the so-called popes responsible for calling the council into
being and implementing its reforms were really anti-popes, paragons of
wretchedness, committed to annihilating the faith they had been entrusted with
preserving. With the hour of judgment rapidly approaching, Schuckardt
claimed, authentic Catholicism resided exclusively with the TLRC, and it was
only members of the TLRC who stood a realistic chance of attaining salvation.[29]

By the mid-seventies the TLRC had outgrown its facilities in Coeur d'Alene,
and in January 1978 Schuckardt shifted the community's center of operations to
a former Jesuit seminary, the Mount St. Michael's Scholasticate, located on the
outskirts of Spokane.[30] New recruits continued to stream into the community for
several years following its move to Spokane, but in 1984 the entire operation
blew up in Schuckardt's face. In April of that year four young men who had
recently broken away from the TLRC told the news media that they had been sexually assaulted by Schuckardt while studying for the priesthood under him at

103

Mount St. Michael's, and several weeks later a longtime TLRC priest named Denis Chicoine claimed that Schuckardt had been sexually abusing seminarians on a regular basis for at least a decade. The heat generated by these accusations proved too much for Schuckardt, and in early June of 1984 he fled Spokane with twenty hard-core supporters and $250,000 in community assets. Denis Chicoine took over as provisional leader of the TLRC, and on June 15, 1984, he obtained a ruling in the Spokane County Superior Court barring Schuckardt's return.

Although Schuckardt was now in exile, his reputation continued to take a hammering in the Spokane area. In 1986 the local diocesan newspaper, *The Inland Register*, published an exposé that depicted life in the TLRC under Schuckardt's command as a daily hell. In the name of Catholic tradition, according to the newspaper, everything from the personal finances to the reading habits of church members was strictly regulated, schoolchildren were routinely force-fed jalapeño peppers for disciplinary reasons, nuns were locked in attics for weeks at a time, and rituals of mortification were administered as a matter of course. In one particularly harrowing account, a young girl told of the punishment she received for vomiting after being forced to eat a batch of rotten carrots.

> Sr. Lucia got the razor strap out and said she'd count to five and if I didn't eat a spoon full of my vomit, then she would give me five whacks on my rear end. I got five spoon fulls down before I threw up again. After this, the other nuns there told Sr. Lucia to move me to another room because they were getting sick watching me.
>
> I went into another room and threw up all over a chair. I was made to kneel by the chair to lick the throw up, but I didn't want to. Sr. Clarita told me to say either "Jesus I love you" and lick the vomit clean or say "Jesus I hate you." I had all I could take, so I said, "Jesus I hate you." Sr. Clarita got on top of me and started punching me in the face for saying what I did.
>
> Finally, because I didn't want to get any more beating (I already had a black eye and a very sore bottom) so I ate the rest of the throw-up up.[31]

After fleeing Spokane, Schuckardt settled near the northern-California town of Greenville and tried to rebuild his ministry. In May 1987 disaster struck again, however, as he and eleven of his followers were arrested by a twelve-member SWAT team on charges of possessing drugs and stolen property. Upon searching Schuckardt's priory following the arrests, investigators apparently turned up a small cache of weapons, a stash of illegal drugs, and a bizarre assortment of church publications, including a pamphlet entitled *Death to the Race-Mixers* and another pamphlet that provided information on such sordid sexual thrills as body dismemberment.[32] Once this business was cleared up, Schuckardt moved his ministry back to the Pacific northwest, and over the past several years he and his followers, now calling themselves the Oblates of Mary Immaculate, have led an entirely clandestine existence in various parts of Oregon and Washington state.[33]

The Mount St. Michael's community in Spokane was initially traumatized by all of these revelations concerning its founder. In 1983 the community consisted of approximately two hundred families, a dozen or so priests, and (remarkably) more than a hundred nuns. In the months immediately following Schuckardt's fall from grace, these numbers dropped significantly. Some people left the community for a more moderate traditionalist organization, others went back to the institutional church, and still others drifted out of organized religion altogether. One of the immediate challenges facing the community in its recovery phase was to come up with a bishop to replace Schuckardt, and the first person they turned to was Fr. George Musey, who had been consecrated a bishop in the Thuc line in 1982. When this didn't work out (Musey apparently wanted more control than the Mount St. Michael's people were prepared to give him), the community enlisted the services of Fr. Robert McKenna, the pastor of an independent traditionalist chapel in Monroe, Connecticut, who had been consecrated by the Thuc bishop Guérard des Lauriers in 1986. For several years McKenna commuted intermittently from Connecticut to Spokane to perform confirmations and ordinations, and during this time the community slowly began to work its way back to health.[34]

This arrangement still left Mount St. Michael's without a bishop fully its own, however, and in 1991 the community asked Moises Carmona Rivera, a first-generation Thuc bishop from Acapulco, to select one of its own priests for consecration. Carmona Rivera selected a Lithuanian-American named Mark Pivarunas, and under his leadership (and also that of Fr. Daniel Dolan, who was consecrated by Pivarunas in 1993) the community has staged an impressive comeback. Today there are approximately 175 families, and six hundred laypeople altogether, in the Mount St. Michael's fold in Spokane, and an additional four hundred laypeople in three parishes the community operates in Omaha, Nebraska, and Tacoma, Washington. Almost all of these people are of working- or lower-middle-class background, and at least 80 percent of them have moved from elsewhere in the country for the sake of worshipping full-time at Mount St. Michael's. The community operates a private school (which is thus far not accredited) with two hundred students at its main complex in Spokane, another school with thirty students in rural Washington, and a seminary in Omaha. In addition to its two bishops, the community currently has a total of fifty nuns, fourteen priests, and eight priests-in-training, all of whom belong to the Congregation of Mary Immaculate Queen, and most of whom were recruited to religious life while students in one of the community's schools. Over the past several years, moreover, Pivarunas and Dolan have initiated an ambitious expansion program, opening new chapels and Mass centers at a dozen locations in the west and southwest.

WHILE MOUNT ST. MICHAEL'S has succeeded in exorcising most of its founder's demons, the theological doctrine that Schuckardt spent years propounding remains the community's most distinctive feature. This is the doctrine of *sedevacantism*, a Latin compound meaning "the chair is vacant." From his earliest days in Coeur d'Alene, Schuckardt was adamant that the papal throne in the contemporary church was unquestionably vacant, and the Mount St. Michael's community has done nothing since his departure to soften this position. Its rationale, in fact, is alluringly simple: if Catholic doctrinal teaching is eternally valid and unchanging, and if the papacy exists in order to preserve it as such, any so-called pope responsible for substantially altering this teaching cannot be regarded as legitimate. Now there is no doubt, the Mount St. Michael's people say, that traditional Catholic doctrine has been fundamentally altered in the contemporary church by the Second Vatican Council, and the implication of this is clear and unavoidable. The popes who have presided over the council and the changes stemming from it must be denounced as false. They are anti-popes, heretics of the highest order.

Above all else, the Mount St. Michael's community bases its sedevacantist case upon the Second Vatican Council's new teaching concerning religious liberty and ecumenism. In its Declaration on Religious Freedom (*Dignitatis Humanae*), the council taught that all people, by virtue of their inherent dignity, must be free to practice the religion of their choice. And in its documents on ecumenism and non-Christian religions, the council affirmed the spiritual value of Protestantism and of non-Catholic religion more generally, and called for a new dynamic of religious cooperation in the modern world. The problem with this, the Mount St. Michael's people claim, is that it directly contradicts everything Catholics were taught prior to the council. Pope Gregory XVI's *Mirari Vos* (1832). Pope Pius IX's *Quanta Cura* and *Syllabus of Errors* (1864). Pope Leo XIII's *Immortale Dei* (1865). Pope Pius XI's *Quas Primas* (1925). Pope Pius XII's *Mystici Corporis Christi* (1943). In various ways, all of these papal encyclicals drove home the same point: the Catholic church alone possesses the fullness of truth and the certain means of salvation, and the only right that must be recognized by the state is that of its citizens to practice Catholicism freely and without impediment. Either this is true, or what the council teaches is true. The principle of noncontradiction precludes the possibility of both being true at the same time. For Catholics still loyal to the traditional truth, there is only one thing to conclude. The council is schismatic, the popes of the council are schismatic, and the entire institutional church is also therefore schismatic. This is a syllogistic imperative—the high road of logical consistency.[35]

Other separatist (or traditionalist) groups, including both the SSPX and the SSPV, have also been deeply troubled by the council's innovative teaching on religious liberty and ecumenism, but most have stopped short of espousing (at least publicly) the sedevacantist position. (At various points in his own traditionalist career, Archbishop Lefebvre was tempted by sedevacantism, without ever finally crossing the line.[36]) From the Mount St. Michael's point of view, this is the consequence of cowardice, or, at the very least, of a fatally flawed logic. The new teaching clearly contradicts what came before it, and Catholics are compelled to take their stand either with or against the so-called popes who have authorized it. There is no middle position. Even worse are Catholic conservatives like E. Michael Jones and James Hitchcock, who complain about the excesses of the council while simultaneously expressing affection and admiration for John Paul II. To the Mount St. Michael's people, this is sheer papolatry. The new teaching on religious liberty and ecumenism to which John Paul II happily subscribes is demonstrably false, and its consequences for the life and mission of the institutional church have been utterly disastrous. And this is even leaving aside the horrors of the new Mass and all of the other lunatic innovations of the past twenty-five years that also enjoy the endorsement of John Paul II. Once again, immutability means yesterday and today and for all time. And the pope who would declare otherwise is not really the pope. It's as simple as that.

———

SITUATED HIGH ON A BLUFF OVERLOOKING northeastern Spokane, the Mount St. Michael's complex began life as a Jesuit seminary in 1916, and today it retains the idyllic charms of a small college campus. A four-story, Tudor-Gothic, brick building at the heart of the complex houses a chapel, a convent, a dormitory, and various meeting facilities, and branching off from it are tree-lined walks that peter out in the surrounding woods. In October 1994 I visited the complex for a week-long conference entitled "Fatima and World Peace," and upon entering the main meeting hall for the first time I was treated to the spectacle of fifty blue-and-white-habited nuns, at least half of whom looked to be under thirty years of age, circulating among the guests. (Long gone are the days when a mainstream women's religious order, such as the Notre Dame Sisters, could muster a similar show of strength.)

I met with Bishop Pivarunas shortly after arriving, and like several other traditionalist bishops currently on the national scene he was disarmingly youthful, almost boyish, in appearance. Pivarunas was born in Chicago in 1959 and raised there in a fairly strict Catholic family of five. His parents were right-wing Republicans, actively involved with the anticommunistic John Birch Society, and apparently just as right-wing in their religious views. His father in particular was convinced that the Second Vatican Council had resulted in a "watering-down of the faith," and when a young priest took to their parish pulpit one Sunday and extolled the virtues of religious tolerance, the entire family stood up and stormed out of church. When Pivarunas was just fourteen he went to a lecture by Fr. Denis Chicoine of the TLRC, and almost immediately afterward he decided he wanted to join the organization himself and study for the priesthood.

His parents were opposed to the idea, mainly because they mistrusted Francis Schuckardt, and the following year Pivarunas ran away from home to join up with the TLRC in Coeur d'Alene.

After the TLRC's move to Spokane, Pivarunas discovered that Schuckardt had deep-seated personal problems, but he never seriously considered leaving the organization. "He didn't touch me, but he was definitely sexually abusing seminarians, usually at his private residence in Spokane, and he was also taking a lot of drugs. His immorality was scandalous, but I continued to regard him as my legitimate bishop." Pivarunas was ordained by George Musey in 1985, the year following Schuckardt's flight, and consecrated a bishop by Moises Carmona Rivera in 1991.

Leaving the institutional church, with its deep history and even deeper symbolism, can be a daunting step, especially for someone zealously committed to the church's traditions, and I asked Pivarunas if he ever had misgivings or moments of doubt concerning his own move. "Not really; I've always been firm in my beliefs," he said. "I'm convinced that John Paul II is a false pope, and my conviction is based on the traditional teachings of the Catholic Church, the teachings that were consistently taught for over nineteen hundred years. Vatican II, and the so-called popes of Vatican II, have no authority to negate these teachings. In any case, you have to keep in mind that it's not us at Mount St. Michael's who have broken with the Church. We're still faithful. It's the entire conciliar Church that has broken with Catholic truth. We don't mind being a tiny minority. We take our inspiration from St. Athanasius, who stood against almost the entire world in the fourth century in opposing Arianism."[37]

Whereas Bishop Pivarunas was forced to run away from home to join Mount St. Michael's, Joseph Berchtold's involvement has been a total family affair. A thin, sallow, solemn man in his mid-thirties, who served as a sort of volunteer guide for me during my time at the complex, Berchtold and his six younger siblings have been mainstays of the Mount St. Michael's community for almost their entire lives. Three of his sisters are currently nuns in the Congregation of Mary Immaculate Queen, and, until his recent defection to a rival organization called the Apostles of Infinite Love, his brother Paul was regarded as one of the community's most promising young priests.

Berchtold's family moved from the Los Angeles area to Colorado Springs when he was seven years old, partly because of his father's poor health, and partly because both of his parents were unhappy with the theological liberalism that was rapidly working its way into the Catholic school system in Southern California after the Second Vatican Council. During their second year in Colorado Springs, his parents came into contact with the sedevacantist teachings of Francis Schuckardt, and were so impressed that in 1970 they joined the Tridentine Latin Rite Church and moved their entire household to the TLRC's satellite community in Rathdrum, Idaho. While their father scraped out a living as a carpenter,

Berchtold and his siblings went to TLRC schools in Coeur d'Alene and Spokane, and after finishing high school Berchtold entered the community's seminary in the hopes of becoming a priest. To the immense disappointment of his family, however, this didn't work out, and after almost seven years in the Mount St. Michael's seminary Berchtold dropped out and tried his hand at a variety of blue-collar jobs. At the age of twenty-seven, he enrolled in North Idaho College in Coeur d'Alene, and he eventually completed his degree at the University of Idaho in Moscow. For the past several years he has tried unsuccessfully to find work, and he is now living in Rathdrum with his father and youngest sister. (His mother died of cancer in 1983 at the age of forty-two.)

Like quite a few other people I interviewed in Spokane, Berchtold is drenched in conspiracy. In addition to being thoroughly committed to the sedevacantist orthodoxy of Mount St. Michael's, he subscribes wholeheartedly to the "Cardinal Siri" theory, is convinced that the Second Vatican Council was a Judeo-Masonic plot to undermine the church, and, at one point in our conversations, he rather ominously confided that he'd be open to joining a Catholic militia in order to defend the faith against the American government. We've already encountered most of these themes among the traditionalists of Berlin, New Jersey, and here too they form a pastiche of conjecture and fantasy rather than a coherent intellectual system. For traditionalists like Berchtold, in fact, conspiracy-talk frequently resembles an exercise in free association: mention of one conspiracy leads to mention of another, and then another, and so forth. In all of this, there is a marked disinclination to separate fact from fancy, or even to care about the difference between the two. Conspiratorial themes from various sources are bundled together, usually without the slightest concern for internal consistency or historical plausibility.

There are several recurrent themes in the conspiracy-spinning of Catholic traditionalists, one of which is an anti-Judaism that sometimes shades into outright anti-Semitism. Anti-Jewish sentiment is not, of course, an exclusive preoccupation of the extreme Catholic right in the United States: it is standard currency within the world of right-wing Protestantism as well, and has received popular expression in books such as Nesta Webster's *World Revolution: The Plot Against Civilization* (1922) and Eustace Mullins's *Secrets of the Federal Reserve* (1954).[38] Many Catholic traditionalists are at least passingly familiar with this literature, but the book that has exerted a far greater influence on them is *The Mystical Body of Christ in the Modern World*, written by an Irish priest named Denis Fahey and first published in 1935. In the final analysis, Fahey claims, modern world history can be understood as a cosmic struggle between the forces of spiritual truth, on the one hand, and the forces of materialism and subversion, on the other. The first camp, he says, is made up almost entirely of zealous Catholics, and the main players in the second camp are diabolical Jews. In virtually every secular enterprise that has helped shape modern history, from Bolshevism to high capitalist finance, it is Jews who have been the principal power brokers; and in every case their ultimate objective has been the destruction of Catholicism and the creation of an anti-Christian world order. In support of his thesis, Fahey even goes so far as to dredge up the infamous *Protocols of the Elders of Zion*, a laughably inauthentic document that was passed off at the turn of the century as a blueprint for a Jewish-Masonic conspiracy to achieve world mastery. It would be extremely difficult today to find mainstream Catholics willing to take Fahey's views seriously; but among traditionalists such as Joseph Berchtold, uninfected by ecumenism and desperate for final solutions, they are received as gospel truth.[39]

The group that is mentioned just as often as Jews in Mount St. Michael's conspiracy-talk (and very often in the same breath) is international Freemasonry. Here too we're on familiar ground. For two hundred years or so prior to the 1980s, Freemasonry was widely regarded by Catholics throughout the world as a sinister and subversive force intent on destroying the church and creating a worldwide secular utopia. Freemasonry, according to its Catholic detractors, was a pivotal (if largely hidden) agency behind both the French and Russian Revolutions, it was responsible for masterminding the overthrow of Catholic regimes in Latin America and elsewhere, and it was the controlling influence behind an international network of spies and agents provocateurs. Not all of these charges, in fact, were entirely groundless; and considering its compulsive secrecy, its ornate ritualism, its penchant for intrigue, and, at points, its virulent anti-Catholicism, Freemasonry was sometimes capable of giving at least an excellent impression of being the church's sworn enemy. Over the years, Freemasonry was condemned by no less than seven popes, and Catholics were forbidden, under automatic excommunication, from joining Masonic lodges. This prohibition was softened somewhat by Pope John Paul II in 1983, however, and in recent decades most American Catholics have ceased to regard Freemasonry as a serious threat.

But not Catholic traditionalists. Once an enemy, always an enemy, they claim, and the worst kind of enemy is usually the one that isn't taken seriously. At precisely the time when most Catholics had ceased worrying about them, traditionalists claim, Freemasons and Jews succeeded in infiltrating the institutional church and in engineering its collapse. "You have to ask yourself why the Church fell apart, so suddenly and so completely," Berchtold said to me. "We know that Freemasons and Jewish leaders have wanted for centuries to bring on a one-world government, and we know that the Church was the only thing really standing in their way. So when the Church let down its guard, they jumped at their chance. How did the Second Vatican Council come about? Because the Masonic-Jewish conspiracy planned it to destroy the Church. And as far as I'm concerned, the popes of the council, from Roncalli [John XXIII] onward, have all been secret Masons."[40]

It's certainly possible, of course, that every pope since John XXIII has been an agent of international Freemasonry intent on wiping out the church. The only problem is, there's no evidence for this. For Berchtold and many other Mount St. Michael's people, however, lack of evidence is only a temporary inconvenience. The conspiratorial truth is glaringly obvious to anyone not yet blinded by materialism and secularism, and its full significance will be revealed to all people in the years ahead. This fascination with conspiracy on the part of Berchtold and other young traditionalists I met in Spokane seems, to some degree at least, a function of their cultural isolation. Outside of Berchtold's time as a college student, Mount St. Michael's is the only world he has known since his earliest childhood. He doesn't read novels or works of secular scholarship, he finds contemporary popular culture shallow and immoral, and although he'd like to get married ("but only to a woman who is a traditionalist and rejects the papal authority of John Paul II and who is modest"), he doesn't date and is still a virgin. Almost all of his time in this culturally sequestered environment, he told me, is taken up with prayer, sleep, the study of religion, and speculation about what has gone wrong with the institutional church since the council.[41]

Even within the Mount St. Michael's community itself, in fact, there's at least some concern that this conspiracy mentality has been taken too far. During my stay in Spokane, I spoke at length with Fr. Casimir Puskorius, a thirty-four-year-old, second-generation Lithuanian-American who is Superior General of the Congregation of Mary Immaculate Queen. Puskorius has been a member of the community since he was ten years old, and his mother and both of his sisters are Mount St. Michael's nuns. (His father died in a car accident in the early seventies, shortly after moving his family to the Spokane area from Los Angeles.) "Yes, we do concoct these conspiracies endlessly," Puskorius said to me. "Some of our people are completely immersed in them. I personally have no stomach for these things. I find most of them ridiculous and even detrimental to faith. It's like some of our people desperately need the conspiracy theories so they can feel in control: 'Yes, something horrible has happened, and we know what it is.' But we don't need to know why things have gone the way they've gone. The important thing is that we do something about it. Some of our people seem to miss this point."[42]

ALTHOUGH MOST MOUNT ST. MICHAEL'S PEOPLE are lifelong Catholics, the community also includes a diverse assortment of converts and religious seekers. One of the most dedicated of these is a thirty-six-year-old, energetic, and extremely likable blue-collar worker named Brian Walker. Raised as a Methodist by his adoptive parents in various parts of the country (his adoptive father worked as a sex-complaints investigator in the federal civil service), Walker left school in the eleventh grade and spent several years bouncing from odd job to odd job. During the late seventies, he traveled back and forth across the country by freight train, taking work wherever he could find it, but through all of this he felt a gnawing sense of spiritual incompleteness.

"I was a total loner, I wasn't liked, and I was considered a goofball by a lot of people," he told me. "I didn't date, I wasn't really doing anything. I was kind of a lost innocent, and there were times when I felt completely depressed. Looking back now though, I can say I was a rebel with a cause. I was desperately search-ing for religious truth, but even more to the point, I was looking for the Catholic religion. When I was a young teenager, about fourteen I think, my parents had taken my sister and myself to Montreal, and we visited cathedrals. This really left an incredible impression on me. I regarded the crucifixes in those cathedrals as the embodiment of triumph. I knew then that this was what I wanted, but for the longest time I didn't have an idea how to go about getting it."

In 1981 Walker hopped a freight train from Seattle, where he'd been staying with his parents, and wound up in Chicago. While wandering the city's streets one evening, he decided to drop into a catechetical center run by the Paulist Fathers, and several months later he was baptized a Catholic. In a sense, however, this was only the beginning of his troubles. Before long Walker discovered (and here is a common refrain among Catholic converts) that the church he'd joined wasn't anywhere close to being the church he'd bargained for. What he'd expected was thundering certitude and worldly defiance, but what he got instead was simpering New Age theology and excuse-me liturgy. "I was unbelievably disappointed with post-conciliar Catholicism," he said. "It was a rip-off, not at all what I had joined the Church for. While I was being prepared for baptism, I used to go into the library of the Paulist Fathers and read these beautiful old cat-echisms with their solid doctrinal teaching. This was what I wanted, and what the modernist priests were now telling me just didn't jibe. This new Catholicism didn't seem much different from the Protestantism I'd grown up with."

Intensely disappointed that the Catholicism he had dreamed of no longer seemed to exist, Walker fell into a deep depression and at times even contem-plated suicide. He went to confession from time to time in the hopes of finding some solace, but he eventually gave up on this when a couple of the priests he confessed his sins to suggested that he see a psychiatrist. "This was just great! This could actually drive someone to suicide," he said. "Catholic priests wanting to send me to an expert in secular humanism when it was secular humanism, especially secular humanism in the Church, that was the problem."

Walker moved back to Seattle in 1985, found a job in construction, and became heavily involved in union activism. Despite his unhappiness with the mainstream church, he continued to attend Mass, and at his local parish he joined a small circle of conservative Catholics for at least a measure of social sup-port. After a while, however, even his conservative friends came to seem wishy-washy to him, and simply going to church became an agonizing experience. In early 1991, just when he was on the verge of giving up Catholicism altogether, he met a woman named Daisy, who told him that there was a traditionalist chapel in Tacoma where "the real Mass was being said." The Tacoma chapel was affiliated with the Mount St. Michael's community, and upon visiting it the following Sunday Walker was immediately smitten.

"This was my moment of liberation, the exclamation point," Walker said to me. "I'd been to a traditional Latin Mass once before, when I was in Chicago again for a week in 1989, and I felt like I'd finally come home. The hymns, the beautiful church and vestments, with the priest facing the altar. It was the first valid communion I'd ever received. So when Daisy told me about the chapel in Tacoma, I said to myself I'm going to the Latin Mass, and I don't care what happens. No more sadomasochism. I wanted out of the torture chamber. Nothing to do any longer with the disgusting, puerile, bland Novus Ordo Mass. I knew from Daisy that the Tacoma chapel was an outlaw chapel, but I wasn't worried about getting excommunicated. I went, and it was absolutely beautiful, and I've been going ever since."

Walker's decision to join the Mount St. Michael's chapel in Tacoma was tantamount to a full-fledged conversion experience. He felt immediately revitalized, his depression evaporated, and, for the first time in his life, he felt absolutely certain of who he was and what his responsibilities were. A large part of his responsibilities over subsequent months involved coming fully to terms with the sedevacantist theology of Mount St. Michael's, and he seems to have learned his lessons well.

"One of the things that had always drawn me to Catholicism was the power and authority of the papacy," he told me. "After I came into Mount St. Michael's, though, I realized I'd been living a lie. I came to the knowledge that the papacy was obviously and absolutely corrupted, and that J.P. II wasn't a true pope. Would a true pope promote something as ugly as the Novus Ordo Mass, or teach such obvious falsehoods as religious liberty and ecumenism? I had been brainwashed into blind obedience to the pope. I liberated myself from all of this. In the final analysis, I made up my mind to follow my own conscience."

Much like the theology that he's embraced, Walker's lifestyle today is austere and reclusive—stripped down to the essentials. He continues to work in the construction industry, but otherwise he spends most of his time at home taking care of his elderly mother and studying religion. He very rarely dates or socializes, and claims still to be a virgin. (He was involved in a fledgling romance with a conservative Catholic woman several years ago, but she broke it off when he converted to Mount St. Michael's.) Like Joseph Berchtold, he is appalled by rock music, Hollywood movies, and virtually every other component of contemporary popular culture. He hopes one day, after his mother dies, to enter the Mount St. Michael's seminary in Omaha and become a priest.[43]

———

THERE IS AN IRONY TO WALKER'S STORY, and to the story of Catholic traditionalism more generally. Like dozens of other people I interviewed in Spokane and Oyster Bay and Berlin, New Jersey, Walker is zealously attached to the traditions of the pre-conciliar church—its doctrines, its rituals and authority, its cultural imperviousness, its statues and hymns and incense—and just as zealously opposed to the council for disrupting these traditions. The council's greatest sin, according to Walker and other traditionalists, was to have Protestantized the church. Whereas Catholicism prior to the 1960s was a religion of obedience and institutional conformity, they claim, the council's teaching on religious liberty and the primacy of conscience has turned it into something barely distinguishable from Lutheranism or Methodism. Now every Catholic is entitled (or at least feels entitled) to disregard the teaching of the church and follow the dictates of her or his own conscience in matters of faith and morals. The inevitable consequence of such a development, according to traditionalists, is religious disunity. Where individuals themselves are the supreme arbiters of faith, what is to prevent groups of them from splintering off from the church and forming competing churches (or sects) of their own? This is precisely what has taken place within the world of Protestantism, traditionalists say, and the council has virtually guaranteed a similar fate for Roman Catholicism.

So how have traditionalists responded to this threat of Protestantization? They have broken off from the institutional church and formed competing groups of their own, and then in many cases broken off from these groups and formed still other ones. And all the while they have justified their actions by appealing not just to the sanctity of tradition but to the sanctity of individual conscience as well. (Walker: "In the final analysis, I made up my mind to follow my own conscience.") While ostensibly protesting the Protestantization of the church, in other words, traditionalists have taken the so-called Protestant principle to its outer limits. Archbishop Lefebvre breaks off from Rome and creates the SSPX, Clarence Kelly and company break off from the SSPX and create the SSPV, Daniel Dolan and company break off from the SSPV and join Mount St. Michael's. Schism leads to schism leads to schism—all in the name of tradition and the unity of faith.[44]

In the summer of 1995 I had an opportunity to discuss this apparent irony with Fr. Anthony Cekada in Cincinnati. Tall, self-confident, and enormously articulate, Cekada is currently associate pastor of the St. Gertrude the Great chapel in Sharonville, Ohio, and much of his life over the past twenty-five years reads like a veritable diary of traditionalist schism and counter-schism.

A third-generation American of Slovenian-Italian background, Cekada was raised in Milwaukee, where his father worked as a chauffeur for the Schlitz beer family. (His mother died of cancer when he was twelve years old.) After completing high school in 1969, Cekada entered St. Francis Major Seminary in Milwaukee and immediately began a one-man protest against, in his words, "the theological and liturgical modernism which the institution was literally drowning in." Within just months of his arrival, Cekada's professors branded him a troublemaking reactionary, and over time the seminary's administration tried to write him off as an emotional misfit. "They psychologized my opposition to theological liberalism," Cekada told me. "They claimed it was a manifestation of deep-seated personal problems. I was too rigid and too immature to function as a priest in the modern Church." On October 31, 1972, while the seminary was preparing for a Halloween dance to be held later the same day ("Talk about cognitive dissonance!" Cekada said), the administration informed him that he was being thrown out, but after he threatened to bring a lawsuit they backed down and worked out an arrangement that permitted him to graduate with a B.A.

Cekada entered a Cistercian monastery outside of Milwaukee in 1973, but he found the atmosphere even here far too liberal for his liking, and after professing his first, or temporary, vows in 1975 his superiors sent him to the ultraconservative Hauterive Monastery in Switzerland. This too fell considerably short of his standards, and in late 1975 Cekada entered Archbishop Lefebvre's seminary in Ecône. Two years later he was ordained a priest of the Society of St. Pius X. "By the time I was ordained, I had come to the conclusion that the new Vatican II system was profoundly wrong and evil and damaging to the salvation of souls," he said. "And I had also concluded, as a corollary of this, that it could not have come from legitimate authority. The true Church does not give forth evil. And because Vatican II produced evil effects, this meant that the popes supporting it were not legitimate. The Church is indefectible, and so I knew that the council and its popes didn't represent the true Church."

After returning to the United States, Cekada taught chant and liturgy for two years at the SSPX's Armada House of Studies in Detroit, and then spent several years teaching part-time at the SSPX seminary in Ridgefield, Connecticut, and performing pastoral work in Oyster Bay. This phase of Cekada's career came to an end in 1983 when he, Daniel Dolan, Clarence Kelly, and six other priests broke with the SSPX and formed the upstart Society of St. Pius V. "Although Lefebvre actually expelled us from the Society, we probably would have had to leave sooner or later anyways," Cekada said. "By this point Bishop Dolan and myself were already convinced sedevacantists, and we regarded Lefebvre as being far too soft and far too open to compromise. We also suspected that he was working on some sort of secret deal with the Vatican which would have sabotaged our entire cause."

Life in the SSPV wasn't quite the paradise Cekada had hoped for either, however, and in July 1989 he and Dolan bolted the organization, and after serving stints as independent traditionalists they both eventually joined forces with the Mount St. Michael's community. "Bishop Dolan and myself developed serious problems with Fr. Clarence Kelly," Cekada said. "He was the Superior of the SSPV, and we found him imperious, dictatorial, and conspiratorial. He seemed to think he was the font of all spiritual wisdom. He tried to turn the convent at Round Top into a cult of personality, and his behavior with some of the nuns was totally grotesque and unfair. Bishop Dolan and myself felt we had no choice but to leave, and it wasn't long before three other SSPV priests joined us."

I asked Cekada whether he and other traditionalists, by virtue of these sectarian fissions, were actually living out the "Protestant principle" they otherwise spent so much energy decrying. "Well, that is very glib, but it doesn't get you very far," he retorted. "The fragmentation of traditionalism is a function of the loss of authority within the Church. I would agree that it's distinctly unedifying, but it's not primarily our fault. We don't have a pope exercising authority and jurisdiction, the Vatican has absconded from responsibility, and whenever there's a vacuum of authority you have to expect that people will run off in somewhat different directions while trying to hold onto the truth. And you have to remember that our primary obligation is to render obedience to the truth, not to a papacy and an institution that have abandoned truth."

And did Cekada ever worry that his own sedevacantist version of the truth might actually turn out to be false? "I quite honestly never worry about that," he said. "If I'm wrong, then God has repealed the law of noncontradiction, and no one has told me about it. It can only be one way or the other. We can't say that Vatican II directly contradicts Catholic truth and tradition and yet uphold the authority of the people who transmit and enforce the teachings of the council. I'm convinced that the council and its popes are totally bogus. What they're preaching is not the Catholic religion."[45]

CONSERVATIVES AND SEPARATISTS/TRADITIONALISTS

Despite their shared abhorrence of theological liberalism, then, Catholic conservatives and traditionalists inhabit vastly different religious worlds. Whereas conservatives—starting with the most obvious difference—look to John Paul II for inspiration and leadership, traditionalists (or separatists) regard the current pope as either a hapless stooge or an outright force of evil. During my visit to Mount St. Michael's in 1994, I sat in on a lecture by a prominent traditionalist from Cincinnati named Timothy Duff, who came as close as possible to depicting John Paul II in demonic terms. "J.P. II is an anti-pope, the greatest anti-pope in the history of the world," Duff said. "He isn't the Antichrist; but he's the closest thing to it, a foreshadowing of it.... Multitudes of souls are being lost today because of the false and satanic religion that J.P. II is portraying as authentic Catholicism." Duff's traditionalist audience greeted these comments with appreciative applause; Catholic conservatives would have been horrified.[46]

Partly because they're so preoccupied with warding off the evil that lurks everywhere in the institutional church, and nowhere lurks more dangerously than in the Vatican, traditionalists have little interest in the kinds of public activism that engage conservatives. They're concerned primarily with cultivating a cloistered virtue; protesting abortion and other secular sins is far less important to them than creating Catholic utopias-in-miniature where the liturgies and doctrines of yesterday might somehow be restored to their full glory. "Yes, it's true that we're not nearly as prominent in fighting abortion as the people you call conservatives," Fr. Anthony Cekada told me in Cincinnati. "But that's because this is all conservatives have left. We still have the Tridentine Mass and the timeless teachings of the Church. This is where we invest our passion and our energy. They have nothing but their pro-life issues."

There's another angle to this as well. Unlike Catholic conservatives, traditionalists are full-blown introversionists. No less than Mennonite Amish or Hasidic Jews, they want to maintain standards of utmost religious purity; and entering the wildly ecumenical milieu of anti-abortion protest would put them at grave risk of contamination. Bishop Daniel Dolan touched upon this theme during a 1994 lecture he delivered at Mount St. Michael's. "We have to be very careful about joining other people in social action, whether on abortion or anything else," Dolan warned his audience. "I've often been scandalized by Novus Ordo Catholics protesting outside abortion clinics. The women are often immodestly dressed, and the women and men alike think nothing of singing Protestant hymns or chanting Protestant prayers. How tragic! If we were to participate in public displays such as this, we would run the risk of corrupting our own faith."[47]

Catholic conservatives and traditionalists differ as well in their degree of estrangement from the modern world. Whereas conservatives have made a kind of grudging peace with America's culture of religious pluralism, traditionalists would like nothing more than to be transported back to Louis XIV's France or Franco's Spain, where Catholicism enjoyed an unrivaled presidency over cultural life and other religions existed entirely at its beneficence. Their great dream is for a restored Christendom, and virtually every major historical development since the French Revolution is seen by them as an unqualified evil.[48]

Furthermore, while Catholic conservatism is an almost entirely lay-centered movement, traditionalism (or separatism) is dominated by priests. It is primarily priests who have provided its intellectual leadership, and priests as well who have presided over its intrigues and internal feuds. In at least one sense, this is readily understandable. Prior to the Second Vatican Council, Catholic priests in the United States and elsewhere enjoyed a highly enviable status: they were custodians of doctrine and practitioners of grace; and, in their highly specialized ritual capacity, they served as signposts of divinity itself. With the implementation of the council and the new Mass, however, this status underwent a marked decline. As Catholic worship took on a more communal character and laypeople assumed a progressively more prominent place in the church's ongoing life, the priesthood suffered an almost tangible loss of mystique and prestige. Not all priests, quite understandably, were pleased with this development, and some— including Archbishop Lefebvre, Gommar De Pauw, and other pioneering traditionalists—committed themselves to a campaign of protest against it.[49]

This is not, of course, to say that Catholic traditionalism is entirely the consequence of status-deprivation on the part of psychologically maladjusted priests.
Many traditionalists have serious theological objections to the council and new
Mass, and many have demonstrated considerable courage in carrying these objections to their logical limit. Still, there seems little question that issues of status
and prestige figure prominently in the traditionalist world. In their chapels and
Mass centers, traditionalist priests command a level of respect and deference that
priests still connected with the mainstream church can only dream of. Among
their parishioners, they are sometimes regarded as superhuman figures, and they
frequently inspire a degree of loyalty normally reserved for the guru or prophet.
For many lay traditionalists, in fact, the traditionalist priest is the very embodiment of Catholicism; the last bulwark between salvation and oblivion.

All of this prestige and deference, moreover, carries with it a certain temptation of power that not all traditionalist priests have succeeded in withstanding.
Many have run their ministries like personal fiefdoms, bringing everything
tightly under their own control and refusing to tolerate even the slightest challenge to their personal authority. In some cases they have brazenly courted episcopal advancement, and in others they've attempted to extend their sphere of
influence by raiding rival traditionalist camps for precious resources.

The dominance of priests in the traditionalist scheme of things can be seen in
other areas as well. Among Catholic conservatives, adherence to the anti-contraceptive teaching of Pope Paul VI's encyclical, *Humanae Vitae*, is regarded as an
absolute necessity of faith—a kind of litmus test of authentic Catholic identity
in the modern world. Catholic traditionalists, in contrast, seem hardly to know
the encyclical even exists. When I asked Joseph Berchtold where he stood personally on *Humanae Vitae*, he gave me a puzzled look and admitted that he'd
never heard of it. And Fr. Paul Baumberger of the Society of St. Pius V told me
that he'd first have to read the encyclical before commenting on it. This apparent
indifference on the part of traditionalists to *Humanae Vitae* is partly because it
was written by Paul VI, a conciliar pope who is regarded by them with particular scorn, but also because the encyclical deals almost exclusively with the question of lay sexuality. And on the traditionalist scale of concerns, this is hardly a
question that warrants top billing. For traditionalists everywhere, the marquee
issue is the Mass, and the star performers are the priests who preside over it. Lay
Catholics exist primarily in order to support the Mass and its priests; and the less
heard from them otherwise, the better.

And this seems especially the case with traditionalist women. Although the
women of Catholic conservatism aren't nearly as prominent as the men, their
prospects for upward advancement aren't entirely closed off. Conservative
Catholic women such as Helen Hull Hitchcock, Anne Roche Muggeridge, and
Janet Smith have risen to positions of intellectual leadership within their movement, and conservative Catholic pro-life activists have grown accustomed to hav-

ing women call at least some of the shots. Catholic traditionalism, in contrast, is unremittingly patriarchal: it is the men—and especially the priests—who call all of the shots. Women are relegated to positions of public invisibility. While undertaking research for this book, for example, I found it virtually impossible to find traditionalist women willing to be interviewed. With very few exceptions, the women I approached begged off and pointed me in the direction of their local priest. Father always knows best. More often than not, conservative Catholic women recognize this to be untrue.

Finally, another note of irony. For all of their right-wing vehemence, Catholic traditionalists aren't really that much different from Catholic liberals in their attitude toward the papacy and papal authority. Since the Second Vatican Council, Catholic liberals have regularly dissented from papal teaching on sexual matters by invoking the primacy of individual conscience and by challenging the scope and legitimacy of papal infallibility. The pope can teach whatever he wants, liberals have said, but whether or not he should be listened to is very much an open question. Although their own quarrel with the papacy has centered on matters of liturgy and doctrine rather than on sexual issues, Catholic traditionalists have adopted almost exactly the same line. The pope (or would-be pope) can change the Mass to his heart's content, or promote innovative teachings on ecumenism and religious liberty, but faithful Catholics are always free to resist his folly. In the final analysis, truth supersedes obedience, and conformity to one's conscience wins out over conformity to Rome. As theories of religious dissent go, Catholic liberals couldn't ask for anything more.[50]

MYSTICAL MARIANISTS AND APOCALYPTICISTS
THE APOSTLES OF INFINITE LOVE

CHAPTER FIVE

AS NAMES OF RELIGIOUS COMMUNITIES GO, the Apostles of Infinite Love sounds like it belongs somewhere in California. The name conjures up images of woolly-minded New Age occultism, or of recalcitrant hippies still living out their sixties dreams. St. Jovite, Quebec, is a long way from California, however, and the Apostles of Infinite Love is a Catholic monastic community with very little sympathy for either New Age falderol or (despite rumors to the contrary) sixties-style hug-fests. Established in Canada in 1962 by Father John Gregory of the Trinity (né Gaston Tremblay), the Infinite Love community is every bit as radical in its own way as the more extremist traditionalist groups discussed in the previous chapter. Like the Society of St. Pius V and Mount St. Michael's, it rejects the legitimacy of both the Second Vatican Council and the so-called popes of the council, but unlike them, it doesn't believe that the papal throne is currently vacant. John Paul II is unquestionably a false pope, the Infinite Love community claims, but this doesn't mean that a true pope doesn't exist somewhere else: somewhere else such as in St. Jovite, Quebec.

Gaston Tremblay was born in Rimouski, Quebec, in 1928, and was raised in an apparently unexceptional working-class Catholic family. He left home at the age of sixteen and moved to Montreal, where he entered the Community of the Brothers of St. John of God, or the Hospitalers, and became known as Brother John Grande. After five years with the Hospitaler Brothers, which he spent mostly as an orderly in a community-run hospice for the chronically ill, Brother John claimed to receive a mystical vision in which "a Pope chosen by God" told him that he was called "to organize a community which would preach the Gospel with the power of the Apostles."[1] Several other visions with similar themes followed this one, and in 1952 Brother John decided to leave the Hospitaler community in order to pursue his new calling.

On October 24, 1952, he met with Archbishop Paul Léger of Montreal and received permission to found a religious community for men that would be based on "strict evangelical poverty."[2] The new community, which was called the Congregation of Jesus and Mary, initially consisted only of Brother John and three disciples, and the small group spent several years wandering throughout rural and small-town Quebec as latter-day mendicants, preaching, begging for food, and sleeping in makeshift hovels. Their rather fearsome appearance in these early years, gaunt and brown-robed and bearded, coupled with their fierce denunciations of clerical wealth and privilege, brought them into frequent conflict with Quebec's Catholic establishment, and over time they were barred outright from two dioceses and dissuaded from visiting several others. The group eventually scrounged up enough money to purchase their own tract of land, and in 1958 they took up residence on an old farm located just a mile outside of the Laurentian resort town of St. Jovite.

For the next several years, Brother John's energy was mostly taken up with the construction of a new monastery for his community, but in March 1961 his life was changed irrevocably when he bumped into an obscure French mystic named Fr. Michel Collin at Montreal's Dorval Airport. Fr. Collin was born in Béchy, a tiny village in Lorraine, France, in 1905, and was ordained to the priesthood in 1933. The priesthood, however, was just the beginning. In April 1935 Collin announced that he had been mystically consecrated a bishop by Christ himself, and later that year he formed a new religious community, the Order of the Mother of God, that he claimed was the fulfillment of a request the Virgin Mary had made during her miraculous apparition at La Salette, France, a century earlier. According to Catholic apparitional lore, the Virgin appeared to two shepherd children at La Salette in 1846 and spoke to them of the horrible catastrophes that awaited both the church and world as divine punishment for their obdurate sinfulness. One of the children, Mélanie Calvat, eventually published a brochure outlining the full content of the La Salette revelation, including the Virgin's request that a new community be established for the purpose of strengthening Catholic faith during the forthcoming days of tribulation. It was precisely this community, Collin claimed, that he had brought into being with the Order of the Mother of God.[3]

On October 7, 1950, Collin received still another ecclesiastical promotion when he was mystically crowned pope under the name of Clement XV. Despite these impressive credentials, however, his community (which he was now calling the Apostles of Infinite Love) had difficulty attracting new members, and by the time he met Brother John it was made up of just a half a dozen or so elderly priests. Their chance (or predestined) encounter at Dorval in 1961 was apparently a moment of mystical déjà vu. Collin, or Pope Clement, claimed that he had seen Brother John several times in visions, and Brother John claimed to recognize Collin as the "Pope chosen by God" from the vision he had experienced more than a decade earlier while still a Hospitaler Brother.[4] After comparing prophetic notes, the two men agreed to merge their respective communities into a single Apostles of Infinite Love, and the following year Brother John traveled to France, where, in rapid succession, he was ordained a priest and consecrated a bishop by Collin.

Word of Brother John's ordination and consecration at the hands of the mystical pope, Michel Collin, spread rapidly through Quebec, and the province's Catholic leadership was clearly not impressed. On May 10, 1962, Bishop Eugène Limoges of the Mont Laurier diocese, which included the St. Jovite area, publicly denounced the Apostles of Infinite Love as a sacrilegious group and warned that any Catholics associating with them would be subject to automatic excommunication.[5] Warnings such as this, however, did not succeed in scaring everyone off. At the time of Brother John's consecration, there were only seven full-time Apostles living at the monastery in St. Jovite. A year later there were more than thirty, and by the spring of 1964 the number had increased to almost ninety. By this time the Second Vatican Council was well under way, the threat of religious change was already in the air, and the St. Jovite monastery seemed to many of those who were drawn to it a refuge of simple and robust piety. (That its leader was a man with a rapidly growing reputation for mystical powers did nothing, of course, to hurt its attractiveness.) Although the monastery didn't actively solicit new recruits, it did everything possible to accommodate anyone who showed an interest in joining. In the summer of 1962, the community began to accept single women as full-fledged members, and the following year it began to take in married couples and entire families with children.

As its population continued to swell during the mid-sixties, the monastery came under increasing attack from the external society. Local clergymen accused it of being a haven for criminal activity, including white slavery and prostitution, and the parents (or grandparents) of some of its members accused Father John of everything from hypnotism to spiritual despotism. These insults and rumors were nothing, however, compared to the campaign of harassment waged against the Infinite Love community by the Quebec civil authorities. On December 12, 1966, Judge Léandre Prévost of the Social Welfare Court of St. Jerome ruled that the monastery was an unsuitable environment for children and that all of its underage residents must be handed over to the custody of the province. When Father John refused to comply with the court order, the provincial police conducted several raids on the monastery and seized a total of seventeen children, all of whom were turned over to the Quebec social welfare bureaucracy. In the meantime, Father John went into hiding with another fifty-five children, and in February 1967 he was listed on Interpol as one of the ten most wanted criminals in Quebec. The saga of "the hidden children of St. Jovite," as it was dubbed in the news media, went on for almost seven months, with the provincial government threatening to shut down the Infinite Love monastery altogether, and Father John vowing, at one point, "We will fight unto death, if necessary, we will let ourselves be cut up into tiny pieces, but we will not hand over our children."[6] In the end, it was the provincial government that blinked first. In December 1967 a judicial delegation visited St. Jovite and determined that conditions at the monastery weren't nearly as bad as the province had been led to believe, and on March 13, 1968, Judge Armand Trudelle of the Quebec Superior Court overturned the December 1966 ruling of Judge Prévost and thereby paved the way for the children's return.[7]

The only thing the Infinite Love community seems actually to have been guilty of during this entire debacle was religio-cultural deviance. Conditions at the monastery were orderly and sanitary, and there was never any evidence of abuse or neglect. The problem was that the monastery was no ordinary community. Its leader was a self-professed mystic who had broken with Rome and who seemed to regard virtually every aspect of the broader culture as irredeemably corrupt. For many representatives of Quebec's political and religious establishment, as well as relatives of monastery residents, this was damning enough.

Although its legal outcome was favorable to the Infinite Love community, the "hidden children" affair generated reams of adverse publicity, including a highly inflammatory article that appeared in the January 27, 1967, issue of *Time* Magazine. Someone who kept particularly close tabs on the affair was Michel Collin (or Pope Clement XV), who was back in France presiding over the European chapter of the Apostles of Infinite Love. While Father John was busy dodging the police in Quebec, Collin apparently began to have second thoughts about his association with the St. Jovite monastery, and in 1967 he claimed to receive a divine revelation that instructed him to bypass Father John as his papal successor. Not to be outdone, Father John had a revelation of his own, in which he presumably learned that he had been divinely chosen to succeed Collin, and on September 10, 1968, he claimed that he had been mystically elevated to the papacy under the name of Gregory XVII. Perhaps sensing that he was outgunned in this duel of revelations, Collin professed to receive some sort of mystical confirmation of Father John's papacy the following May, and immediately afterward he sent the following note of reconciliation to St. Jovite:

> 4:00 p.m. Call after call, impossible to reach you. May the world know that I ask forgiveness of God, of everyone. Heaven spoke wondrously on May 8, 1969. Be with us in total union for all that regards the Holy Church, mystical universal Pontiff, to help, complete, substitute for, replace me according to the views of God and the mysterious times that are coming. Gregory XVII, God bless you, dear Father and Brother.[8]

After Father John's elevation to the papacy, the Quebec Apostles decided that the time had arrived to extend their presence beyond the rural confines of St.

Jovite. In 1970, accordingly, they opened a mission in Montreal and then spent several years vigorously recruiting new adherents throughout the Caribbean. They received a chilly reception in Haiti, but during the early to mid-seventies they succeeded in establishing missions in Guadeloupe, Puerto Rico, the Dominican Republic, and Guatemala. The Guadeloupe mission was easily the most successful of these, and for a period during the mid-seventies (before pressure from the local government forced it to shut down) it attracted thousands of pilgrims on a weekly basis for a full slate of traditional Catholic devotions.[9] Having established a decent beachhead in the Caribbean, the Apostles next set their expansionist sights on North America, and during the late seventies and early eighties they opened new mission centers in Toronto, Winnipeg, Vancouver, Brooklyn, and Paterson, New Jersey.

Throughout all of this expansion, the St. Jovite monastery remained the primary center of operations for the Apostles and their made-to-order pope. And Father John, or Father Gregory, as he was now sometimes called (eschewing pontifical formality, he generally preferred not to be addressed as Gregory XVII), was by no means inactive. At some point during the early seventies, he apparently received a revelation that mandated the ordination of women, and over the next several years many of the community's nuns also became priests. In 1975, moreover, he issued a 270-page encyclical entitled *Peter Speaks to the World*, which spelled out his views on everything from juvenile delinquency to the approaching apocalypse.

Although the encyclical today comes across as downright stodgy at points, with homilies against drinking, dancing, smoking, professional sports, and even mixed swimming, it also includes several fairly progressive sections on economic justice and the rights of labor. (In contrast to most leading traditionalists, Father John is no doctrinaire anticommunist.) Its most important sections, however, are those dealing with Father John's papacy and with the role of the Apostles of Infinite Love in the economy of salvation. Like Michel Collin before him, Father John explicitly links his papacy to the famous Marian apparition that allegedly took place at La Salette, France, in 1846. While speaking with the two shepherd children at La Salette, Father John says, the Virgin Mary warned that the day was coming when "Rome will lose the Faith and become the seat of Antichrist." And with the rise of theological liberalism and false ecumenism after the Second Vatican Council, according to Father John, this day has now arrived. The entire institutional church under Rome has fallen into apostasy, and a new church, headed by Gregory XVII, has been raised up to preserve authentic Catholicism. Regardless of how small this new church might be, or how fiercely persecuted, Father John says, it will persevere in truth until the very end.

When God chastised the world by the Flood, only a tiny portion of humanity was spared by entering Noah's Ark. Thus, the True Church of Jesus Christ, which God has charged Us to direct, is the Ark of the new times raised up by Providence to save a portion of Christendom. "Fight, children of light," said Our Lady of La Salette, "you little number who see; for behold the time of times, the end of ends."[10]

Although the encyclical was one of Father John's first major achievements as pope, the Apostles of Infinite Love weren't given much opportunity to savor it. In 1976 a fire destroyed most of the St. Jovite monastery, and while the Apostles were hard at work rebuilding it they once again ran into trouble with Quebec's civil authorities. And once again, the trouble started out as a custodial tug-of-war involving some of the monastery's children.

In 1970 a married couple from Ontario named Bill Currier and Carmen Sabourin joined the Infinite Love community with their three children. They had a fourth child shortly after joining, and in 1971 Bill Currier was ordained a priest by Father John. (By this time, Father John had extended the privilege of ordination to married Apostles.) For the most part, the couple seemed model citizens of the community, but in 1973 Currier left without warning and returned to Ontario, and three years later he petitioned Quebec's Family Court for exclusive custody of his children. On August 19, 1976, the court ruled in Currier's favor, but Carmen Sabourin, possibly with the connivance of Father John, insisted that the children were far better off staying with her at the monastery, and she refused to surrender them to her husband. Currier eventually gained physical custody of his three younger children (the oldest, by then of legal age, decided to stay in the monastery as a monk), but in the meantime Father John was tried on charges of contempt of court and illegal sequestration, convicted, and sentenced to two years in Ste. Anne des Plaines Penitentiary in Montreal.[11]

Father John was released from Ste. Anne des Plaines on March 25, 1981, after serving six months of his sentence, only to find that his community was still the subject of intensive controversy. Picking up where they'd left off in the wake of the "hidden children" affair, the Canadian and American news media were once again portraying the Apostles of Infinite Love as a public menace. The group's leader was a power-crazed tyrant prepared to go to any lengths—even kidnapping and forcible confinement—to keep his charges in line. And rank-and-file Apostles were lip-synching zombies, spiritual losers who'd turned over their minds and wallets to Father John and his henchmen in a wacky quest for immortality. As is usually the case with such matters, former members of the community were only too willing to feed the media a steady diet of atrocity tales. Mind-numbing regimentation . . . sexually predatory monks . . . sadistic nuns. There seemed no limit to the community's sinfulness.[12]

BY THE LATE EIGHTIES, the controversy arising from the Currier case had mostly worn itself out, and since then the Infinite Love community has enjoyed a period of relative calm. In September 1995 I visited the St. Jovite monastery for the first time, having been warned beforehand by representatives of two anti-cult organizations that I could expect to find barbed wire and guard dogs, which were presumably useful not just for keeping enemies out but also for keeping itchy members in. I found the monastery about a mile along a sparsely traveled rural road running west from the town of St. Jovite. At its main entrance was a small, brown-shingled gatehouse with a window slot on the side from which a sister-sentry monitored incoming traffic. When I identified myself, the sister lowered a chain that was strung across the front drive and permitted me access to the monastery's grounds. (In terms of security measures, this humble arrangement seemed a far cry from razor wire and German shepherds.) Immediately beyond the gatehouse, and off to the left, stood a jumble of huts and house-trailers, which serve as accommodation for monastery residents known as Third-Order Disciples. These are laypeople, either single or married, who belong to the community but are exempted from the religious vows of poverty, chastity, and obedience. (Partly because of the turmoil that has accompanied the community's various legal run-ins, the number of Disciples in full-time residence at the monastery has dropped precipitously in recent years. Today there are only twenty adult Disciples and fifteen children in residence; in the late seventies, there were sixty adults and more than a hundred children.) The main monastery building itself, and also an adjacent convent, both large cinder-block structures that were rebuilt almost entirely from scratch following the fire of 1976, stood another fifty yards or so back from the road. Dominating the entire scene was an illuminated bell tower, about seventy feet high, with an immense bronze Sacred Heart statue perched at the top. (On the public road leading to the monastery, slightly less than half a mile away, there was also a small Infinite Love mission compound, consisting of a small chapel and several simple wooden domiciles, with a total of ten nuns and novices in residence.)

In addition to the lay Disciples and their children, the monastery is currently home to about two hundred priests and religious brothers and sisters, all of whom belong to the Order of the Magnificat of the Mother of God, which is the official name for the specifically monastic division of the Apostles of Infinite Love. (The order has approximately three hundred members worldwide.) Slightly more than half of this number are women, and slightly more than half are under forty years of age. Brother Apostles, as male members of the order are called, are tonsured and wear a brown robe and hood; Sister Apostles wear a blue robe and veil, and a white collarette. Like the Shakers and several other nineteenth-century utopian groups, the Magnificat Order practices a strict community of goods. Newcomers to the order are required to turn over their worldly assets to the larger community, and all material resources are shared in common. Also like the Shakers, the order enforces a rule of strict sexual segregation: brothers and sisters live and labor as two distinct communities, with separate quarters reserved for all activities.

127

The monastery has a small farm nearby on which it produces most of its own food, and it also runs a print shop that produces religious calendars and other items (including a monthly magazine called *Magnificat*), which are sold door-to-door by Apostle Sisters in various locales throughout North America. Economic support for the community also comes from people known as *tertiaries*, who are lay adherents living and working in the outside world.[13]

The Infinite Love community has become increasingly circumspect in its dealings with outsiders in recent years, and the terms of my visit were carefully laid out right from the start. Shortly after arriving, I met with a Fr. Simon in a small reception room located just off the monastery's main vestibule. Forty-fiveish, witty and articulate, and enormously self-assured, Fr. Simon serves as one of the community's principal liaisons with the outside world. I asked if I might learn something of his own personal background.

"Probably not," he said.

"This information is a secret?"

"No, but it's against our community regulations to discuss our pre-conversion lives."

"But I'm interested in how you, and others in the community, came to be here. I suspect that your personal narratives might prove illuminating."

"Maybe so. But we find this sort of thing completely irrelevant and uninteresting. It was customary prior to the council for monastic orders to have regulations against self-disclosure. And this is exactly what we have here."

Principled (or strategic) silence of this sort is, of course, entirely reasonable. Religious devotees should feel no obligation to discuss their private lives with outsiders, and in a compulsively confessional age such as ours, rules against self-disclosure might actually be seen as virtuous in their own right. Enemies of the Infinite Love community, however, regard the matter in an entirely different light. They say that community adherents are prevented from discussing their past lives mainly because they have been psychically stripped of those lives by Father John and his chief lieutenants. Far from being agents of discretion, adherents are victims of mind control and cultic repression.

It isn't surprising to hear accusations of mind control and cultic repression coming from the anti-cult establishment, but the very same accusations are also regularly raised against the Apostles of Infinite Love by Catholic traditionalists. With the possible exception of the Second Vatican Council, in fact, there is nothing that traditionalists of all stripes hate more than the Infinite Love community. And for the most part, this may be described as a hatred of the "almost-the-same" variety.[14]

While the Infinite Love community is strikingly similar to traditionalist groups in some respects, it is regarded by them as infuriatingly different in others. Like the Society of St. Pius V and Mount St. Michael's and so forth, it completely rejects the authority of the council and the popes of the council, but unlike them, it doesn't feel irrevocably bound to the traditions and disciplines of the pre-conciliar church. The community ordains married men and, even more scandalous, both single and married women; and it celebrates the Tridentine Mass in French and English rather than in Latin. Moreover, while traditionalists have been engaged in a frantic scramble to come up with bishops of their own, the Infinite Love community has trumped them all by coming up with its own pope. Indeed, Father John, as Gregory XVII, has given the Infinite Love community a seductive allure that even some traditionalists have found difficult to resist. At present, roughly two-thirds of the community's full-time members are American, and a significant number of these have defected from traditionalist groups in the United States in order to join Father John in St. Jovite. To Catholic traditionalists in general, the Infinite Love community is like a maddeningly precocious and wayward sibling who somehow makes one's own achievements look meager in comparison.[15]

While continuing our conversation over a bread-and-soup supper in an adjoining room, Fr. Simon spoke of his community's tortured relations with Catholic traditionalists. "It's safe to say that traditionalists resent us as much as, if not more than, anyone else," he said. "They are spiteful and narrow, terribly circumscribed and prejudiced. We frustrate them tremendously because we're not a traditionalist community like them. We don't have a strict Tridentine Mass—we have a variation of it—and they can't get beyond this. And, of course, they can't get beyond our ordination of women."

In any event, Fr. Simon added, there probably wasn't enough time remaining on the historical clock for the Infinite Love community to mollify all of its enemies. "The last thing we can worry about now is what traditionalists think of us. We are currently living in the End Times. We are experiencing the beginning of the chastisement. The dénouement will likely take place around the year 2000. Of course, this depends on the response of men and women. It's within our power to reduce the level of suffering the world is facing, but I wouldn't be overly optimistic about this. Our track record is pretty horrible. We are now in a period of general chastisement—a purgation of the world. There will also be a second chastisement, which will be directed at the wicked who remain on the earth."[16]

―――――――――

HERE WE ENTER THE DEEP REACHES of Catholic apocalypticism. The Infinite Love community is just one of many groups on the far fringes of the church that live and breathe end-time prophecy. Taken together, all of these groups constitute a kind of pre-millennial underground within the broader Catholic world. Rather than the popes of Rome or the traditions of the past, they take as their final authority the words of woe, or apocalyptic warnings, that have been issued by Catholic mystics and seers throughout the ages. Anna-Katarina Emmerick, the eighteenth-century German stigmatist; Nostradamus; Mélanie Calvat, the seeress of La Salette; Lucia dos Santos of Fatima fame—it is these people, and dozens like them, who are the true authorities of faith. Through Marian apparitions and other mystical revelations, they have been given prophetic insight into the final drama of world history, and only those who heed their warnings stand a realistic chance of salvation.

And how exactly, according to these mystics and seers, will the final drama of world history be played out? The challenge here, of course, is in the correct reading of their prophecies, and the Infinite Love community and its competitors on the current apocalyptic scene haven't always read them the same way. Nevertheless, most Catholic apocalypticists would agree that the prophetic evidence points to the following three-stage scenario:

1. *The first chastisement.* This stage begins with a great collapse of faith, or great apostasy. Most Catholics throughout the world abandon traditional doctrine and morals and throw themselves into heresy and hedonism. An anti-pope is installed in Rome, and the authentic Catholic church is reduced to a small and persecuted remnant. Communism (or some functionally equivalent force) assumes iron-fisted control of almost the entire world, but a Great Pontiff and a Great Monarch, both directly appointed by God, rise up and lead a Catholic counterforce into battle. In the meantime, however, the world is ravaged by a series of horrible disasters and plagues, some of which may be the result of a comet striking the earth. There are floods, earthquakes, droughts, and epidemics. Countless people die, and the earth's resources are vastly depleted, but the Great Pontiff and Great Monarch eventually triumph and establish a new Christendom.

2. *Period of peace and virtue.* With the establishment of a renewed Christendom, there is a brief period of peace and prosperity on earth. The Great Pontiff reigns over the spiritual realm, the Great Monarch over the temporal, and traditional Catholic beliefs and values flourish. The church receives millions of new converts, and its religious authority is uncontested.

3. *The second chastisement.* This Catholic utopia, however, doesn't last. Over time, there is a widespread return to infidelity and wickedness, and a second period of war and calamity brings a final end to world history.

Although they mostly agree on this rudimentary end-time framework, there's also much that Catholic apocalypticists disagree on. Some believe that the first chastisement is already well under way, and that there's little hope of either reversing it or of softening its effects. Others believe that with massive conversion and repentance the first chastisement might still be postponed, or its severity mitigated. The Infinite Love community takes the more pessimistic view: the doomsday clock is already winding down, and there's virtually no chance of turning it off. The community also holds that Father John, or Gregory XVII, is the Great Pontiff directly chosen by God, and it recently published a 950-page book of prophecy entitled *Thou Art Peter* in an effort to cinch its case. Didn't Mélanie Calvat, the seeress of La Salette, once claim that "The great Pope [of the end-time] will not be Roman"? And who possibly besides Father John could the nineteenth-century prophet known as the Monk of Padua have had in mind when he declared: "You are the Angelic Shepherd of Rome, O benevolent Doctor, O most indulgent Father. Hail Gregory XVII, Father most holy, necessary Shepherd"?[17]

Of course, passages such as these, and they are piled up by the dozen in *Thou Art Peter*, would not likely convince anyone of Father John's mystical papacy who wasn't already convinced (or wanting to be convinced) of it. As is so often the case with religious affairs, it is belief that comes first. The evidence (such as it is) serves merely as convenient corroboration.

———————

SR. MICHELLE, FOR ONE, certainly requires no further convincing. Blue-and-white-habited and bespectacled, with sharp features that somehow manage at the same time to be warm and inviting, Sr. Michelle first joined the Infinite Love community in 1963, when she was twenty-three years old, and today she serves as assistant to the Mother Superior of the Magnificat Order. Sitting in the same reception room where I first interviewed Fr. Simon, she told me that her belief in Father John (or Fr. Gregory) hasn't wavered in the thirty-odd years since she met him. "I have personally been involved with so many of our community's struggles," she said. "The persecutions . . . the constant attacks in the media . . . the false accusations. I've testified on behalf of Fr. Gregory in court, and I've been thrown in jail for my loyalty to him.[18] I don't have personal doubts now, and I never have doubted him. I made my decision to follow Fr. Gregory a long time ago. When I first met him, I knew that he had been called to save the Catholic faith. And now I also know that he is the true pope. The fundamental Catholic religion has been betrayed in Rome. Our community, with Fr. Gregory leading us, represents the authentic faith."

This personal testimonial notwithstanding, Sr. Michelle was almost as guarded regarding the details of her life as Fr. Simon was his. "We want to discourage gossip and idle curiosity," she told me. "Humanly speaking, people want to talk about themselves, but we regard this as completely unimportant. The first apostles gave testimony to Jesus; they didn't talk about their personal lives. And neither do we."

One aspect of her personal life that Sr. Michelle didn't mind talking about was the priesthood. Of the approximately150 women who belong to the Magnificat

Order, roughly fifty (including several who are married) have been ordained by Father John. Sr. Michelle was ordained twenty years ago, and she regards the Infinite Love community's openness to women priests as one of its greatest strengths. "Ever since I was very young, I'd always yearned for the priesthood, and I'm very grateful to the community for recognizing the priestly vocations that some women truly have. Of course, to traditionalist Catholics, this is the ultimate scandal. I think this is the main reason, even more than Fr. Gregory's papacy, why they're horrified by us. It's important to recognize that myself [sic] and the community's other women priests don't regard ourselves as part of the feminist movement, and we're not trying to take over from the brothers. God has decided the time has come for this. I think God has decided to make women priests because men haven't done their jobs."

One can never tell exactly where mysticism or personal charisma might lead, of course, and this is one reason why, historically, the institutional church has tried to keep the Father Johns of the world at bay. Having direct access to divine will gives the mystic, or the charismatic personality, a license for innovation that neither papal authority nor the force of tradition can effectively control. As Father John once told a Swiss journalist, the issue of women priests was decided for him in the course of his direct dealings with God: "Despite the fact that I am very conservative, and that at first I was really perturbed over the idea of having to ordain women, I understood that the hour for this development had struck and that it was the Will of God. I asked the Good Lord for several proofs that these ordinations were really in conformity with His Will, and I got them."[19]

This experiment with women priests has not yet, however, reached the point of full equality. The priest-nuns of the Infinite Love community say their Masses privately, generally only in the presence of other women, and community-wide liturgies are still presided over exclusively by men. I asked Sr. Michelle why this discrepancy in privilege between male and female priests at St. Jovite was still in force. "I don't regard saying Mass in public as a privilege," she said. "It's more of a penance. And anyways, it's the place of women to be more discreet. This doesn't make us inferior. A young and beautiful sister would be a distraction up front saying Mass. There would be a temptation to pay more attention to her than to the Mass. I'm not suggesting I'm personally so young or beautiful, but this is one of the main reasons for the difference in ministry between our brother and our sister priests."

At this point, our conversation was interrupted when Fr. Simon entered the room followed by Father John. I hadn't anticipated meeting Father John on this visit, but I recognized him easily from photographs I'd seen at the monastery and in various newspapers. He was short and a bit stocky, with a rough-and-tumble gray beard, deep-set brown eyes, and small, fragile-looking hands. He was dressed in an ordinary monk's robe, and could easily have passed as just another rank-and-file brother. (I learned later that he only wears his papal whites and insignia of office on formal occasions.) He apologized to Sr. Michelle and me for breaking in on our conversation and asked if he could join us.

For the next four hours, first in the reception room and then over another bread-and-soup supper in the monastery's basement dining hall, Father John conducted a rambling monologue that covered the highlights of his ministry over the past twenty-five years. Speaking in the rough-hewn patois of rural Quebec, with his hands clasped and head lowered, he seemed gracious and relaxed and very much in command. He began by telling me about his lengthy imprisonment in Montreal in 1980 and 1981. During his first several weeks in jail, he said, the constant blare of rock music from transistor radios nearly drove him mad, but he eventually developed a taste for the music and even joked with the prison guards about starting up his own rock band. The prisoners treated him well, and seemed pleased to have a pope as a fellow inmate. He helped them compose love letters to their wives and girlfriends, and when they complained about conditions in jail, he would say to them: "Nonsense! We are guests of the Queen. We have everything we need here . . . food . . . shelter . . . clean beds . . . well, perhaps not quite everything."

I asked Father John about his history of visions and private revelations. What was his mental state when he experienced them? He said that he normally fell into a trance-like state that was accompanied by a sense of immense physical heaviness. He didn't deliberately try to cultivate visions; they usually came to him quite unexpectedly. Neither he nor anyone else in the community, he said, doubted that these visions and revelations were of divine origin. He also said that John Paul II, his papal competitor in Rome, fully recognized the authenticity of these visions but was prevented by the Vatican's power structure from publicly endorsing them.

Although clearly not a legitimate pope, Father John said, John Paul II was basically a decent man who was simply out of his depth in dealing with the spiritual crisis currently facing the church. Paul VI, however, was a different story entirely. During his misbegotten tenure in Rome, according to Father John, Paul VI did everything possible to turn Catholicism into a merely secular religion. Indeed, Father John claims to possess conclusive evidence, which he is not yet at liberty to reveal, that Paul VI was a fifth column planted inside the Vatican by international Freemasonry for the purpose of destroying the divine, transcendent character of the church.[20]

Father John told me that he is deeply disappointed with Catholic traditionalists for refusing to accept the legitimacy of his papacy. He agrees with traditionalists that the Second Vatican Council was a disastrous undertaking for the church, but he thinks that on other critical counts they've completely missed the point. Would God really allow the church to go more than twenty years without a valid pope? he asked. Isn't it about time that traditionalists recognized that the authentic Catholic hierarchy has been moved from Rome to North America? It seems strange, Father John said, that traditionalists should be so close to the Infinite Love community in some ways, and yet so far apart in others.

FR. NICHOLAS GRUNER AND †HE FATIMA CRUSADE

So close, and yet so far apart. As Father John suggested, the Infinite Love community has a great deal in common with traditionalist (or separatist) groups such as the Society of St. Pius V and Mount St. Michael's. Like them, it completely rejects the authority of the Second Vatican Council and the popes of the council; and like them, it is adamantly opposed to almost every aspect of the modern secular world. In other respects, however, the Infinite Love community is vastly different from such groups. Whereas traditionalists take their stand with the doctrines and rituals of the pre-conciliar church, the Infinite Love community bases itself on the mystical legacy of La Salette, the visions of Father John, and the conviction that mundane history is on the verge of crashing to an apocalyptic end. This is not, of course, to say that Catholic traditionalists have no interest themselves in prophetic visions or doomsday reckoning. The critical difference is that for traditionalists this is a decidedly secondary interest, a kind of spiritual avocation; for the Infinite Love community, there is nothing more important.

Fr. Nicholas Gruner also holds much in common with Catholic traditionalists. So much, in fact, that he has sometimes (as we saw in the previous chapter) been featured as a guest speaker at traditionalist conferences. In the final analysis, however, Gruner's traditionalist credentials are every bit as shaky as Father John's. Rather than seeking salvation through the doctrinal teachings and liturgies of the Catholic past, Gruner hinges absolutely everything on the famous Marian apparitions of Fatima. It is only through Fatima, he contends, that final salvation may be obtained, and only through Fatima that world peace in the historical present may be achieved.

Of the dozens of Marian apparitions that have been reported worldwide over the past two hundred years, none has packed nearly as much dramatic punch as Fatima. Secret messages, apocalyptic countdowns, cloak-and-dagger intrigue within the highest echelons of the Vatican: not even Hollywood could ask for better material than this. In its basic outline, the Fatima story runs as follows:

In 1917, from May 13 to October 13, the Virgin Mary made six miraculous appearances to three peasant children, Lucia dos Santos and her younger cousins Jacinta and Francisco Marto, in the small Portuguese village of Fatima. Word of the Fatima apparitions spread rapidly throughout Portugal, and during the Virgin's final appearance on October 13 many of the seventy thousand pilgrims on hand claimed to witness the sun actually trembling and dancing in the afternoon sky. The two younger childen, Jacinta and Francisco, both died just a couple of years after the apparitions, and in 1925 Lucia dos Santos joined a women's religious order called the Sisters of St. Dorothy. Even while living as a cloistered nun, however, Lucia remained the center of considerable attention. During her first five years in the convent, she received several additional visitations from the Virgin Mary, and at the climax of the last one, on June 13, 1929, the Virgin told her: "The moment has come in which God asks the Holy Father in union with all the bishops of the world to make the consecration of Russia to my Immaculate Heart, promising to save it by this means."[21]

This wasn't the first time, as it turns out, that the Virgin Mary had spoken with Lucia about the consecration of Russia. On July 13, 1917, during one of her appearances at Fatima, the Virgin had communicated a three-part secret to Lucia and her two cousins which the children refused to reveal to their interrogators. The so-called Fatima secret was kept under tight wraps for more than twenty years, but in a memoir that she wrote at the request of her religious superiors in August 1941, Lucia disclosed the contents of its first two parts. The first part of the secret, according to Lucia, consisted of a horrifying vision of hell, and in the second part the Virgin spoke the following words:

> God wishes to establish in the world devotion to my Immaculate Heart. If what I say to you is done, many souls will be saved and there will be peace. The war is going to end; but if people do not cease offending God, a worse one will break out during the pontificate of Pius XI. When you see a night illumined by an unknown light, know that this is the great sign given you by God that He is about to punish the world for its crimes, by means of war, famine, and persecutions of the Church and of the Holy Father.
>
> To prevent this, I shall come to ask for the consecration of Russia to my Immaculate Heart, and the Communion of reparation on the First Saturdays. If my requests are heeded, Russia will be converted, and there will be peace; if not, she will spread her errors throughout the world, causing wars and persecutions of the Church. The good will be martyred; the Holy Father will have much to suffer; various nations will be annihilated. In the end, my Immaculate Heart will triumph. The Holy Father will consecrate Russia to me, and she will be converted, and a period of peace will be granted to the world.[22]

Lucia's 1941 memoir seems to have been taken quite seriously by church officials, and on October 31, 1942, Pope Pius XII consecrated not just Russia but the entire world to Mary's Immaculate Heart. By the mid-forties, there was mounting pressure on Lucia to reveal the third part of the 1917 secret, and in 1944 she committed it to writing and sent it in a sealed envelope to the bishop of Fatima-Leiria, Dom José Correia da Silva. The bishop apparently didn't want to take the risk of reading the secret himself, however, and after failing to entrust it to a higher authority he deposited the sealed envelope in a safe at his chancery office, where it remained for more than ten years.

Lucia, in the meantime, was adding several twists to the plot. In February 1946, while being interviewed by a Dutch priest named Fr. Jongen, she indicated that the Virgin Mary didn't want the third part of the Fatima secret made public until 1960. In the same interview, she also indicated that Pope Pius XII's

1942 consecration of the world to Mary's Immaculate Heart fell far short of what the Virgin had actually requested. "The exact petition of Our Lady," Lucia reportedly told Fr. Jongen, "was for the Holy Father to make the consecration of Russia to Her Immaculate Heart, commanding that at the same time and in union with His Holiness, all the bishops of the Catholic world should do it."[23]

In 1957 Bishop da Silva finally arranged to have the envelope containing the secret sent to the Vatican's Sacred Congregation for the Doctrine of the Faith, and two years later it was delivered, still sealed, into the hands of Pope John XXIII. John XXIII apparently read the secret, but 1960 came and went without it being made public. In later years, John XXIII's papal successors also seem to have read the secret, but they too decided to keep it under wraps. On May 13, 1982, and then again on March 25, 1984, John Paul II became the second pope to consecrate the world to Mary's Immaculate Heart, but like Pius XII forty-two years earlier, he neglected to make specific mention of Russia or to undertake the consecration in absolute unison with all the bishops of the Catholic world.[24]

Although the Fatima apparitions were declared to be authentic by the bishops of Portugal as early as 1930, it wasn't until the early 1950s, and the onset of the Cold War that they became widely known in the broader Catholic world. With its call for the consecration of Russia, in fact, Fatima was regarded by many American Catholics in the fifties and sixties as the West's best hope for neutralizing the military might of the Soviet Union and halting the spread of communism. If Catholics everywhere were faithful to Fatima, the reasoning went, Russia would be converted and a period of miraculous peace would descend upon the earth. It was also during the fifties and sixties that the so-called "third secret of Fatima" became a topic of fevered speculation within certain sectors of the American church. Did the secret warn of some evil plot that was being hatched against Catholicism from within the church itself? Did it speak of an impending nuclear war in which entire nations, possibly even the United States, would be annihilated?

For the most part, however, devotion to Fatima among American Catholics during the fifties and sixties was a relatively staid affair. In 1947 a New Jersey–based priest named Monsignor Harold Colgan founded an organization called the Blue Army of Our Lady of Fatima, and over the next ten years the Blue Army developed into one of the leading Marian organizations in the world. In small, parish-based cells located in virtually every diocese throughout the United States, members promoted a Marian piety centered around the Brown Scapular of Our Lady of Mount Carmel, the rosary, and prayer for the conversion of Russia.[25] The Blue Army reached its height of popularity during the late fifties and early sixties, but like almost every other Marian apostolate in America it fell into a state of steady decline in the years following the Second Vatican Council. In the newly modernized Catholicism that was coming into being in the wake of the council, Marian devotions were increasingly seen as mawkish and freighted with superstition, and reformers were quick to dismiss them as relics of a benighted and best forgotten past. While devotion to Fatima continued throughout the seventies and eighties, it gave every appearance of being a cause whose time had come and gone.

OVER THE PAST TEN YEARS, no one has worked harder at restoring a sense of relevancy to Fatima than Fr. Nicholas Gruner. Gruner was born in Montreal in 1942 and was raised in a fairly affluent Catholic family as the fifth of seven children. After graduating with a degree in accounting from McGill University in 1964, he spent a year traveling in Europe and then returned to Montreal to study for the priesthood. In 1971, after having shifted his theological studies to Rome, Gruner met two young American men who invited him to join them on a trip to Fatima. Before returning to Rome, the three men went to visit a priest named Fr. Breno Zecatti, who lived in the Italian Alps about forty miles north of Bologna. Fr. Zecatti was a well-known exorcist in the area, and over the years he'd also built up a considerable reputation as someone with remarkable powers of spiritual discernment. Gruner's companions were told by Fr. Zecatti that they were destined for the priesthood, and Gruner himself was told that he had a special calling to promote devotion to the Virgin Mary.

Gruner was ordained in the Italian diocese of Avellino by Bishop Pasquale Venezia in 1976, and the following year he received permission from Bishop Venezia to seek out a bishop who would be willing to incardinate him in a North American diocese.[26] In August 1977, after spending several months in futile pursuit of a bishop willing to take him on in the United States, Gruner was summoned to the Ottawa area by a woman named Anne Cillis, whom he knew from his seminary days in Montreal. Cillis had just recently come into possession of the Canadian Pilgrim Virgin statue, which was one of seventy Fatima statues blessed by Pope Paul VI in 1967, and she wanted to know if Gruner would assume responsibility for it as part of a new North American Fatima ministry. For Gruner this was an easy call. By this point in his life, he already had an intense Marian piety. He'd been praying the rosary daily and wearing the Brown Scapular since 1965; and, in any event, hadn't Fr. Zecatti, the Italian exorcist, already assured him that he possessed a special calling to promote devotion to the Virgin Mary?[27]

Gruner accepted Cillis's offer and immediately began touring North America with the Pilgrim Virgin statue in an effort to heighten popular devotion to Fatima. It didn't take long for him to become a fixture on the Fatima circuit, and in 1978 he expanded his ministry by launching a quarterly magazine called the *Fatima Crusader*. At the outset, the *Crusader* was an uneventful eight-page, black-and-white affair mostly taken up with sweetly pious (and eminently forgettable) pieces on the lives of the three Fatima seers and the spiritual benefits of the rosary. It was sent free of charge to Fatima devotees throughout North America, most of whose names were culled from the Blue Army's mailing list, and was financed entirely through the donations of readers. The *Crusader* staggered along for several years in almost complete obscurity, but in the early 1980s Gruner hit upon the issue that would catapult it to instant prominence.

By the summer of 1982, the consecration of Russia which the Virgin Mary had requested during her July 1917 appearance at Fatima was hardly a burning issue among American Catholics. Pope Pius XII, in October 1942, and Pope John Paul II, in May 1982, had both consecrated the entire world to Mary's Immaculate Heart, and it seemed that nothing more needed to be said (or done) about it. During the first several years of the *Fatima Crusader*'s publishing life, in fact, Gruner himself saw little reason to treat the consecration as a pressing concern. In the late summer of 1982, however, he came across an article by a Scottish Catholic named Hamish Fraser which caused him to change his mind.

Contrary to popular belief, Fraser wrote, the consecration of Russia demanded by the Virgin Mary at Fatima was still waiting to be done. Both Pius XII and John Paul II had failed to carry out their consecrations in unison with every bishop throughout the Catholic world, and both had neglected to make specific mention of Russia. In Pius XII's case, according to Fraser, this failure to comply with the Virgin's specific demands may simply have been an oversight, but in the case of John Paul II, a far more insidious dynamic was at work. As much as he probably wanted to, Fraser said, John Paul II was prevented from ordering the bishops to join him in publicly consecrating Russia out of fear of provoking an open rebellion within the church. The Virgin Mary had called for the consecration in the first place, according to Fraser, in order to prevent Russia from spreading its communistic errors throughout the world, but since the Second Vatican Council an alarming number of bishops and church bureaucrats had actually undergone conversions to communism. And regardless of what the Virgin (or the pope) might want, Fraser said, it was highly unlikely that these bishops and bureaucrats would agree to participate in a public consecration that singled out communism for special criticism.[28]

In Gruner's view, this was quite possibly the story of the century. The Virgin Mary had appeared at Fatima with a program of salvation for the entire world, but conspiratorial forces within the church itself were doing their utmost to block its implementation. As unpalatable as the story might be to the Catholic hierarchy, Gruner felt, it was imperative that it be broadcast as loudly and widely as possible, and in late 1982 he turned the *Fatima Crusader* into an instrument for telling the full, unexpurgated truth about Fatima. And as is quite often the case, the full, unexpurgated truth turned out to be extremely profitable. In 1983, as the *Crusader* hammered away relentlessly at the consecration issue, donations poured into Gruner's Fatima ministry at an unprecedented rate, and the *Crusader*'s circulation more than doubled, from twenty thousand to almost fifty thousand. A year later, as Gruner ratcheted up the polemical heat several additional notches, the magazine's circulation soared to 100,000, and with the help of a wealthy benefactor from California, it was converted into a full-color, forty-page production. And this was still just the beginning. Within the next several years, the *Crusader*'s circulation increased to more than 400,000, and Gruner's ministry grew into a $5-million-a-year enterprise.

Any good conspiracy story, of course, must have its share of behind-the-scenes intrigue, and during the mid- to late eighties the *Fatima Crusader* regularly churned out more intrigue than its readers could possibly have asked for. To start with, there was the so-called Vatican-Moscow accord of 1962. Since the early seventies, a number of right-wing Catholic publications in Europe had been contending that Pope John XXIII and Nikita Khrushchev had entered into a secret (and still binding) agreement on the eve of the Second Vatican Council, with John XXIII promising to go soft on Soviet communism in return for Khrushchev's promise to go soft on Catholics living behind the Iron Curtain. When Gruner, in the mid-eighties, first heard reports of the Vatican-Moscow accord, he was immediately convinced they must be true. Finally, he reasoned, all the pieces of the puzzle were coming together. In addition to everything else that was standing in the way, the consecration of Russia demanded by the Virgin at Fatima was being held back by a secret agreement that never should have been struck in the first place. And to make matters worse, communist sympathizers inside the Vatican, led by Secretary of State Agostino Cardinal Casaroli, were doing everything in their power to keep the agreement in place.[29]

As Gruner and his *Crusader* staff railed against the Vatican-Moscow pact and other related evils throughout the late eighties, they succeeded in giving the Fatima cause a new (and decidedly sexier) lease on life. Far from being the object of a merely grandmotherly piety, Fatima was now fully caught up in the mysterious world of Vatican Ostpolitik, clandestine deal-making, and geopolitical brinkmanship. To many of the *Crusader*'s readers, all of this was undoubtedly heady stuff: in return for their support of Gruner's Fatima ministry, they were being given a privileged window into the inner workings of the most critical historical developments of the age. And the most critical development of all, as the *Crusader* consistently reminded its readers, was the mounting military might of the Soviet Union. In an endless parade of articles bearing such red-banner headlines as "URGENT! COMMUNISM IS ADVANCING," "NUCLEAR ADVANTAGE OF RUSSIA OVER U.S.A. NOW 6 TO 1," and "THE GREAT SOVIET DECEPTION," the magazine tried desperately to set the record straight: perestroika was a hoax, Gorbachev was no better than Stalin, and, despite all the sweet talk coming out of Moscow, communist Russia was setting the stage for a final military assault on the entire free world. Not that any of this should have been surprising. The Virgin Mary had warned at Fatima that Russia would spread error and misery throughout the world unless her requests were granted; and now, more than seventy years later, the Virgin was still waiting.[30]

Determined not to keep her waiting any longer, Gruner tried to pressure the pope into action by sponsoring a letter-writing campaign to the Vatican and, for added effect, publicizing the names of several high-ranking cardinals who presumably agreed with him that the consecration of Russia had not yet been properly carried out. At least one of these cardinals, however, saw the matter in an entirely different light. In a letter to Gruner dated April 15, 1988, Edouard Cardinal Gagnon, president of the Vatican's Pontifical Council for the Family, declared that he was far from amused at having his name and picture featured in the *Fatima Crusader*. Contrary to what the *Crusader* had reported, the cardinal said, his own position on the consecration was exactly the same as the pope's, and neither the pope nor anyone else in the Vatican needed to be lectured by Gruner on the true meaning of Fatima. "It would be a great act of pride from a son of the Church to pretend he knows the will of God and in particular the revelations of Fatima better than the Pope. The Pope has talked with Sister Lucia and is responsible enough to know what he has to do. . . . The Pope has the privilege of infallibility and a special gift to lead the Church. Private revelations can help him but are not binding on him, and much less the interpretations given to such revelations. . . . Furthermore it is a strange notion of the functioning of the Magisterium, to think that the Holy Father is like an elected member of a democratic parliament and makes his decisions according to the number of letters he receives." If Gruner didn't tone down his act in the near future, the cardinal added, he risked "bringing upon [his] apostolate a condemnation from the highest Church authorities."

Gruner's response to Cardinal Gagnon, which he published in the *Crusader* for the edification of his readers, was a masterpiece of righteous indignation. However much he now wanted to deny it, Gruner said, the *Crusader* had the word of unimpeachable sources that the cardinal had previously admitted in private conversation that the consecration was still waiting to be carried out. And what crime had he himself committed, Gruner asked, in encouraging his supporters to voice their concerns to the Vatican? Both the First Vatican Council (1870) and the Second Council of Lyons (1274) affirmed that all Catholics have the right of direct appeal to the pope, and for the cardinal to suggest otherwise in this case was "an inexcusable and grave injustice." Moreover, Gruner added, the pope himself was undoubtedly aware that the consecration of Russia had not yet been carried out in the precise manner requested by the Virgin, but was prevented from ordering that it be done so by obstructionist forces within the church itself. Closing on a note of defiance, Gruner wrote: "Your judgments and your letter to me and your remarks to others in the Church is [sic] no doubt doing harm to this work of Our Lady. . . . If I am wrong tell me what specifically I have done; if I am not wrong, why do you persecute me? If I am not wrong, then you do wrong to attack me and my work. If you have done wrong then you owe it to Our Lady to repair the harm you have done. Would you believe it if I told you that I write this in a spirit of fraternal charity?"

Cardinal Gagnon's response to this tirade seemed almost the Vatican equivalent of throwing in the towel. In a letter to Gruner dated October 7, 1988, the cardinal wrote: "In the light of the content of your long letter . . . I see that there is no reasonable way to convey my views to you. . . . I believe that you are undermining the confidence of the faithful in the Holy Father by suggesting that he is weak and that the apocalyptic content of your magazine, more exaggerated with each issue, is spreading fear and anxiety among them. . . . I do not support your apostolate or the organization functioning from it. You are not to use my name henceforth in any publication of your organization."[31]

While engaged in this long-distance sparring match with Cardinal Gagnon, Gruner was also forced to contend with several additional problems. One of these concerned his own increasingly beleaguered standing as a Roman Catholic priest. According to church law, a priest is supposed to be attached to the authority of a particular bishop, but in 1989, more than a decade after leaving Italy to find a bishop willing to incardinate him in a North American diocese, Gruner was still functioning as a free agent. After failing, in the early eighties, to hook up with a friendly bishop in the Ottawa area, he established new headquarters in Fort Erie, Ontario, and an outreach office just outside of Ogdensburg, New York, but he was hardly given a hero's welcome in either place. In 1985, the bishop of Ogdensburg, Stanislaus Brzana, publicly advised his flock against supporting Gruner, and in 1987 Bishop John Fulton of St. Catharines, whose diocese included Fort Erie, demanded that Gruner pledge allegiance to him and abandon his Fatima ministry. Gruner rejected these demands, and when the Canadian Apostolic Pro-Nuncio, in September 1989, summoned him to a meeting in Ottawa to discuss his irregular status, Gruner simply refused to go. Two months later, at the urging of the Vatican's Congregation for the Clergy, the new bishop of Avellino, Gerardo Pierro, advised Gruner in writing that he faced possible defrocking unless he took immediate steps to straighten out his situation. Gruner shrugged off this threat, however, and when the Archdiocese of Toronto, in a June 1990 announcement, condemned him for operating "without any canonical approval and in disobedience to his legitimate superiors," he responded by filing suit for defamation of character and informing the *Toronto Star* that he expected to receive a "princely sum" as settlement.[32]

Although this ecclesiastical pressure undoubtedly complicated Gruner's life, it didn't really slow him down. In 1988 he launched a daily radio program, "Heaven's Peace Plan," that was slotted on forty-three stations in the United States and Canada, and he followed this up the next year with a weekly television show called "Fatima: The Moment Has Come." Henceforward Fatima devotees in more than twenty states could tune in on Sunday mornings and catch Gruner in conversation with Don McAlvany, a self-proclaimed Soviet expert, on the true meaning of perestroika; or with Robert Morris, a right-wing geopolitical analyst, on the rising tide of international communism; or even with Fr. Paul Leonard, Gruner's corpulent sidekick, on the iniquitous Vatican-Moscow accord.

Of course, all of this programming was enormously expensive, and during the late eighties Gruner unleashed a high-powered fundraising campaign that, for sheer chutzpah, would have made Oral Roberts blush in appreciation. After signing on with a direct-mail expert based in Atlanta, Gruner's ministry bought and rented and borrowed mailing lists from virtually every right-wing Catholic organization in North America, and then sent out personalized pitch letters on a bimonthly (and sometimes monthly) basis.

> Dear Michael . . . You are so important! I am writing you today—as one of Our Lady's dearest ones—to plead urgently for your help in bringing this wonderful program to millions of souls across America. . . . Our bank account is now practically empty. . . . Please say a Hail Mary with me now that you and all of Our Lady's children will respond generously FROM THE HEART to this desperate appeal. . . . Our Lady's FULL Fatima message is our only hope. If She is not heard in time then the whole world including the United States will be enslaved by Communist Russia and many entire nations will be annihilated. PLEASE HELP NOW. It is almost too late. (July 13, 1989)

> Dear Michael . . . As you probably know, the Apostolate and I have been under extremely heavy attack by powerful forces seeking to silence the Fatima Message forever. . . . OUR LADY'S APOSTOLATE IS FACING A LIFE-OR-DEATH CRISIS. . . . Please do not desert us in this desperate time of need. We urgently need your prayers and LARGEST POSSIBLE SACRIFICES today as we battle against those who would silence the Message of Fatima forever. Our debts are over $200,000 at this time. This is truly a "make or break" time. . . . Please, I beg you with all my strength to help Our Lady now! (October 24, 1989)

> Dear Michael . . . After working so hard and accomplishing so much this year, it is very difficult to have to tell you that we are now facing a life-or-death financial crisis. . . . But put simply, the great victories we have won over the last year in the battle for Our Lady have not come cheap. . . . It has cost literally hundreds of thousands of dollars to bring the Fatima Message to you and millions of others through Our Lady's magazine, radio program and new weekly TV series. . . . With God's help and yours, we have somehow managed to hang on. . . . With every passing day, you can see how close we are moving to that terrible chastisement Our Lady warned us of at Fatima. . . . With every Rosary I pray and in every single Mass, I am asking Almighty God to give you the means to help us with the LARGEST POSSIBLE OFFERING you can make. . . . I pray that this will not be the LAST letter I ever send to you. The survival of Our Lady's Apostolate is at stake today. (December 8, 1989)

But, of course, it isn't the last letter that Gruner sends. Every month brings a fresh financial crisis to his ministry . . . there are urgent projects (books, pilgrimages, worldwide conferences) that desperately require funding . . . finances are perpetually at an all-time low . . . and the specter of historical disaster is always looming just ahead.

During the late eighties and early nineties, Gruner even succeeded in turning his ongoing difficulties with the institutional church to strategic marketing advantage. He was the heroic truth-teller, the martyr, the honest broker of Fatima, under constant attack from every imaginable angle. When Cardinal

Antonio Innocenti, the Prefect of the Congregation for the Clergy, wrote from the Vatican in August 1989 to tell Gruner that he might be suspended from the priesthood for his disobedience, it merely gave Gruner an opportunity to play out his tortured martyr routine at full length on the *Crusader's* pages. "You accuse me of disobedience. This is a sacrilegious and slanderous lie," Gruner's open-letter response to the cardinal began. "It is a lie against a sacred person, myself a Catholic priest, therefore it is sacrilegious. It is slanderous because it is false and gravely damaging to my reputation. . . ." And then, several pages of wounded feelings later: ". . . you are not acting like a pastor but like a wolf; you are on a witch hunt, you have held a kangaroo court and passed sentence on me, without a hearing, or a chance for me to face my accuser . . . is this justice Vatican style?" And finally, the coup de grâce: "Such injustice as you perpetrate against me is an obvious attempt to silence the only voice speaking out loudly and clearly the full message of Our Lady of Fatima, especially that part which clearly shows the obligation of the Pope and the Bishops to obey Our Lady of Fatima and consecrate Russia to Her Immaculate Heart. It is to silence us from denouncing the Vatican-Moscow Agreement that you unlawfully inflict upon us this heinous and callous injustice. . . . Since you refuse to follow the dictates of morality and due process of law in your dealing with me you have resorted to this unconscionable and lawless abuse of authority against me."[33]

Another problem that Gruner was forced to contend with during the late eighties and early nineties (and one that proved a bit more resistant to stage-managing) was the dramatic collapse of the Soviet Union. As the Berlin Wall came down, and as much of the former communist world embraced the principles of free markets and open elections, Gruner's apocalyptic warnings of a forthcoming era of worldwide communist enslavement came to sound increasingly hollow. Indeed, the Blue Army, which remained Gruner's chief competition on the North American Fatima scene, took the collapse of the Soviet Union to mean that the consecration of Russia had in fact been properly carried out by John Paul II and that the era of subsequent world peace promised by the Virgin Mary at Fatima was now in process of being realized.[34] To concede this, of course, would have meant the end of his ministry, and Gruner instead opted for a policy of straight denial. Despite all the media hoopla over the supposed demise of communism and end of the Cold War, he insisted, nothing had changed except the color of the uniforms. Russia was still a force of apocalyptic reckoning, and the consecration requested by the Virgin had still not been properly carried out. "We might only have as little as 6 months to 3 years left before Russia enslaves the whole world," Gruner wrote in the Summer 1990 issue of the *Crusader*.[35]

As the months passed, however, and the dismantlement of the Soviet Union continued, Gruner seems to have recognized the need to broaden his rhetorical focus. While his money-flogging remained as shameless as ever ("And with all my strength, I beg you to ask Our Lord and Our Lady to guide your hand as you write your check today"), he now began to treat communism as if it were just one of many evils on the Fatima hit list.[36]

> In the last year, the tide of crime, poverty, drug-addiction, AIDS, divorce, pornography and abortion has risen to unprecedented heights, relentlessly destroying more and more of our families and making our cities virtual war-zones. . . . And worst of all this year, we've watched as our Holy Catholic Faith continues its headlong retreat. More parishes and schools closed, more declines in Mass attendance and confessions, more lapses in faith, more confusion, more calls for "reforms" . . . ONLY Our Blessed Mother has remained true. And ONLY the Message She gave us at Fatima can save us from total disaster. (*Crusader*, Summer 1991)

> Looking at the situation in the Church, can any of us really be surprised that our streets are filled with drug-crazed gangs? Or that our prisons are full to overflowing? Or that our politicians are corrupt? Or that 75 percent of our families are torn asunder by divorce and disharmony? . . . The Mother of God, the crowned Queen of Heaven, came to Fatima to offer us the solution to all the many problems confronting our Church, the world, our nation and particularly our families. (*Crusader*, Fall 1991)

> From the Middle East to Yugoslavia to Haiti, conflict after bloody conflict continues to erupt. Millions of lives continue to be lost. Despite promises of peace, our world grows less and less secure as political chaos spreads across the earth. (*Crusader*, Winter 1992)

Drug addiction, family breakdown, abortion, war, political corruption . . . and, while we're at it, add the United Nations and secular humanism to the list. Without ever renouncing his long-standing position on the imminent threat of a global communist takeover, Gruner now generalized his appeal to virtually every evil under the sun. Fatima was the all-embracing panacea—the supernatural solution to every imaginable grievance and affliction. And to fuel the action even further, there was always the famous Third Secret.

Since the start of the Second Vatican Council thirty years earlier, the Third Secret had practically become a dead issue within the American church, but in the early nineties Gruner did his utmost to bring it fully back to life. In June 1990 he placed a full-page advertisement in the *New York Times* calling on Pope John Paul II to carry out the consecration of Russia requested by the Virgin Mary, and also "to publicly reveal to the world the full text of the Third part of Our Lady of Fatima's Secret (as She asked be done in 1960). . . ."[37] And later the same year, as part of what he called the "Free Sister Lucy" campaign, Gruner encouraged his supporters to pressure the Vatican into permitting Lucia to speak openly about the Secret. In the summer of 1991, moreover, he sent copies of *The Third Secret*, a nine-hundred-page exposé written by a self-appointed Fatima expert from France named Frère Michel de la Sainte Trinité, to every bishop in the Catholic world. According to Frère Michel's research, the secret almost certainly referred to a horrible apostasy that would strike the church toward the close of the century. Bishops and cardinals would turn against the faith, perversion would run rampant, and communism would invade the highest reaches of the church's authority structure. Frère Michel was convinced, and Gruner with him, that this period of apostasy was already well under way.[38]

———————

IN SEPTEMBER OF 1992 I stopped by Gruner's head office, a converted factory located on the fringes of Fort Erie, to meet with him for the first time. Gruner escorted me into a small conference room, and after a couple of minutes we were joined by Fr. Paul Leonard. (Fr. Leonard took a seat directly across from me, and then sat with his arms folded for the entire meeting, without saying a word.)

When I had previously seen him on television, Gruner had always struck me as somewhat bewildered and ineffectual, as someone who might have trouble, in the outside world, making a simple subway connection. In person, however, he was aggressive and self-confident—even to the point of arrogance. He characterized his opponents in the Vatican as "theological pygmies," and claimed that E. Michael Jones, Alphonse Matt, Jr., and other leading Catholic conservatives were "unlearned and naive." "Instead of attacking me," he said, "all of these people should admit that what I'm telling them is over their heads and that they can't see it because of their stupidity and ignorance." Despite the unremitting persecution he faced, Gruner said, he always attempted to comport himself "respectfully and graciously, without going out of the way to besmirch anyone's reputation." His opponents, however, were a different story entirely. "They're intractable, they make complete fools of themselves all by themselves. They certainly don't need my help for this. Left to themselves, they never cease their erring ways."

Since the inception of his ministry in the late seventies, Gruner has performed a curious balancing act. Despite his personal disgust with the church's current leadership, he has been forced to tread carefully (or, at least, more carefully than he might prefer) so as not to risk alienating his supporters, many of whom probably still feel some allegiance toward the Vatican and especially John Paul II. While harshly criticizing the Catholic hierarchy, therefore, he has always stopped just short of fully renouncing it. And while tending to portray John Paul II as weak and gullible and misguided, he has reserved his most scathing judgments for the pope's chief lieutenants in the Vatican. I asked Gruner whether he might eventually reach the point of breaking away altogether from the institutional church.

"There is a ridiculous amount of misunderstanding on this point," he answered. "Despite what my enemies claim, I have always acted as an absolutely loyal Catholic. There are some people who think I don't have the right to criticize the Vatican. But this is preposterous. The very best Catholic theologians, saints such as Aquinas and Bellarmine, taught that Catholics have the right and the responsibility to insist that their leaders preach the truth. And just because I have the courage to exercise that right doesn't mean that I'm disloyal or that I'm

145

perpetrating schism. But let me also say this: the pope is not God. We must never confuse what popes say with the authentic, eternal magisterium of the Church. Popes can certainly teach falsehood, and when doing so they must be reproached. You have no idea the persecution I've suffered just for stating simple truths such as this."

And was Gruner prepared, regardless of the persecution he might suffer, to carry on with his Fatima crusade? "The only way my numerous enemies could possibly cause my downfall is through economic pressure," he said. "It's only in the economic area that I'm vulnerable. In terms of integrity and fidelity to the truth, I am unimpeachable and impregnable. And so this is why the bishops and the Blue Army and E. Michael Jones and all the others are trying to wipe out my economic support. They know they can't touch me otherwise. They claim that I'm disloyal to the pope, or that my credentials as a priest are in question, all in an effort to turn my supporters away from me. But they won't succeed in this. I know that ultimately, despite all the persecution, my position, which is the position of Our Lady of Fatima, will triumph."[39]

———

THE MONTHS THAT FOLLOWED MY INITIAL VISIT with Gruner in Fort Erie proved extremely rocky for him. In October 1992 he sponsored a week-long symposium in Fatima, the "Fatima Peace Conference," to which every bishop in the Catholic world was invited. Although Gruner's ministry was picking up the complete tab for travel and lodging, only a smattering of bishops bothered to show up, and on the second day of the symposium Gruner was physically assaulted in the Sacristy of the Fatima Shrine. Shrine officials claimed that Gruner had staged the incident himself as a publicity stunt, but Gruner charged that it had been ordered by the shrine's rector, Msgr. Luciano Guerro, in an effort to scare him off. To add insult to injury, Gruner had managed to arrange a private meeting with Sr. Lucia at her convent in Coimbra on the third day of the symposium, but it was abruptly canceled at the last moment. Sr. Lucia was apparently too ill to meet with Gruner at the appointed hour—but not so ill that she couldn't meet with Corazon Aquino fifteen minutes later.[40]

All of this was inconsequential, however, compared to the bombshell that came out of Coimbra the same week. On October 11, Anthony Cardinal Padiyara, the archbishop of Ernakulam, Kerala, India, and one of Gruner's staunchest supporters in the Catholic hierarchy, visited Sr. Lucia in her convent and asked if the consecration performed by John Paul II on March 25, 1984, had satisfied the specific request made by the Virgin Mary at Fatima. To the surprise of the cardinal, and several other witnesses, Sr. Lucia's answer seems to have been an unequivocal "yes." For Gruner, this was just about the worst development imaginable. For years he had been pounding away on a single theme—that the consecration demanded by the Virgin had not yet been properly carried out—and if

Sr. Lucia, the last surviving seer of Fatima, were permitted to speak freely, she would unquestionably declare this to be the case. But now Sr. Lucia had apparently spoken, and in the process she had undercut Gruner's entire ministry.

In the view of Gruner and his closest allies, something was clearly amiss here. For over sixty years, Sr. Lucia had insisted that the consecration called for by the Virgin at Fatima must make *specific mention of Russia* and must also be undertaken by the pope *in temporal unity with every bishop in the Catholic world*. Why should Lucia now say something completely different? To this question, there seemed only one satisfactory answer: Lucia had been brainwashed; her mind had been taken over by forces of iniquity within the Vatican and quite possibly within her own convent as well. In the Winter 1993 issue of the *Crusader*, Gruner assigned his heaviest hitter, Fr. Paul Leonard, to the case.

"Why has Sister Lucia made such a fool of herself?" Leonard wrote. "It is very easy to apply brainwashing techniques on a person who lives in a cloistered environment—especially when the subject is of a very advanced age. . . . People who have been subjected to brainwashing or sensitivity training are often known to repudiate with enthusiasm the things that have been most sacred to them. . . . Under normal circumstances . . . it would be inconceivable that Sister Lucia would discredit her own statements and disparage her own writings as she is now apparently doing. Her present state of mind is in itself a strong indication that Sister Lucia has been mentally abused by her superiors who have subjected her to mind control. She has been 'trained' to say that the consecration of Russia is already accomplished, that Russia is converted and whatever else the Ostpolitik-minded officials of the Vatican want her to say."[41]

This episode, it might be supposed, should have finally depleted Gruner's store of credibility. How much cognitive dissonance, after all, could his supporters be expected to put up with? Worldwide communism was more powerful than ever. . . . The Soviet Union wasn't really in tatters. . . . His own priestly credentials were absolutely shipshape. . . . Sr. Lucia, the ultimate authority on world peace and salvation, was being kept silent. . . . And now that she was speaking, but saying the wrong things, Lucia was obviously a victim of mind control. . . . (Or, as a subsequent issue of the *Crusader* proposed, this was quite possibly an imposter Lucia.[42]) Rather than cashing in their chips, however, the great majority of Gruner's supporters seemed content to wait out the game. Indeed, it seems highly unlikely that most of them even experienced Gruner's frantic maneuvering and frequent about-faces as cognitive dissonance. What they craved wasn't logical consistency, or historical plausibility, but rather the promise and anticipation of miraculous intervention.

———

IN COMPARISON WITH THE INTENSIVE LEVEL of commitment demanded by groups such as the Apostles of Infinite Love and Mount St. Michael's, in fact,

Gruner offers his supporters a relatively cheap ride. Not much more is expected of them beyond making financial contributions and attending the occasional public lecture, and in return they're given the satisfaction of participating, however vicariously, in a spiritual struggle of cosmic importance.[43]

In May 1993 I sat in on a lecture given by Gruner at the Skyline Hotel on the outskirts of Toronto. Altogether about three hundred people were in attendance, and probably as many as one hundred of them had driven to Toronto from Ohio and New York State for the occasion. Roughly two-thirds of the audience were women, at least two-thirds looked to be over fifty years of age, and the overwhelming majority were white.

Gruner's talk, which he delivered from a small stage flanked by the Pilgrim Virgin statue (or at least a reasonable facsimile of it), was standard *Fatima Crusader* boilerplate. He decried the moral decadence and violence of the contemporary world, and blamed it all on communists, militant atheists, and secular humanists. ("They are enemies of our souls, and they all have the same goal. They want to corrupt Christian hearts; they want to make Christians drink in vice through their senses.") He insisted that communism was not only stronger than ever but was actually on the verge of attaining world domination. ("Whatever the Soviet Union calls itself today, it is still continuing to arm itself while we disarm. Despite all the propaganda, nothing has changed. The United States is the number one nation on the list for enslavement and annihilation, and Canada isn't far behind.") However much his enemies hated to admit it, Gruner said, Fatima remained the last authentic hope for world peace. ("The grace of peace has been entrusted exclusively to the Immaculate Heart of Mary. The great tragedy is that our enemies continue to suppress the Fatima messages, and many of our worst enemies are wearing priest's robes and bishop's hats. But this shouldn't surprise us. The Third Secret of Fatima predicted a horrible period of apostasy within the Church, and this is the period that we are now living in.") He defended himself against his detractors within the church ("I'm certainly not perfect. I'm not the saint I'm sometimes made out to be. But why are they so intent on persecuting me? I'm only telling the truth about Fatima") and even found time to protest the current liturgical practice of receiving communion in the hand ("This is a sacrilege even worse than abortion").

Gruner is hardly a dynamic public speaker, and his hour-and-a-half talk was punctuated only once or twice by applause. During the lengthy question-and-answer period that followed, I struck up a conversation with a forty-year-old woman named Judy, who had slipped into the hotel lobby for a cigarette. Twice divorced and the mother of two teenagers, Judy had driven more than two hours from Western New York just for the lecture, and she seemed to think the trip had been well worthwhile. "Fr. Gruner's terrific," she said. "This is the third time I've heard him speak, and he always gives me a lot to think about."

I asked Judy how she had first come into contact with Gruner's ministry.

"About three years ago, my mother gave me a couple of Fr. Gruner's magazines, and months went by before I read them, but I eventually did read them," she said. "I had been sort of involved with the New Age scene for a few years, looking for something, some sort of spiritual meaning, I guess, and I decided to check the magazines out. I was raised a Catholic, but I had stopped going to church when I was a teenager. But Catholicism never really leaves you, and I thought reading them might put me back on track. And all I can say is that I was just blown away. I knew that there were problems with the Church, but I had no idea they were so severe. Catholicism has lost a lot since I was a kid, and Fatima is the only way to get it back."

Despite her expressions of enthusiasm for Gruner, Judy isn't much more than a casual consumer of his Fatima ministry. She admits to not reading every new issue of the *Crusader*, she attends Mass and prays the rosary only sporadically, and she continues to dabble in astrology and other forms of New Age spirituality.

Helen, a fifty-one-year-old lifelong Catholic from the Rochester area, who joined me for a cup of coffee after the proceedings had wrapped up, seems to have invested much more heavily in the ministry. A homemaker and the mother of three grown children, Helen reads the *Crusader* zealously, prays the rosary daily, and makes regular contributions to Gruner's cause. When she was first introduced to the *Crusader* by her sister in the late eighties, Helen told me, she felt an immense sense of relief and gratitude. "I felt like this magazine had been written for me," she said. "It answered so many of my questions. For a long time I knew in my heart that the Church was in a terrible mess, but I just couldn't put my finger on what had gone wrong. My kids are basically very decent people, but none of them has even thought about going to Mass for years now. I used to think there might be something wrong with them, but the truth is that it's the Church that has the problem."

I asked Helen if she could specify what she felt was wrong with the contemporary church. "Well, that's a tough question," she answered. "Everything seems to be wrong with it. There's no mystery or faithfulness or beauty any more. And I truly believe it all comes down to Fatima. Fr. Gruner is right on the money here. Our Lady came out of love for us to warn of the terrible things that were going to take place in the Church and the world. And the Church has turned its back on Her and tried to stifle Her message. And now look at what the Church is doing to Fr. Gruner! He's probably one of the most pious and holy priests alive today, but because he's taken the side of Our Lady of Fatima the Church is attacking and persecuting him and trying to discredit him."

As the examples of Judy and Helen would seem to bear out, a great deal of Gruner's support is made up of the vaguely disaffected; that is, Catholics who feel aggrieved with the contemporary church without always knowing exactly why. Their children (or grandchildren) may have stopped attending Mass; their own sense of spiritual equilibrium may have been thrown out of kilter by the changes brought about by the council; or they may simply have found compensation for personal loneliness in the sort of mail-order fellowship that Gruner specializes in.

It seems likely as well that at least some of Gruner's supporters have been attracted by the allure of magical certitude. For generations prior to the council, much that counted as popular devotionalism in the Catholic world carried the strong imprint of magic. Holy pictures and statues; votive candles, relics, and medals: all of these objects were thought to possess a supernatural efficacy or potency. If approached properly, with the right piety and incantations and so forth, they could (presumably) assist in bringing about a miraculous healing or some other tangible benefit. As Catholicism in the United States and Canada became more modernized and more rationalized in the years following the council, however, the magical dimension of popular devotionalism was gradually suppressed. And for many people, this was undoubtedly experienced as a great loss. Their church was now less mysterious and less enchanted than before, and considerably more remote from the concerns and desires of everyday life.

If nothing else, Gruner has helped to restore in the lives of his supporters something of this same sense of magical enchantment. Indeed, with his insistence on precise formulas (Russia *must* be specifically mentioned in the act of consecration), and also the precise mechanics of ceremony (the consecration *must* be performed by every bishop in the world at exactly the same time), he recalls to mind the Malinowskian magician preparing spells and rituals so as to ready his tribe for battle. It may not be sound religion, but as an ongoing drama it's tough to beat.

AND AS TIME WENT ON, Gruner somehow managed to keep the drama pulsing. In addition to his now-or-never fundraising tactics ("I am crying as I write this letter of introduction to this issue of The Fatima Crusader which may possibly be the last") and his blow-down-the-door attacks against the Blue Army and other competitors, he continued to uncover new conspiracies of evil.[44] America's cities were teeming with Satanists. The New Age movement was setting the stage for a one-world government and one-world religion. The federal government and federal law enforcement agencies were determined to reduce America to a repressive police state. And as a backup, there was always Russian communism, which was still alive, and still gathering strength.[45]

Gruner also remained active on the international scene. In November 1994 he sponsored another worldwide bishops' conference, this time in Mexico City, in an effort to win some more high-ranking converts to his cause. Thanks to the "sinister machinations" of Vatican bureaucrats, however, only a handful of bishops wound up attending, and Gruner was once again forced to take his case directly to John Paul II in Rome.[46]

In a two-page open letter that appeared on July 12, 1995, in *Il Messaggero*, Rome's largest daily newspaper, ten of Gruner's top supporters told the pope that "In the last 18 years, despite constant opposition from radical modernists and anti-Marian forces within the Church, [Fr. Gruner] has succeeded in creating one of the largest lay Apostolates in the world, bringing together nearly 500,000 individuals in a community of prayer and sacrifice dedicated to promoting the *full and complete* Message of Fatima." Tragically, the letter went on, it has been some of the pope's very closest advisers who have spearheaded the opposition against Fr. Gruner and his Fatima ministry. "Our hearts remain indissolubly united with yours, Holy Father, but we fear that you are being deceived and misled by those in whom you have placed your trust. . . . After the bitter experiences of the last two Conferences, it now seems undeniable that there exists a small group of Vatican officials who have become so confident of their unbridled power that they will use *any* means (including lies, slander and libel) to silence anyone promoting the *full* Fatima Message. Thus, Holy Father, we are obliged to appeal to you directly in this public letter, trusting as always in your probity and fairness."[47]

The open letter to the pope, which cost 250 million lire to publish, drew a magisterial "no comment" from the Vatican, and upon returning to North America, Gruner was dealt still another piece of adversity. In May 1995 the Supreme Tribunal of the Apostolic Signatura, the church's highest administrative court, had reviewed his case, and the verdict was now official: Gruner was commanded to abandon his North American Fatima ministry and to return immediately to the jurisdiction of his bishop in Avellino, Italy.[48]

When I visited Gruner again in Fort Erie several months afterward, he seemed slightly more subdued but by no means resigned to defeat. "Vatican courts and Vatican bureaucrats can give me all the ultimatums they want," he said, "but this doesn't make the final difference. In Catholic tradition, every Catholic has the right to appeal directly and personally to the pope. This is exactly what I intend to do. And I have heard from high-ranking inside private sources that the pope agrees with me."

I asked Gruner whether the various setbacks he'd suffered over the past ten years—from the downfall of Soviet communism to his own repeated run-ins with ecclesiastical authority—were finally exacting an economic toll on his ministry. "I find it interesting that you naively speak of the 'downfall' of communism just when communists are being voted back into office in Russia," he said. "I still regard communism as a menace, and I believe that we're in greater danger than ever. And obviously my readers agree with me. We're still putting out five hundred thousand magazines per issue, and we still have one hundred thousand financial supporters. Our rate of growth has leveled off, but we're more than holding our own. I employ fifty people on a full-time basis here. The ministry is still very successful, and that's because we're the only voice truly representing Our Lady of Fatima in the world today."[49]

In the view of some of Gruner's detractors, however, there's a far more obvious explanation for the success of his ministry: old-fashioned chicanery. Despite his professions of sincerity, they claim, Gruner is nothing more than a skillful manipulator who has made a profitable career out of exploiting the fears and anxieties of gullible and emotionally hard-pressed Catholics. And how does he respond to such charges? "I've heard it all before," he told me. "I'm supposed to be ripping people off, fattening my own bank account. This is ridiculous. I don't need to do this. I'm well taken care of financially from my parents' legacy. My salary is $500 per month, exactly the same as it's been since 1979. I'm not saying I'm not ambitious. I have initiative, and I regard this as a Christian virtue. I'm motivated entirely by love of God and by truth. If we love justice and hate iniquity, we're compelled to do everything possible to spread the full Fatima message. The peace of the world and the salvation of millions of souls hinges on the truths of Fatima. What I'm doing is a matter of life and death."[50]

VERONICA LUEKEN AND THE BAYSIDE MOVEMENT

December 7, 1995. Despite the frigid temperature and the bone-biting winds gusting in off Long Island Sound, the three hundred pilgrims who were assembled on the grounds of the 1964–65 World's Fair, in Queens, New York, seemed perfectly at home. Bundled up in blankets and shawls and parkas, they swapped stories of supernatural healings, showed off their latest miraculous photographs, and passed around Thermoses filled with hot tea. As the winter darkness descended, they drew themselves into a rough semicircle around a portable shrine that had been set up on the same site where the Vatican Pavilion had stood thirty years earlier. At the center of the shrine, flanked by two porcelain angels on bended knee, and surrounded by banks of lit candles and bouquets of roses, stood a large, illuminated, blue-and-white statue of the Virgin Mary. The shrine was cordoned off by twenty men wearing white berets, and at the prompting of a young man standing at a microphone, the entire crowd began to recite the rosary.

Hail Mary, full of grace, the Lord is with thee . . . As the pilgrims filled the air with a sonorous chorus of Hail Mary's and Our Father's, late rush-hour traffic pounded away on the Long Island Expressway to the immediate south. Just two hundred yards beyond the shrine were green highway signs for the Van Wyck Expressway and the Whitestone Bridge . . . *Blessed art thou among women, And blessed is the fruit of thy womb, Jesus* . . . Every fifteen minutes or so the chorus of prayer was momentarily drowned out by the roar of jets taking off from LaGuardia Airport. Police and ambulance sirens wailed somewhere off in the distance . . . *Holy Mary, Mother of God, pray for us sinners. . .* Most of the pilgrims knelt on the cold, frozen ground as they prayed. Some sat in lawn chairs that they had brought with them onto the grounds. At least twenty people stood on the perimeter of the crowd with Polaroid cameras snapping photographs. Occasionally someone would walk right up to the front of the shrine with a camera and start shooting. . . . *now and at the hour of our death. Amen. . .*

The rosary recital lasted a full three-and-a-half hours, and the winds became increasingly more bitter as the evening wore down. (I made three trips to my car to jot down field notes with the heater blasting. Everyone else stuck it out in the cold for the duration.) Although their features were difficult to make out in the dark, roughly two-thirds of the pilgrims looked to be over fifty years of age, and slightly more than half were women. Half a dozen African-American women knelt in a prayer knot at one end of the semicircle. Among the younger pilgrims, there were several scruffy-looking men in their early to mid-twenties with scraggly long hair and jeans. One of them came up to me halfway through the vigil and launched into an incoherent tirade about demons and exorcism. A middle-aged man wearing a white beret, whom I recognized from a vigil I'd attended several months earlier, gently steered him away and then said to me: "He's one of the crazy ones. We get all kinds coming out here. You'd be better off talking to someone who knows what's going on."

At one point, I found myself standing beside a sixtyish man who was wearing only a tweed jacket, sweater, and fedora as protection against the cold. I introduced myself, and after a couple of minutes he was joined by a woman of about the same age who wanted to show him a photograph she'd apparently just taken. The man took a penlight from his jacket pocket, shined it directly on the photograph, frowned, and then tried several different angles. Finally, he thought he saw something interesting.

"Do you see this?" he asked the woman.
"Where?"
"Over here—at the upper left—in the sky above the shrine."
"What is it?" she said.
"It looks like strange lights."
"You're right. I hadn't noticed it."
The man trained his light on the photograph again and asked me if I saw anything interesting.
"I'm not sure," I said.
"Well, we'll have to examine it more closely later. I only wish Veronica was still here so I could show it to her."

When the last decade of the rosary had finally been recited, the pilgrims lined up to kiss a crucifix that was strung around the neck of the statue of the Virgin Mary. A shrine attendant wiped the crucifix with a fresh tissue after each kiss, and every pilgrim took her or his tissue away as a sacred souvenir. While watching this spectacle, I was approached by a friendly young man in his mid-twenties named Jim. Jim told me that he had graduated with a degree in chemistry from Pomona Polytechnical in California several years earlier, and that he'd been working full-time for the shrine ever since. He also told me that the crucifix the pilgrims were lining up to kiss had been directly kissed by the Virgin Mary herself during one of her own visits to the shrine years before.

While the shrine was being dismantled and loaded onto a van, I struck up a conversation with a middle-aged woman named Anne, who was enshrouded in blankets and sweaters and scarves. Anne told me that she lived in New Jersey, just an hour's drive away, and that she'd been attending prayer vigils at the fairgrounds on a regular basis for more than a decade. "But it's just not the same without Veronica," she said. "Veronica's the reason we've all been coming. I can't tell you how much I miss her."[51]

VERONICA LUEKEN, the woman behind the prayer vigils at the old World's Fair grounds, died of congestive heart failure on August 3, 1995, and many of the pilgrims in attendance on that wintry night in December were still in a state of mourning. For more than twenty years, Veronica (as she is still fondly referred to by her admirers) had been the star attraction of the vigils. Upon arriving at the shrine with her husband, Arthur, she would fall like clockwork into an ecstatic trance and begin receiving messages from the Virgin Mary, Jesus, and other heavenly beings. The messages would be tape-recorded on the spot and then transcribed and sent out to Veronica's thousands of followers across North America. Among other things, the messages dealt with end-time prophecy, with the cultural evils of the modern world, and, most of all, with the plague of apostasy that had befallen the Catholic church in the wake of the Second Vatican Council. For Veronica's followers, the messages were a holy testament, an apocalyptic gospel of salvation and damnation, and Veronica herself was the great prophetess of the last days. As Anne from New Jersey rightly pointed out, it was mainly because of Veronica that people had been coming out to the fairground vigils for the past two decades, and now that Veronica was gone many of her followers were no longer certain where to turn.

As befits a prophetess of the last days, the story of Veronica's private life is a confusing tangle of rumor and innuendo, half-truths, and wishful thinking.[52] She was born Veronica Kearn on July 12, 1923, in Jamaica, Queens, and her childhood seems to have been marked by a fair bit of turbulence. Her mother remarried when Veronica was a young girl, and she was adopted by her stepfather whose surname was MacDonald. The MacDonalds were lower-working-class, and Veronica left high school prior to graduation and worked at a variety of jobs, including a stint during her late teens as a dancer at the Roxy Theater in Manhattan. As a young woman, Veronica was very attractive, with a sweet face and thick black hair, and she seems to have dreamed of making a career for herself as an entertainer in Hollywood. In the late forties she met Arthur Lueken, a construction worker from Indiana, at the skating rink in Flushing Meadow Park, and the couple was married shortly afterward at a Catholic church in Queens. Over the next fifteen years Veronica had five children, and, after several changes of residence, the family finally settled, in late 1965, into a five-room apartment in the Bayside Hills section of Queens.

It's at this point that the story grows considerably murkier. According to several accounts, the Luekens were hit with a run of bad luck shortly after their move to Bayside. Complicating an already overcrowded domestic situation, Veronica's brother, who was suffering from multiple sclerosis, moved into the family apartment in 1966, and he was soon followed by her stepfather, who was out of work and homeless. (Veronica's mother had died in 1954.) In the meantime, Arthur fell ill and lost his job, and the oldest child, Butch, left home and spent a year as a yoga devotee in California. In an effort to make ends meet, Veronica apparently began to tell fortunes out of the apartment, and over a period of several months she built up a fairly steady clientele.

Arthur eventually recovered from his illness and returned to work, and on June 5, 1968, while driving him to his new job at a construction site in Queens, Veronica heard on the car radio that Senator Robert F. Kennedy had just been shot. Veronica joined in the prayer sessions that were being conducted over the radio for the dying senator, and suddenly, quite out of the blue, she was overcome by a powerful fragrance of roses. The fragrance returned several more times over the next couple of days, and Veronica became convinced that St. Thérèse of Lisieux, who reportedly had had a special fondness for roses, was mystically communicating with her. Two months later, on August 6, Veronica experienced a miraculous vision of St. Thérèse while dusting in her bedroom, and the saint kept her awake for three days and nights dictating poetry and messages of supernatural salvation. St. Thérèse continued to visit Veronica over the next two years, and in the spring of 1970 the Virgin Mary also appeared to her with a special promise. Starting on June 18, the Virgin said, she would appear to Veronica on the eve of every major Catholic feast day on the grounds of St. Robert Bellarmine's, Veronica's parish church in Bayside. On June 18, Veronica waited in the rain until almost midnight, kneeling by a statue of the Virgin Mary on St. Robert's front lawn. When the Virgin finally appeared, she told Veronica that she wanted the statue consecrated to her as a national shrine under the title Our Lady of the Roses, Mary Help of Mothers. The Virgin also said that a miraculous spring of water would soon emerge at the shrine, and that the grounds of St. Robert's would eventually be the site of one of the most important basilicas in the Catholic world.

By this stage of the game, many of the people closest to Veronica were hard-pressed to explain what was going on. Veronica had apparently been prescribed diet pills early in 1968, and some of her neighbors and family members suspected that the visions and mystical communications were nothing more than a hallucinatory side effect. Arthur, for his part, was convinced that Veronica had gone completely mad, and he apparently succeeded at some point after her initial encounter with St. Thérèse in persuading her to seek psychiatric counseling.

None of this, however, seems to have mattered much to the crowds that began showing up at St. Robert's for the Virgin Mary's regularly scheduled appearances. Although no one other than Veronica was capable of actually seeing or hearing the Virgin, the apparitions were soon drawing as many as five hundred pilgrims and curiosity-seekers at a time. The messages that Veronica received on the grounds of St. Robert's during these early years varied in content from the fantastical and apocalyptic to the kitchen-table practical. In addition to telling Veronica that the Antichrist was now living in the United States (May 19, 1971) and that a "fiery ball of redemption" was on the verge of striking the earth (June 17, 1971), the Virgin also took the trouble to remind her to collect money from her followers for stamps and other ministry-related expenses (August 21, 1972).[53]

Not that money for stamps was a frivolous consideration. By the summer of 1972, Veronica was printing up condensed versions of her mystical messages on an old mimeograph machine and sending them out to her steadily expanding circle of followers. And while the cost of these mailings was at least partly offset by private donations, Veronica was clearly in need of some sort of institutional support.

Institutional support came Veronica's way a year later, as it turns out, and from a quite unexpected source. In the summer of 1973, leading members of the Pilgrims of Saint Michael (or White Berets), a Roman Catholic lay order based in Rougemont, Quebec, began attending the vigils at St. Robert's, and they were obviously deeply impressed. By almost any standard, the White Berets were a highly unusual group. Their order had been founded in 1934 for the purpose of advancing the economic principles of "Social Credit," but since the mid-sixties they had gone off in an increasingly eccentric direction. They were convinced that the machinery of international finance was controlled by a satanic elite called the Illuminati, and also that world history was soon destined for an apocalyptic conclusion. They were also deeply immersed in the world of Marian apparitions, and over a number of years they had been looking for an apparitional phenomenon that they could adopt as their own and take a hand in actively promoting. The ongoing apparitions at St. Robert's seemed to fit the bill perfectly, and in late 1973 the White Berets undertook a massive public relations campaign on behalf of Veronica and her mystical visions and locutions. In their French-language quarterly, *Vers Demain*, its English-language equivalent, *Michael Journal* (which boasted a combined circulation of almost ninety thousand), and an array of pamphlets and broadsheets that were distributed abroad, the Berets set about publishing the full text of Veronica's messages and promoting her as the greatest seeress of the age.[54]

In several other respects, however, 1973 proved a rather difficult year for Veronica. To begin with, there was the controversy that grew out of the so-called miraculous photographs, or "pictures from heaven." In late 1970, several of Veronica's followers had started taking Polaroid photographs during the apparitions at St. Robert's, in the hope of capturing some sign or token of the Virgin Mary's presence. The practice soon caught on, and by mid-1971 it had developed into a full-blown ritual, with dozens of people snapping photographs at the vigils and then later bringing them to Veronica for an authoritative interpretation. For the most part, the miraculous photographs belonged to the realm of pure Rorschach: they featured streaks of light or splotches of color that could have meant anything under the sun—or nothing at all. Occasionally, however, the cameras seemed to catch something rather more tantalizing—a vague outline of the Virgin perhaps, a tracing of letters, or even the glimmering features of a deceased relative. In the most famous case of all, a photograph that was taken on September 14, 1971, appeared with the caption "JACINTA 1972" eerily scrawled across its upper face. Jacinta, the youngest seer of the redoubtable Fatima apparitions, had apparently prophesied, shortly before her death, that 1972 would be a year of immeasurable suffering for the church, and it appeared that she was now transmitting the same message to Veronica and her followers through the miraculous medium of photography.[55]

Not everyone was as fully enamored of the miraculous photographs as the Bayside pilgrims, however, and during the spring and summer of 1973 the Queens District Attorney's office conducted an investigation into Veronica's ministry for possible fraud. Suspicious that the photographs may have been contrived in order to jack up recruitment and fundraising for the ministry, investigators collected a sample of them and sent them off to the Polaroid Corporation for analysis. On September 12, Polaroid reported back to the D.A.'s office that in most cases the strange effects that appeared on the photographs were likely the result of overexposure, camera tipsiness, and other kinds of amateur bungling, but that in several others a "more sophisticated process of tampering" may have been involved.[56]

In the end, the D.A.'s office elected not to bring charges against Veronica, but in the meantime the Roman Catholic Diocese of Brooklyn was conducting its own investigation. During the summer of 1973, a committee of five priests, including the pastor of St. Robert's, Msgr. J. Emmett McDonald, and the diocesan chancellor, Msgr. James King, examined transcripts of Veronica's mystical messages and concluded that they were the product, at the very most, of a "highly fertile imagination." On September 20, Msgr. King informed Veronica in writing that the diocese would be forced to take decisive action if she persisted in holding her vigils on church grounds. Veronica refused to back down, however, and when crowds continued to flock to St. Robert's for the vigils, the diocese, on November 27, removed the statue of the Virgin Mary from the church's front lawn. But this, as it turns out, was only a minor inconvenience: without missing a beat, Veronica arranged to have a duplicate statue brought to the grounds for the vigils, and the crowds kept coming.[57]

Veronica suffered a terrible blow several weeks later when her youngest child, Raymond, was killed in an apparent hunting accident in upstate New York. Of her five children, Raymond had been Veronica's closest confidant and easily the most supportive of her mystical ministry, and at the vigil that took place on February 1, 1974, just three days after his death, she claimed to receive a vision of him entering heaven.[58]

By the summer of 1974, the vigils were regularly attracting anywhere from fifteen hundred to two thousand pilgrims at a time, and the controversy surrounding them was becoming increasingly more intense. On September 17, the Brooklyn diocese proclaimed that Catholics were forbidden to attend the vigils, and three months later the parish staff of St. Robert's fenced off the church property and forced the pilgrims onto the street. Still undeterred, Veronica and her followers moved their shrine to a nearby traffic mall, but this only brought them into open conflict with the local community. Incensed with the traffic congestion and incessant chanting that were regular features of the vigils, Bayside homeowners banded together and finally, in April 1975, succeeded in obtaining a court order prohibiting Veronica and her followers from congregating in the neighborhood. In an attempt to work out some sort of compromise solution, officials from the parks and police departments proposed to Veronica that she henceforth hold her vigils in Flushing Meadow Park, at the site of the old World's Fair Vatican Pavilion, and on May 18, 1975, the Virgin Mary appeared to Veronica in her living room and announced that this new location would be acceptable.[59]

The move to the old World's Fair grounds brought a measure of peace to Veronica's ministry, but it wasn't long before controversy struck again. In the spring of 1977, Veronica informed her followers that the Virgin Mary had appeared to her with a fashion ultimatum: all male devotees of the Bayside apparitions were henceforth to wear white berets, and all female devotees blue ones. The problem with this was that both male and female members of the Pilgrims of Saint Michael, who were Veronica's biggest boosters at the time, had been wearing white berets for decades, and this new fashion directive seemed to them entirely unreasonable. When Veronica (and the Virgin) refused to grant the Pilgrims a special exemption, they withdrew their support of the apparitions and returned to Canada in a huff.[60]

Veronica was tremendously perturbed by this disloyalty, and she immediately took steps to bring her ministry under more rigorous control. In the summer of 1977 she and Arthur (who was now, at least outwardly, a believer in the apparitions) and several of their closest allies presided over the formation of a lay community of men that was entrusted with promoting the ministry and ensuring that it remained safely within Veronica's orbit. Veronica appointed a Canadian and one-time White Beret named Frank Albas as director of the community, and during the autumn of 1977 Albas recruited a dozen young men who were eager to put their entire lives at Veronica's service. Following a directive from the Virgin, the community was christened the Lay Order of St. Michael, and right from the start it adopted an ethic of strict, quasi-monastic asceticism. Community members (or full-time shrine workers, as they were more commonly called) lived together in a communal apartment in the Bronx and commuted daily to Queens where they put in fourteen-hour days transcribing Veronica's divine messages, answering mail, and taking calls from people anxious for more news on the approaching chastisement. By early 1978, Veronica's ministry had grown to the point where it was able to purchase a substantial printing facility in Queens, and the full-time workers were given the added responsibility of producing the shrine's various promotional materials, including a newly established newspaper called *Roses*, which was charged with keeping track of the Virgin Mary's ongoing communications.

KEEPING TRACK OF THE VIRGIN MARY'S COMMUNICATIONS in those days was by no means an easy task. Throughout the 1970s, the Virgin appeared with remarkable frequency to Veronica, and she seems never to have been at a loss for words. In many of her messages, in fact, the Virgin demonstrated a rather surprising penchant for colloquialism. She mimicked the glossolalia (or speaking-in-tongues) of Catholic charismatics ("bla-la-la-la-la-la-la"); she told Veronica that she had been chosen as a seeress because she was incapable of "keep[ing] her mouth closed"; and she criticized the American Catholic bishops for playing "a cat-and-mouse game" with Veronica and for repeatedly "passing the buck" on matters of vital spiritual importance. At other points, the Virgin's utterances seemed lifted straight out of some Hollywood B-movie lexicon. She told Veronica that UFO's were "transport ships from hell"; that zombies ("animated by demons") were roaming the earth; and that the "Son of Sam" serial killer (David Berkowitz) was really "Satan in a human body."[61]

As might be expected, however, the Virgin Mary's most startling scoop concerned the leadership of the Roman Catholic Church. During an extended appearance on September 27, 1975, the Virgin let Veronica in on a secret that she had also recently confided to Clemente Dominguez Gomez, the self-styled visionary and prophet of Palmar de Troya, Spain (see above, pp. 99). Several years earlier, according to the Virgin, three of the most powerful bureaucrats in the Vatican had carried out one of the most monstrous conspiracies in the history of the church. In an effort to bring about the final destruction of Roman Catholicism, Cardinals Jean Villot, Papal Secretary of State, Giovanni Benelli, Deputy

Secretary of State, and Agostino Casaroli, Secretary for the Council of Public Affairs, had poisoned and imprisoned Pope Paul VI and installed an imposter in his place on the papal throne. The imposter was a professional actor who had been surgically remade into an exact double of Paul VI, and even members of the pope's own family had been taken in by the scheme. As the Virgin herself put it to Veronica:

> My child, I bring you a sad truth, one that must be made known to mankind. Our dear, beloved Vicar, Pope Paul the Sixth, he suffers much at the hands of those he trusts! My child, shout it from the rooftops! He is not able to do his mission. They have laid him low, My child. He is ill, he is very ill!!!
>
> Now there is one ruling in his place, an IMPOSTER created from the minds of the agents of Satan. Plastic surgery, My child, the best of surgeons were used to create this IMPOSTER. Shout it from the rooftops! He must be exposed, and removed!
>
> Behind him, My child, there are three who have given themselves to Satan. You do not receive the truth in your country, and in the world. Your Vicar is a prisoner!!!
>
> Agostino Casaroli, you shall condemn your soul to Hell! Giovanni Benelli! What road have you taken? You are on the road to Hell and damnation! Villot, leader of evil! . . . You consort with the Synagogue of Satan. . . .
>
> The Anti-Christ, the forces of evil, have gathered, My children, within the Eternal City. You must make it known to mankind, that all that is coming from Rome, is coming from darkness. . . .
>
> The appearance in public is not Paul the Sixth, it is the imposter Pope. Medication of evil has dulled the brain of the true Pope. . . . They send into his veins poison, to dull his reasoning and paralyze his legs. . . .
>
> My children, you must now pray for the light. You must know the truth. All that is given to you is being sent from the traitorous hearts of those who have seized power in the Eternal City of Rome. My child, you will be mocked with this message, you will be scorned by many, but you bring the truth!
>
> It is the diabolical plan of Satan to have the hates of the world turn to the Vicar, Pope Paul the Sixth, in Rome. The plan of Satan is to heap upon his shoulders all the error and wrong-doings. However, those he has trusted, have betrayed him, and have now assumed complete control of his mission. . . .[62]

The imposter-pope theory rapidly became a signature theme of Veronica's ministry, and during the late seventies and early eighties no effort was spared in driving it home. In addition to the Virgin Mary's running commentary on the topic, the shrine's promotional literature regularly featured photographs of the real Paul VI and the imposter Paul VI in incriminating juxtaposition. As observers of the photographs could readily see for themselves, the imposter's nose was shorter and rounder than the real pope's, and his ear structure was completely different. And then there was that telltale mole. . . . All in all, the best plastic surgeons in the world seem to have been strangely inept.[63]

As outrageous as the imposter theory might seem, it went a long way toward helping Veronica and her followers make sense of the disturbing changes that were unfolding in the church in the wake of the Second Vatican Council. And what's more, unlike the sedevacantist theories discussed in the previous chapter, it had the particular advantage of relieving the papacy of direct responsibility for these changes. It wasn't Pope Paul VI, after all, who had banished the beloved Tridentine Mass or implemented the new policies on ecumenism and religious liberty, but rather the cosmetically flawed stooge who had taken his place on the papal throne. And because the pope himself was blameless in all of this, there was no reason for faithful Catholics to give up on the institutional church. Mount St. Michael's and other traditionalist groups were wrong to think that the church was beyond redemption: the challenge was to stay and fight for its salvation from within.

In a series of messages that she delivered to Veronica during the late seventies and early eighties, in fact, the Virgin Mary made it abundantly clear that staying and fighting from within was also her preference. "We do not wish that you break apart into small groups of discord," the Virgin told Veronica in November 1979. "No schisms must take place in My Son's Church. For all who are baptized a Roman Catholic must die Roman Catholics to enter Heaven." And then again almost three years later: "Remember, My child and My children, no matter how rough the road gets, you will stay within your parish church. And by good example and many prayers you will bring the priesthood back into the light."[64]

Despite counseling them to remain in their local parish churches, the Virgin Mary certainly didn't want Veronica and her followers to accept all of the liturgical changes that had come about in the years following the council. In several communications to Veronica during the late seventies, the Virgin condemned the new liturgical practice of receiving communion in the hand rather than on the tongue, and on July 14, 1979, she also told Veronica that her followers should always receive the sacrament while kneeling. And over the next ten years, in fact, this would become a chief identifying mark of Baysiders (as Veronica's followers were popularly dubbed) in Catholic parishes throughout the United States and Canada. In small groups of five or six, they would defy the current liturgical conventions by insisting upon kneeling for communion—with hands folded in prayer and tongues extended.[65]

The topic that the Virgin Mary seems to have spent the most time discussing with Veronica during the seventies and early eighties was the approaching chastisement. In the very near future, the Virgin told Veronica, there will be a Great Warning, in the form of some horrible natural catastrophe, that will result in immense suffering throughout the world. Veronica and her followers will be spared the worst effects of the catastrophe, but in the meantime they must prepare for it by storing water, blankets, food, and blessed candles in their homes. The warning will be of short duration, and will be followed by a celestial miracle that will provide added inducement for people to surrender their hearts to God.[66] In all likelihood, however, the great majority of people will persist in wickedness, and God in turn will unleash a furious chastisement upon the world. The chastisement will take place in two distinct stages. First, there will be a major global conflict (World War III) in which countless people will die, and then virtually the entire world will be destroyed by a great comet (or Ball of Redemption). Over the years, the Virgin Mary gave Veronica numerous glimpses of the devastation that almost certainly lay ahead. "I see a great light, a flash! It's so hot, this flash! Oh, there's a large ball of fire. Oh, it's very hot, and it's whirling through the sky, and it's shooting off sparks behind it. . . . Now the waters, the waters are rising very high. I can see the waters. Oh! Oh! Oh, the waters have come in. They're so high! And I see some cities. I see a large city, and the waters are now—oh, they're pounding against the ground. And now I see the build-ings—they're falling! Now the ground is cracking, and the buildings are falling into the holes. Oh! Oh! Oh!" (June 16, 1973) And again: "Now I notice that there is a tremendous ball now setting out in the sky by the sun. . . . And it's heading now over towards the earth again. It's hit it once, and something hap-pened. And now it's heading for another part of the globe. It's turned its course completely around and is striking the globe; I can see now the whole underside of the globe in flames." (April 14, 1984)[67]

Nevertheless, as Bayside promotional literature has usually been at pains to point out, there remains a slight chance that none of this will come to pass. "The length, timing, severity, or even occurrence of this Chastisement is totally depen-dent on man's response. . . . A full restoration to godliness and traditional values in all spheres of life would stay God's holy wrath."[68] And toward this end, Veronica and her followers have been given a momentous role. They are the Disciples of the Latter Days, the chosen few who have been charged with the responsibility of preaching the necessity of conversion to the entire world. "Shout the Message from Heaven from the rooftops!" the Virgin exhorted them in March 1977. "Do not slacken in your mission from heaven." And later the same year: "You will be called fanatics! You will be called insane! You will be laughed at with derision! Accept it, My children, for as My Son was rejected, you too will be rejected."[69]

For enduring all of this persecution, however, Veronica and her followers will be richly rewarded. As the day of the chastisement approaches, the Virgin promised in December 1976, the Disciples of the Latter Days will be miraculously raptured to a place of safekeeping. "I give you great grace of heart, My children, to know that many shall be taken from your earth before the great Chastisement. It will be of great mirth, My child, to reveal to you that there will be much consternation and conflicting thought when these beloved children disappear from the earth. Many of your news medias shall state that they have been carried off by flying saucers. Oh no, My children, they were carried off into a supernatural realm of the Eternal Father to await the return of My Son upon earth."[70]

BY THE LATE 1970S, the Lay Order of St. Michael (or full-time workers) had completely taken over the day-to-day running of the shrine, and Veronica was able to dedicate herself almost entirely to her ongoing visions and locutions. In addition to the Virgin Mary, Jesus and St. Michael and several other heavenly beings had also started making frequent appearances to her at the shrine, and the full-time workers were forced to rig up a system of lighting so that pilgrims could keep track of the incoming celestial traffic. A flashing blue light signaled that the Virgin Mary was on the grounds, and a flashing red one signaled the arrival of Jesus.

By this time also, the ministry had developed a fairly rigid hierarchy of both status and authority. At the top were Veronica and Arthur, Veronica's longtime confidante and personal secretary Ann Ferguson, and Frank Albas, who served as both director of the shrine and rector of the Order of St. Michael. Next in line came the full-time workers who were responsible for both promoting the ministry and safeguarding its orthodoxy. (The sacred messages were supposed to mean exactly what Veronica said they meant—nothing more, nothing less.) After the workers were the people known as *organizers*. These were especially dedicated devotees of Veronica from outside the New York City area who were responsible for organizing prayer vigils in their local communities and also arranging pilgrimages to the old World's Fair grounds. By 1980 there were organizers in almost all fifty states, seven Canadian provinces, and more than a dozen other countries worldwide. And finally, there were the rank-and-file adherents who supported the ministry through their prayers and their (mostly) modest financial donations.

These modest donations eventually added up, and by the early eighties Veronica's ministry was a flourishing concern, with an operating budget of more than $50,000 per month and a mailing list of almost sixty-thousand names.[71] Pilgrims from throughout North America were arriving by the busload for the Holy Eve vigils, and Veronica's closest followers seemed justified in thinking she would go down in history as one of the most famous visionaries of her time.

Below the surface, however, not everything was quite so upbeat. After a decade serving as the voicebox of the Virgin Mary, Veronica's mystical celebrity seemed to be taking a toll on her. Her physical health was poor and getting worse, and during the early to mid-eighties she grew increasingly fearful for her personal safety. Convinced that mysterious enemies were plotting her assassination, she withdrew into the privacy of her home and refused to meet with anyone outside of her inner circle. As the decade wore on, moreover, Veronica found attending even the fairground vigils a difficult chore, and as often as not the pilgrims showed up only to learn that their seeress had decided to stay at home.

And then there were the troublesome rumors. According to some reports, the

Luekens' marriage had turned nasty, and both Veronica and Arthur had actually been hauled away in handcuffs following one of their more violent exchanges. According to others, Veronica had finally lost all grip on reality, and she was seeing a psychiatrist two or three times every week. Still more disturbing were the reports of financial malfeasance. In early 1980, with Arthur once again out of work, the Luekens had somehow managed to come up with $89,000 in cash for the purchase of a new home in Terryville, a small town on Long Island's North Shore. And exactly how, considering their presumably meager circumstances, were they able to afford twice-yearly (and sometimes thrice-yearly) vacations?

One of the people who played a leading role in spreading these negative reports was a heating contractor and suburban New Yorker named Dan Callegari. During the late seventies both of Callegari's in-laws had become involved with Veronica's ministry, and shortly afterward a special Bayside recruiting team targeted his wife. "My in-laws got sucked in, and then Veronica's people started working on my wife," he told me during a recent interview. "As soon as I would leave for work, they'd come over and begin indoctrinating her. These were Veronica's professional recruiters. They specialized in bringing people in. It took a couple of weeks, and then she was completely changed."

The recruiting team responsible for bringing Callegari's wife into the Bayside fold apparently advised her to seek a divorce unless Callegari himself also came to see the light. Living with an unbeliever in these dangerous times, they told her, was an exceedingly risky business. In an effort to preserve his marriage, Callegari feigned conversion, but his subterfuge was soon exposed. "I made a show of joining, but there comes a point when you just can't be one of them," he said. "I guess it was pretty obvious I wasn't really buying into their foolishness about Balls of Redemption and zombies and imposter popes and whatever, and so they insisted that my wife divorce me. We hadn't been married in the Church, and so they claimed it wasn't a valid marriage in the first place."

Callegari had always suspected that Veronica was a fraud, and now he set out with a vengeance to prove his case. With the help of several friends, including a retired New York City police detective and former Bayside devotee named Hank Cinotti, he spent months tracking Veronica and Arthur's movements and spying into their personal finances. And at the end, he told me, he and his friends had unearthed enough dirt to sink a ship. "Veronica was a complete phony. Without a doubt, she was making at least $100,000 a year personally off the ministry. And Arthur was always in it just for the money. There used to be a petition sack at the vigils, and with their prayer petitions people would always throw in a little money. Two bucks. Five bucks. Ten bucks. You'd be amazed at how fast it all adds up. Then at a certain point Arthur would pick up the sack and carry it to his car and put it in the trunk. Then a few minutes later they'd both leave the vigil and stay at a hotel. Veronica was also quite the performer. In preparation for the vigils, she would put on makeup so she'd look white as a ghost. And lots of times, she'd be brought up to the shrine in a wheelchair. Meanwhile, we'd watched her load the wheelchair into the trunk of her car all by herself half an hour earlier. Everything about her ministry was completely bogus. They made such a big deal about the 'JACINTA 1972' picture. This was supposed to be a great miracle. But we found the guy who took the picture, and he admitted that he'd written the words on the negative before he pulled the Polaroid photo apart. The whole thing, from beginning to end, was nothing but a scam."[72]

Ben Salomone, one of the friends who assisted Callegari in his investigation, disagrees that Veronica's ministry was nothing but a scam. In his view, the entire enterprise was a demonic conspiracy aimed at stealing the souls of distressed Catholics from the church, and when I contacted him by telephone in February 1996 and asked for his impressions of Veronica, he became openly agitated. "You have no idea what you're getting involved with," he said. "This whole thing is from the devil. Just hearing you mention Veronica's name fills me with dread. There's no way I want to go back to those days."

For almost an entire decade, however, until his excommunication from the Bayside ministry in the early eighties, Salomone was one of Veronica's most loyal soldiers. It was Salomone who arranged for the manufacture of the Our Lady of the Roses medal, which Baysiders are supposed to wear to ward off evil, and Salomone and his son John who served as Veronica's chief bodyguards throughout the formative years of her ministry. "I first heard of Veronica in 1970 when someone showed me some of the miraculous photographs," he told me. "And back then she was a very good woman. She was very poor but also very kind and she would share with anyone. And I was forty years old and very confused and very disturbed over what was happening to the Church after Vatican II. And so were all of Veronica's followers. And Veronica gave us great stuff. The rosary at the vigils was absolutely beautiful. And there were the statues and the visions and the messages. Veronica gave us a sense of spiritual euphoria. We were so unhappy with the way the faith was being destroyed after the council, and Veronica came and filled the vacuum. We all loved her for this."

Salomone's love for Veronica began to break down in the late seventies over an accumulation of troublesome details. Why had Veronica been spotted dining out at local restaurants after ordering her followers to barricade themselves into their homes in preparation for the Great Warning? And why did the Lueken household boast three TV sets and a cable subscription to the Playboy Channel when Veronica had repeatedly condemned television? And why was there so much secrecy over the disbursement of ministry monies? When Salomone finally worked up the nerve to raise some of these issues with Veronica, she banished him from the shrine and advised him that his entire family was condemned to hell.

After his banishment, Salomone joined Dan Callegari in investigating Veronica, but he never came to doubt her supernatural powers. "The problem is that her powers were straight from Satan," he told me. "Veronica was used by satanic forces to fill the vacuum after Vatican II. So beware! A certain freelance newspaper reporter once called asking for information on Bayside. I gave her the information, and right after that she and her boyfriend and her newspaper editor drowned. So beware! If you're going to be snooping around Bayside, you have to protect yourself spiritually. I can't believe you haven't been smart enough to protect yourself spiritually. I can't talk about this any longer, but before I hang up I'll tell you one thing. Get invested with a miraculous medal and wear it constantly. And carry a bottle of holy water with you at all times, and bless yourself frequently with it during the whole day. This is the only way you will survive."[73]

Someone else who became a major thorn in Veronica's side during the early to mid-eighties was a Canadian woman (and sometimes Gruner supporter) named Anne Cillis. In a recent telephone interview, Cillis told me that she first became actively involved with Veronica's ministry quite by accident. During the early seventies, while running a traditionalist Catholic newspaper called *The Canadian Layman* from the Ottawa area, Cillis kept hearing from people with marvelous tales to tell about Bayside. They told her of rosaries turning to gold, of miraculous healings and conversions, and of the rapidly approaching days of tribulation. Finally, in early 1977, Cillis decided to check out the action for herself, and she came away favorably impressed. "I went to Bayside for a vigil, and I must say that Veronica and her messages initially struck me as being perfectly legitimate. There seemed to be an aura of genuine holiness surrounding the proceedings. Still, I resisted flinging myself fully into it at first, and for a while my involvement remained quite marginal."

Cillis's involvement might have remained marginal were it not for Veronica's flap with the Pilgrims of Saint Michael. When the Pilgrims pulled out of the ministry and took their newspapers with them, Cillis was asked by several of Veronica's people if a new publication she had just started, *Sancta Maria*, could be used to help promote the divine messages in Canada. Cillis agreed, and over the next several years she and Veronica developed a fairly close acquaintance. After a while, however, Cillis began to suspect that something was seriously amiss. According to her version of events, Veronica was the antithesis of what one would expect of a religious visionary. She was preoccupied with the celebrity culture of Hollywood, and she seemed far more passionate about the latest tabloid gossip than about Catholic theology. Even more disturbing, in Cillis's view, was Veronica's apparent fascination with spiritualism and the occult. She spoke endlessly about ghostly visitations and communication with the dead, and, in one particularly chilling episode, she phoned the Cillis household early one morning and spent several minutes perfectly imitating the voice of a close friend of Cillis who had recently passed away. All of this eventually proved too much for Cillis to handle, and in 1986 she published a sizzling exposé of Veronica's ministry entitled *Bayside Backstage*, in which she accused the seeress of everything from witchcraft to outright charlatanism.[74]

At roughly the same time, moreover, Veronica was also facing accusations of spiritual plagiarism. According to several of her critics, Veronica's routine was a note-by-note ripoff of an apparitional performance that had been playing regularly in rural Wisconsin for more than thirty years. Since 1950, the Virgin Mary had reportedly been appearing on a weekly basis to a woman named Mary Ann Van Hoof in the small town of Necedah, about eighty miles east of La Crosse, and the similarities between Necedah and Bayside seemed too close to be written off as mere accident. In both cases, the Virgin had defied apparitional protocol by continuing to appear over a span of many years rather than, say, for just a week or a month; and in both cases her messages were rambling and slang-ridden rather than (as at Lourdes or Fatima) succinct and epigrammatic. At both Necedah and Bayside, the Virgin spoke frequently of the communist menace to America, and at both places as well she commanded that a national shrine be built in her honor. And there was more. Mary Ann Van Hoof had apparently been tutored in spiritualism by her mother, and Veronica seems to have had more than a passing interest in the subject herself. And both women claimed that they had received the stigmata, or wounds of Christ, as authenticating marks of their ministries. (In Veronica's case, the stigmata were presumably carved into her feet by the legendary Italian mystic Padre Pio while she was at home sitting on her toilet.)

Veronica was certainly aware of Necedah prior to launching her own ministry, and it's quite possible (though the evidence here is flimsy) that she also took the trouble to meet personally with Mary Ann Van Hoof at several points during the 1950s and sixties. Might it not also be possible, her critics asked, that Bayside had been modeled directly after Necedah? For profit? Or for self-aggrandizement? Or both?[75]

As if all of this weren't enough, Veronica was also forced to deal with renewed pressure from the institutional church. On November 4, 1986, Francis John Mugavero, bishop of the Brooklyn diocese, issued an official declaration in which he tried to settle, once and for all, the spiritual status of Veronica's ministry. By all available evidence, the bishop wrote, both the apparitions and the messages associated with the ministry were entirely devoid of credibility, and the people responsible for promoting them were deliberately "acting against the judgment of legitimate Church authority." Speaking firmly, but without directly threatening either excommunication or ecclesiastical interdict, the bishop went on: "Because of my concern for their spiritual welfare, members of Christ's faithful are hereby directed to refrain from participating in the 'vigils' and from disseminating any propaganda related to the 'Bayside apparitions.' They are also discouraged from reading any such literature."[76]

No amount of ecclesiastical arm-twisting was about to halt the show, however, and the Virgin Mary continued her extended engagement at Bayside through the rest of the decade and into the nineties. And there were very few subjects along the way that failed to elicit her concern. The Virgin condemned homosexuality and abortion, modern biblical criticism and genetic engineering, secular humanism in education and secular humanism in the news media, and moral permissiveness in all of its contemporary guises. She pontificated on UFOs and world peace and international finance, and warned that America faced the worst effects of the impending chastisement unless the nation radically changed its ways. She lamented the current condition of the church, and especially its priesthood, but praised the papacy of John Paul II. And she even found time to rail against the United Nations and the threat of one-world government.[77]

At times, moreover, the Virgin and Veronica worked in tandem, putting on what amounted to extended performance pieces, as in the following morality play about the decline of the Mass:

VERONICA: Our Lady is placing Her hands upon Her eyes, and She's pointing over to the left side, Her right side. I see the inside of a church. There is service going on. But however, what are they doing? They are skipping, like frolicking down the aisle. As I watch I see—it is the priest, I believe, behind the altar. He's motioning to two children to come out of the pews and go to the rear of the church. The children are hastily—almost running to the back of the church, and I see they are picking up something. Oh, it is the ciborium and the plate. Oh!

OUR LADY: "Now what are they doing, My child?"

VERONICA: They are taking it up to the altar. Now the priest and the other man—

OUR LADY: "The deacon, he is called, My child, the deacon."

VERONICA: They are giving these over to them, and the priest is now going back to his station behind the altar. Now all of a sudden he raises his hand, and a young—oh, a young woman is coming out of the pew. But oh, my goodness me! She has on a pair of shorts, and she's heading for the altar.

Now Our Lady is pointing. The woman starts to sing. Her music is not oneof the church, or those accepted by God. And as she sings, the priest stands behind the altar. And in his eyes—

Is he admiring her or admonishing her?

OUR LADY: "It looks, My child, like he is admiring her."

VERONICA: The shorts she is wearing are most revealing and immodest, Our Lady said. Now that woman is now going to sit at the side of the altar, and as she crosses her legs it is a most horrible infringement on the sacred rites, for it—

It is almost embarrassing, Blessed Mother, for me to look. Must I see it?

OUR LADY: "Yes."

VERONICA: The shorts are no longer shorts. They're almost gone! And, and I can see the expression on the priest's face as he's observing this. Now also, there are two young girls about fourteen years of age sitting at the side of the altar as the priest goes forward to consecrate the host—

OUR LADY: "My Son's Body."

VERONICA: Now as I watch I notice now after the consecration that the priest is now taking his place on the right side in the altar at the last pew over to the right, and the deacon is going over to the left. And now—I don't believe it!

Oh, I see it, Blessed Mother! There are two young girls. Our Lady, how old are they?

OUR LADY: "Fourteen years old."

VERONICA: And Our Lady is saying:

OUR LADY: "Veronica, don't close your eyes. Open them and tell Me what you see."[78]

———————

AND EXACTLY WHO ARE THE PEOPLE who take melodrama of this sort seriously? In the autumn of 1993, at a restaurant in midtown Manhattan, I met with my first Baysider, a slight, earnest young man of twenty-three who also happens to be a graduate student in history at a fairly prestigious East Coast university.

Joseph (who has asked that I conceal his real identity) still lives with his Irish-Italian parents in the same Queens apartment where he was raised. He is an only child (a sister died in infancy before he was born), and both of his parents have been on disability pension for more than a decade. His mother suffers from various physical ailments, including a heart condition, and his father has been diagnosed as schizophrenic. The family is quite poor, and for several years now they've been forced to go without either a car or a telephone.

Although he had a sense growing up that his father was mentally disturbed, Joseph's childhood was generally happy. He was a fan of Spiderman Comics and the New York Yankees, and he enjoyed the early morning Masses that he and his mother made a point of attending almost daily. When Joseph was seven years old, his maternal aunt began attending Veronica's fairground vigils, and after several months his mother decided to join her. "My aunt led the way, and then my mother started going, and then the whole family. And as I recall, it was very beautiful for us. My parents were very religious, and although they tried hard to accept the changes that came in with the council, they were also very disturbed by some of them. They were very impressed that Our Lady was telling Veronica that we should stay in our own parishes but not give in to such truly irreverent innovations as receiving communion in the hand. And they also knew that there were miraculous healings taking place at the shrine."

Joseph attended the vigils faithfully with his parents for seven or eight years, but then went through a rather mild period of adolescent rebellion. "I didn't lose my faith, but I was too busy as a teenager to go regularly, and I think I wanted to strike out a bit on my own. Not that I committed serious sins. I stayed clear of drugs and alcohol; I saw the negative impact of this all around me. I really didn't have any girlfriends to speak of" (Joseph later told me that he's still a virgin) "and I didn't get involved with gangs. I listened to my own music and sort of did my own thing, but after a couple of years, when I was seventeen or eighteen, I gave this up as penance and went back to the shrine. I realized it was time for me to take responsibility for spreading the faith."

On the strength of both need-based and merit-based scholarships, Joseph was able to put himself through college, and he consistently scored top grades in all of his subjects. Nevertheless, he found college an almost entirely negative environment for his religious convictions. "Usually I didn't speak of my involvement with Bayside, but whenever I did, I was ridiculed," he told me. "One of the most important lessons I learned at college was that we have to expect to suffer for our beliefs. And I suffered quite a lot. I had no support, I was very lonely, and I always knew there was an underlying hostility against me."

I asked Joseph whether his college experiences had ever caused him to doubt the validity of the Bayside messages. "I was faced with personal doubt from time to time," he said. "And whenever this happened, I would make a personal investigation. I'd reread the messages to make sure they jibed with traditional Catholic teaching. And this usually cleared my mind. I continue to believe in Our Lady of the Roses because it continues to appear true to me, and because no one has been able to prove it false to me. I remain convinced that Veronica is a legitimate seeress."

And what would it take to convince Joseph otherwise?

"If Veronica started claiming she was God's daughter, or making other kinds of extravagant claims that were in violation of Catholic teaching, then that would indicate to me that Bayside might be wrong."

And might not the imposter-pope theory qualify as just such an extravagant claim?

"I admit that this is a stumbling block for a lot of people, but once you examine the evidence it makes very good sense. And Veronica wouldn't deceive us about something that important. But there's something else as well. One of the things that has led me to believe that Bayside is true is the constant suffering of Veronica. She lives as an invalid, and she offers her sufferings up to God. We believe Veronica is a victim soul."

Although Joseph believes that the institutional church is currently in horrible shape, he completely rejects the traditionalist, or separatist, option. "The point is to stay in the Church and at the same time fight the small battles from within to restore it to holiness," he said. But the days for fighting such small battles, he went on, are rapidly drawing to a close. "The chastisements are imminent. We fully believe that the world is due very shortly for a great catastrophe. This is what Our Lady has revealed through the apparitions. Unless mankind repents and turns around, a lot of heavy stuff is going to be happening."

Living in the shadow of doomsday has not, however, kept Joseph from planning for his future. He intends to complete his graduate studies, and he hopes afterward to secure a teaching position at a college in the metropolitan New

York area. I asked if he'd ever considered the possibility of ordination. "I've never felt personally called to the priesthood, and Bayside people have great difficulty with this anyways," he said. "We're committed to staying with Rome, and so we can't go into traditionalist seminaries. But almost all of the seminaries still connected to Rome are hopelessly infected by liberalism and modernism, and so we can't go into them either. Someday, I'd like to be married with kids, unless God calls me to something else. Whatever God ordains. In the meantime, I'm called to keep faith with the total Bayside gospel."[79]

Not all of Veronica's followers, as I would soon discover, are quite as scrupulous as Joseph about observing the total Bayside gospel. In June 1995 I attended the shrine's Silver Anniversary celebration at a posh restaurant overlooking Flushing Meadow Park. At least twelve hundred people had paid the $32 admission price, and the restaurant's huge banquet hall was filled to overflowing. They had come from Texas and Florida and California and at least two dozen other states, and from countries as far away as Nigeria, the Philippines, and Ireland.[80] There were speeches and hymns and prayers, there was congratulating and reminiscing, and, most of all, there was the cult of Veronica. Slides of Veronica. Photographs of Veronica. Tributes to Veronica. Anecdotes about Veronica. And when Michael Mangan, the current shrine director, announced that Veronica wouldn't be personally attending because of illness, the crowd moaned in disappointment.

Before dinner I sat for a while with an Irish-American woman named Patricia, who had flown in from Los Angeles just for the anniversary celebration. We talked about New York City, which she enjoys visiting for its rich cultural life, she told me several amusing stories about her teenage son's latest romantic escapades, and only then did the conversation turn to the shrine. Patricia told me that she first started following Veronica's career in the late seventies, following the death of her first-born son, and over the next several years she gradually became a devotee. "I'll admit I was a bit suspicious at first—all this talk of imposter popes and killer comets—but after a while it really grew on me," she said. "I don't know, at a time in my life when I really needed help and consolation, Veronica was there for me. The regular Church, with its sterile approach to everything, just wasn't offering me much."

And what of those imposter popes and killer comets?

"Oh, I don't believe in much of that," Patricia answered. "Look, Veronica's a holy woman, but she's not perfect. I think she gets carried away with herself sometimes, as holy people generally do. She probably thinks she hears things she's not really hearing, but this doesn't mean she doesn't have a special relationship with heaven. I'm convinced she does. She really couldn't just be putting on an act, you know. So I read her messages for the things that make sense to me and the things I find inspiring. And the rest of it isn't harmful. Even where it's wrong, it's at least good fun. We're not obliged to accept the whole package."

After dinner, proceedings moved to a hotel on the LaGuardia Airport strip, where there were more speeches, more prayers, a special slide show featuring some of the more famous miraculous photographs, and a short film about Veronica's life and tribulations. I visited a room that was being used as a temporary gift shop. Back issues of *Roses* stacked on tables. Brown scapulars of Our Lady of Mt. Carmel. Footprints of the Virgin Mary laminated in plastic. Piles of rose petals, also laminated in plastic, that had been "blessed by JESUS and MARY on [the shrine's] sacred grounds for cure and conversion." I picked up a piece of literature and read that the actress Susan Hayward had been miraculously cured of inoperable brain tumors in 1973 when Veronica sent her some rose petals. Hayward refused to acknowledge the source of her cure, however, and two years later she fell ill again and died. "Shortly thereafter, Our Lady revealed to Veronica that Miss Hayward was suffering in purgatory."[81]

"Have you tried them? They really work, you know." I had been approached by two young women, one very tall and the other considerably shorter, who had seen me examining the rose petals. The taller woman told me that she always carried petals with her and that she'd found them useful for fighting off everything from common colds to depression. Her friend said that the two of them had come to the shrine's anniversary celebration from the midwest, where they live, and that they planned to visit Europe for the apparitions at Medjugorje in the near future. I asked if they were taking steps to prepare for the coming chastisement. The taller woman said that she had heard something about this, but wasn't yet sure whether she believed it.

And so it went. In almost every case, the people I met that evening seemed selectively committed to the Bayside gospel. They knew only part of it, or cared about only part of it. Some of it they held onto for dear life, and some they seemed to value primarily as a form of religious entertainment. No one doubted that Veronica was a holy woman, or that she was truly in touch with divine and redemptive forces, but very few seemed to think that this meant accepting everything she said absolutely literally.

For the most part, the true believers of Veronica, the stewards of the full Bayside gospel, are the shrine's full-time workers and organizers. Shortly before the anniversary celebration wrapped up, I met an organizer named Marsha, who lives on Long Island. In her early forties, dark-haired, and attractive, Marsha assured me that she subscribes wholeheartedly to the complete package. The imposter pope, the great ball of redemption, the rapture: all of this, she said, is teaching that has been transmitted directly from heaven. Marsha wouldn't agree to a lengthier interview with me at some future date, but she decided nevertheless to close out our brief conversation that evening with an impassioned harangue. "We are the most despised group in America," she exclaimed. "The media, religious leaders, the so-called intelligentsia—everyone laughs at us and holds us in contempt. Why? They should be thanking us. We're the only group that's warning the country of the horrible catastrophes that lie ahead. And we're the only group actually trying to hold back these catastrophes. And believe me, America will be hit the hardest. America will pay for its sinfulness. And the government will pay the most. We're under constant surveillance from the government because we're not afraid to preach the truth. The government right now is plotting to create a repressive police state in America that will eliminate religious freedom. And they're also completely committed to the creation of a one-world government. And the government will do anything to exterminate religious groups that disagree with it. Look at what they did to the Branch Davidians at Waco. This was a complete massacre. We have irrefutable evidence that government agents started the fire that killed the Davidians, and all they've been doing ever since is covering up their crimes. And they could easily try to silence us the same way. And how do I know that you're not a government agent?"[82]

About a month after the anniversary celebration, I met with a full-time shrine worker named William Dykes at a local Queens diner. (Dykes had insisted on a neutral site: the full-time workers' residence and workshop, he told me, were both strictly off limits to outsiders.) Tall, lean, and red-complexioned, with an alert and expressive face, Dykes was born in Washington, D.C., in 1955, and was raised as the second oldest of eight children in a middle-class neighborhood in Richmond, Virginia. His Scottish-Irish father and German-American mother were both devout Catholics, and the family closed off each day by praying the rosary together.

During his late teens Dykes experienced what he describes as a minor crisis of faith. He stopped going to Mass, and his prayer life almost completely dried up. "I didn't reject the Church; I just got bored and slid away and stopped living the faith," he said. "I wasn't receiving the sacraments, and I was committing some mortal sins. Looking back now, I think if I had died right then, I would have gone to hell." Dykes attended Virginia Commonwealth University for two years, and in 1979 he moved to Los Angeles where he worked for a stretch as a singer-guitarist in a folk rock band. In 1986 he became engaged to a young woman from Virginia, but three months before the scheduled wedding his parents (who were by then also living in Los Angeles) invited him to a Bayside informational meeting that was being held in a local elementary school. "This was in July 1986. I was thirty-one years old. My parents had become involved with Bayside the year before, and I think that I had always been searching for truth. Attending this meeting was like getting hit with a ton of bricks. When I heard about the messages and the apparitions, I just knew it was the truth. And I also knew that this was how God was bringing me back to the faith."

For Dykes's birthday that year, his parents sent his fiancée and him on a trip to New York City for one of Veronica's fairground vigils, and hence came the moment of reckoning. "This was the parting of the ways," Dykes told me. "My fiancée thought that Bayside was absolutely kooky, but I went for it lock, stock, and barrel. In my heart I knew it was true; I knew these messages were from Our Lady in heaven. A short time after the trip, my fiancée and I broke up for good." Several weeks after the breakup of his engagement, the shrine (at his mother's suggestion) contacted Dykes and asked if he'd like to move to New York and become a full-time worker. Dykes jumped at the opportunity, and in the autumn of 1986 he joined the Lay Order of St. Michael.

And for the past nine years, the Order of St. Michael has been Dykes's life. With twelve other young men, he leads a spartan existence of work, prayer (three rosaries per day), mandatory celibacy, and mandatory secrecy. "We live in a rented house in Queens now, but we don't give out our address," Dykes said. "It's vitally important that we maintain our privacy. We don't want girls coming, we don't want strangers coming, and we also don't want many of the people who claim to be Baysiders coming. Some of the people who come out to the vigils are crazies and kooks. Some of them are into the occult and a dozen other things. We have to protect our privacy against them. But most of all, we don't want our enemies to know where to find us. There are powerful forces, and I'm talking in the media, in the Church, and especially in the government, that are determined to destroy us. We have to protect ourselves against these forces in any way we can."

I asked Dykes whether dedicated Baysiders might some day take up arms as a kind of Catholic militia.

"Absolutely not," he answered. "That is not our mission. But we are absolutely sympathetic to most of the goals and concerns of the militia groups that are around the country today. We agree with them that the federal government is committed to curtailing our constitutional freedoms and instituting a police state. And we believe that the federal government is responsible for the Oklahoma City bombing. The bombing was a government conspiracy designed to provide an excuse for destroying the militias and groups such as ourselves. If you knew, Michael, what was really happening in the United States and your country [Canada], you'd be brought to your knees in tears."

"Tell me more."

"There are Russian troops being trained in Canada and the United States. Why Michael?"

"I don't know."

"We're getting ready for something."

"But what Bill?"

"Something far worse than you'd ever imagine, Michael."

"Don't be so evasive."

"Okay. We're going to be invaded, Michael. We're being set up for the imposition of one-world government and one-world religion."

"Is this a Bayside doctrine?"

"No, this is something I'm saying to you personally, Michael."

"But Marsha said the same thing after the anniversary banquet."

"So?"

"Is this something that all of the full-time workers and organizers would subscribe to?"

"Absolutely, it's part of the message."

"Then it is a doctrine?"

"Yes. It's one of the messages from Our Lady. 'When the Church and the world become one, know the end is near.' This is something we all believe in. Do you know about Fr. Gruner, Michael? He also knows that the end is near. Russia still hasn't been consecrated. Our Lady of Fatima has been ignored, and now Our Lady of the Roses is being ignored. But this only makes our job of spreading the truth of Bayside that much more urgent."

Dykes fully recognizes that this won't be an easy job. Even within his own family the truth of Bayside has had difficulty registering. Both of his parents and his older sister Peggy are heavily involved with the shrine, but of his six other siblings, only the youngest has taken the slightest interest. And resistance to Bayside within the broader Catholic world remains as strong as ever. "There's no question that we're regarded as absolutely the wackiest of all groups within the Church today," Dykes said. "This is partly because of the spiritual blindness that has overcome the Church, and also because Bayside deals with private messages and private revelations. And also because Veronica is a woman."[83]

ON AUGUST 3, 1995, just one week after my meeting with William Dykes, Veronica Lueken died. In a letter sent to her followers the next month, the full-time workers pointed out that "the time of her death coincided exactly to the minute (EDT) with that of Robert Kennedy. . . ." The workers also pointed out that "August 3 in the traditional Catholic calendar is not designated as a feast day for any saint in the Church—it's an open slot. All indications are that Veronica Lueken will eventually be canonized a saint of the Roman Catholic church. Already the faithful throughout the world are praying to her and invoking her intercession under the title, 'Veronica of the Cross.'" (This is the title that the Virgin Mary presumably awarded Veronica in June 1980.[84])

Canonization or not, the biggest challenge for the shrine at present is simply to carry on without the physical presence of its seeress. And the early indications show cause for concern. At the time of Veronica's death, the shrine's mailing list consisted of 35,000 names in the United States and roughly 55,000 worldwide. About 30 percent of this total actually supported the shrine with financial donations. Just four months after her death, however, donations had dropped off by almost 50 percent, and attendance at the vigils had declined even more dramatically. The apparitional field is intensely competitive these days, and at least some of Veronica's onetime supporters appear to have decided to take their business elsewhere.[85]

In December 1995 I had an opportunity to discuss life-after-Veronica with Michael Mangan, the current director of the shrine, at the same local diner in Queens. Mangan was tall and suave, with a slightly pockmarked face and a hint of a Boston accent, and, like many other Baysiders, he wore a St. Benedict's medal and a crucifix on top of his shirt and a Brown Scapular underneath.

Mangan was born in 1959 and raised in the Boston area as the second youngest of eight children. His father, who died in 1991, was a sales representative for a manufacturing firm, and both of his parents were fairly strict Catholics. Although he himself was very religious as a child, Mangan told me, he fell away from the faith almost completely during his mid-teens, and it was Bayside that brought him back. "I was leading a very sinful life. I don't want to go into the details, but I wasn't living the faith. But when I was seventeen, in December 1976, I had a conversion through Bayside. My twin sister's fiancé's mother had been attending the vigils, and she told me about Veronica and the messages. I was mesmerized; I was attracted like a magnet. I was thirsty for truth, and I sopped it up like a sponge. I knew this was grace, I responded to it, and I was transformed. I didn't join the shrine right away, but I started studying the messages, and I went back to praying the rosary and receiving the sacraments."

After graduating high school, Mangan enrolled in the Culinary Institute of New York in Hyde Park, and whenever possible he took the train from Poughkeepsie to New York City for Veronica's fairground vigils. At the age of nineteen, he began to feel the stirrings of a religious vocation, and in the summer of 1978 he visited the Society of St. Pius X seminary in Armada, Michigan, to explore the possibility of becoming a priest. After less than a week, however, he came to the conclusion that the SSPX was hopelessly off base. "The rector at the time [Fr. Donald Sanborn] told me that I wasn't permitted to speak about Bayside. In their eyes, Bayside was completely beyond the pale. The rector was also ridiculing Pope Paul VI, and I knew from Bayside that Paul VI wasn't to blame for all the problems that had befallen the Church. They were the fault of an imposter pope. I also knew from the Bayside messages that the new Mass was valid and that we were supposed to stay in our parish churches, not separate and start our own little churches. Needless to say, I didn't stick around for long."

Following this misadventure, Mangan took a job at a restaurant near Boston, but in October 1978, he received a call from the shrine inviting him to join the Lay Order of St. Michael and become a full-time worker. He accepted the offer the same month, and seven years later he replaced Frank Albas (who had by then left the Bayside ministry under dubious circumstances) as director of the shrine and rector of the St. Michael's community. When I met with him, Mangan had been involved with the ministry for eighteen years, and he told me that he had never once over this span been tempted to leave. "But this doesn't mean I haven't been faced with trials and tribulations along the way," he said. "For a long time now my own family has been bitterly divided over the shrine. My mother and three of my sisters support our work, but my other four siblings are vociferous opponents. They think I'm crazy. . . . And it hasn't been easy dealing with the constant contempt. We are regarded by most Catholics as the lowest of the low. Our apostolate is totally derided. And now that Veronica's passed away, some of our own so-called supporters are showing their true colors. They've turned their backs on the shrine and they've run off in a hundred different directions. They've forgotten the messages. They've even forgotten the chastisement. How could they forget this?"

Mangan himself clearly hasn't forgotten, however, and he spoke with great conviction on the horrors that lay ahead. "First we will have the Great Warning, and then the chastisement. The chastisement will have two parts, and altogether it will last six days. First there will be a nuclear war. Nations will disappear in seconds. This will last three days. Then there will be a cleansing comet, the Ball of Redemption, that will eradicate the remaining evil in the world. The comet will cause plagues and floods, and altogether three-quarters of the world—more than four billion people—will perish. But the righteous will be preserved throughout all of this destruction. While retaining their bodies, they will be raptured—miraculously transported—to a safe place somewhere in the sky. After six days Christ will return, and the Church will be restored to glory, and God's kingship will be restored on earth. For a generation or two there will be a Roman Catholic paradise on earth, but then people will start slipping away again, and there will be another great war which will bring about the end of the world. And then there will be the Final Judgment. If people turn away from evil, all of this can be postponed. But we shouldn't be optimistic about this. Evil is increasing rather than decreasing. We fully expect that the chastisement will take place before the end of this century. In other words, sometime in the next four years."

Nevertheless, for all of his doomsday convictions, Mangan remains enormously optimistic about the future of the Our Lady of the Roses shrine. He told me that the shrine will eventually be far bigger, and more prestigious, than even Lourdes and Fatima. He said that a huge basilica will be built on the grounds of St. Robert Bellarmine's parish church. Healing waters will flow, and millions of pilgrims will come. The Lay Order of St. Michael will be approved by the church, and Mangan himself will be formally installed as its rector. "Nothing or no one can stop what we've started here," he told me. "God is with us, Our Lady is with us, and Veronica is with us. This is only the beginning."[86]

CONCLUSION

CHAPTER SIX

DESPITE THEIR MANY DIFFERENCES, all of the groups and individuals discussed in the previous pages—from Mount St. Michael's to Bayside, from E. Michael Jones to Fr. Nicholas Gruner—hold at least one fundamental belief in common: since the Second Vatican Council, mainstream Catholicism in the United States (and elsewhere) has fallen into a state of profound crisis. In the space of just thirty years, the mainstream American church has lost its passion and its zeal, its self-confidence and sense of direction, and, most important of all, its privileged claim to ultimate authority. Indeed, as the mainstream church, with its bishops and priests, its nuns and theologians, has fallen more and more under the spell of the dominant secular culture, in their view, the task of preserving (or retrieving) ultimate Catholic authority has been entrusted almost entirely to small bands of the stalwart faithful.

Precisely what counts as ultimate authority, however, is the issue upon which these groups and individuals have been most emphatically divided. Catholic conservatives—whether intellectuals like James Hitchcock or anti-abortion firebrands like Joseph Scheidler—have elected to take their final stand with Rome and the papacy of John Paul II. In the view of Catholic separatists (or traditionalists), in contrast, the papacy itself has become a renegade institution, and the only guarantee of truth and salvation in these troubled times is the immutable wisdom of the Catholic past. And Catholic Marianists, for their part, have looked for ultimate authority instead in the miraculous realm of mystical visions and end-time prophecy.

Mainly because of their passionate commitment to anti-abortion activism, Catholic conservatives have thus far wielded a far greater public presence than either separatists or Marianists. Over the past twenty years, conservatives have

179

taken the lead in street protest against abortion, they've consistently denounced their bishops for moral cowardice on the issue, and, in the process, they've entered into strategic alliance with conservative Protestants and other denizens of America's religio-political right. On the whole, however, this has been a rather more fragile alliance than is generally recognized. Unlike their Protestant counterparts, Catholic conservatives have shown only a modest interest in the issue of school prayer and hardly any interest at all in the controversy over evolutionary theory. And conservative Protestants, for their part, have sometimes been downright bewildered by the enthusiasm that their Catholic allies have shown for *Humanae Vitae* and its condemnation of artificial contraception.[1]

Far from entering into public controversy over issues such as abortion, Catholic separatists have thus far been concerned with cultivating a strictly introverted piety. Turning their backs on the broader society (and especially the broader church), they have committed themselves to the task of creating religious enclaves of moral and spiritual perfection. And in this respect at least, separatists have been far more American than most of them would probably care to acknowledge. With their perfectionist aspirations, their cultural exclusivity, and their spiritual elitism, separatists are participants in an American tradition of religious utopianism that extends at least as far back as Plymouth Rock. While the content of their theology is self-consciously Tridentine, its practical mode of expression calls to mind the experimental utopias of Shakers and Mormons and of counter-cultural communitarians of almost every imaginable ideological stripe.[2]

If Catholic conservatives are the moral puritans of the American Catholic right, and Catholic separatists the moral perfectionists, Catholic Marianists may be described as the moral catastrophists. As punishment for its rampant infidelity and sinfulness, Marianists claim, virtually the entire world stands on the brink of apocalyptic damnation: the Virgin Mary has delivered the verdict personally through her specially appointed seers, and the chances of having the sentence either commuted or deferred must be considered exceedingly slim. As is generally also the case with Catholic separatism, Marianist movements tend to be stratified according to level of commitment. It is the priests, both male and female, who are the true aficionados of the Infinite Love community; the Lay Disciples and third-order adherents exist primarily in order to furnish economic and moral support. And it is the full-time workers who are the true custodians of Veronica's mystical legacy; ordinary Baysiders should merely do as they're told and be thankful for the salvation that awaits them. Apocalyptic Marianism of the sort discussed here, moreover, may be seen as a peculiarly Catholic counterpart to Protestant millenarianism and dispensationalism. With their overarching fatalism, their theories of divine election, and, of course, their predictions of imminent catastrophe, the apparitional teachings of Bayside and Fatima bear more than a passing resemblance to the Adventist and Darbyite theologies that have long been fixtures on the American religious landscape.[3]

As for the future, much depends, of course, on the ability of these various groups and movements to retain the allegiance of their younger generations. Over the past twenty years, Catholic conservatives have partly addressed this concern by opening several independent colleges with curricula heavily slanted toward Thomistic philosophy, and a significant number of younger conservative parents have decided that educating their children at home is preferable to sending them into the far riskier environment of the local parochial school.[4] For the foreseeable future at least, conservative activists can be counted upon to continue their trench warfare against abortion, and while isolated individuals might be tempted into violence, the overwhelming majority will in all likelihood retain their commitment to pacifism.

Catholic separatists have already dedicated enormous resources to building up their own schools and churches and seminaries, and their efforts in this regard show no sign of slowing down. Indeed, if separatists could ever curb their tendency toward self-cannibalization and perhaps negotiate a measure of internal consensus, they might at some point actually succeed in converting their fractured movement into a significant denomination: a kind of traditionalist Catholic equivalent to Protestant fundamentalism. But there's also another, rather more ominous possibility. Over the years, as we've seen, Catholic separatists have stockpiled conspiracy theories with a vengeance, and in the process they've borrowed freely from the conspiratorial repertoire of the extreme political right in the United States, including the contemporary militia movement. With their talk of one-world governments and repressive police states, in fact, separatist groups such as Mount St. Michael's have sometimes come perilously close to sounding like Catholic militias in the making. This isn't to suggest that such groups will ever reach the point of actually taking up arms against their enemies, but only that such a development is not beyond the realm of possibility.[5]

Although Catholic Marianists are no strangers themselves to conspiracy theory, the particular groups discussed here will likely be hard-pressed over the next several years simply to survive. The Infinite Love community is currently facing yet another media-fomented scandal (this time over allegations of sexual abuse), Gruner's Fatima ministry is steadily losing ground in its ongoing conflict with the Catholic hierarchy, and the Bayside movement is still trying to cope with the loss of its seeress. Of course, even if these groups were to disappear overnight, it wouldn't likely take long for them to be replaced by new ones. In an age of deadened ritual and flaccid theology, almost anyone professing mystical powers or a special relationship with the Virgin is guaranteed an audience, and quite possibly a following.[6]

To this point, I've deliberately avoided referring to the various groups under discussion—whether conservative, separatist, or Marianist—as *fundamentalists*. In the view of more than a few scholars of religion, in fact, the very idea of a distinctly Catholic fundamentalism is a conceptual lost cause, a contradiction in terms. The fundamentalist label should be restricted, they insist, to only those movements of religious protest against the modern world which take some sacred text or scripture (the bible or Koran or Torah, for example) as their ultimate source of authority.[7] And since Catholics (unlike Protestants or Muslims or Jews) arguably don't have a sacred text to which they pay *absolute* homage, they can't, by definition, become fundamentalists. To my mind, however, this smacks of definitional dogmatism. Definitions in the social sciences and the humanities serve very much as investigative lenses: if focused too narrowly or too tightly, they may unduly circumscribe scholarly vision and thereby block out lines of prospective research. In its scholarly usage, moreover, *fundamentalism* is a heuristic concept—an ideal-typical construct—meant to facilitate comparison between movements of perhaps only distant resemblance. The value of the concept, its utility for cross-cultural comparison, suffers when it is forced to bear too much descriptive specificity. Why not, then, admit into the fundamentalist fold movements of religious protest which take something other than sacred scripture (visions, ritual, tradition, or even the papacy) as their primary source of ultimate authority? If fundamentalism is defined inclusively in this way, it makes sense to speak of a distinctly Catholic fundamentalism, or, better, of a Catholic fundamentalism made up of three analytically distinct types: the conservative, the separatist, and the Marianist/apocalyptic.[8]

However they might be classified, the groups that we've examined here seem unquestionably a product of the enormous changes that have taken place within the American Catholic church and the broader culture over the past thirty years. With their samizdat publications, their conspiratorial certitudes, and (in some cases) their thaumaturgical thrills, they have functioned for their participants as both vehicles of protest against these changes and as conventicles of spiritual consolation. They belong to the underground of American Catholicism, and just as much to the cultural underground of America itself. Their futures and, in some cases, their very survival may be in doubt, but the religious hopes and grievances they represent are not likely any time soon to fade quietly into the night.

NOTES

Chapter 1

1. Dennis P. McCann, *New Experiment in Democracy* (Kansas City: Sheed & Ward, 1987), pp. 9–36. See also John C. Farina, *An American Experience of God: The Spirituality of Isaac Hecker* (New York: Paulist Press, 1981).

2. See John Tracy Ellis, *The Life of James Cardinal Gibbons, Archbishop of Baltimore, 1834–1921*, 2 vols. (Milwaukee: Bruce Publishing, 1952); James Hennesey, S.J., *American Catholics: A History of the Roman Catholic Community in the United States* (New York: Oxford University Press, 1981), pp. 196–205; and Jay Dolan, *The American Catholic Experience: A History from Colonial Times to the Present* (Garden City, N.Y.: Doubleday, 1985), pp. 235–40.

3. John Tracy Ellis, ed., *Documents of American Catholic History* (Milwaukee: Bruce Publishing, 1956), p. 556.

4. McCann, *New Experiment in Democracy*, pp. 64–65. Some of the responsibility for the retrenched Catholicism that came into being in America during the early decades of the twentieth century belongs also to Pope Pius X's 1907 anti-Modernist encyclical *Pascendi dominici gregis*. For a discussion of Modernism, anti-Modernism, and *Pascendi*, see Gabriel Daly, *Transcendence and Immanence: A Study in Catholic Modernism and Integralism* (Oxford: Clarendon Press, 1980); Lester R. Kurtz, *The Politics of Heresy: The Modernist Crisis in Roman Catholicism* (Berkeley: University of California Press, 1986); and R. Scott Appleby, *Church and Age Unite! The Modernist Impulse in American Catholicism* (Notre Dame, Ind.: University of Notre Dame Press, 1992).

5. On so-called "immigrant Catholicism" in America in the decades prior to the Second World War, see Dolan, *The American Catholic Experience*, pp. 127–320.

6. See McCann, *New Experiment in Democracy*, pp. 64–90.

7. See John A. Ryan, *Social Doctrine in Action* (New York: Harper & Brothers, 1941). On Dorothy Day and the Catholic Worker movement, see Mel Piehl, *Breaking Bread: The Catholic Worker and the Origin of Catholic Radicalism* (Philadelphia: Temple University Press, 1982); on Thomas Merton, see Dolan, *The American Catholic Experience*, pp. 450–51; and on Murray, see Donald E. Pelotte, *John Courtney Murray: Theologian in Conflict* (New York: Paulist Press, 1976).

8. John Tracy Ellis, "American Catholics and the Intellectual Life," *Thought* 30 (Autumn 1955): 351–88. See also Michael V. Gannon, "Before and After Modernism: The Intellectual Isolation of the American Catholic Priest," in John Tracy Ellis, ed., *The Catholic Priest in the United States: Historical Investigations* (Collegeville, Minn.: St. John's University Press, 1977), pp. 337–55.

9. Garry Wills, *Bare Ruined Choirs* (Garden City, N.Y.: Doubleday, 1972), pp. 15–16, 19.

10. Andrew M. Greeley, *The New Agenda* (Garden City, N.Y.: Doubleday, 1973), pp. 42–43.

11. Cited in Bill McSweeney, *Roman Catholicism: The Search for Relevance* (Oxford: Basil Blackwell, 1980), p. 137. See "Pope John's Opening Speech to the Council," in Walter M. Abbott, S.J., ed., *The Documents of Vatican II* (London: Geoffrey Chapman, 1966), pp. 710–19.

12. McSweeney (*Roman Catholicism*) is one of the very few scholars who has managed to write about the council from a posture of genuine neutrality.

13. Ibid., p. 140.

14. Cited in McSweeney, *Roman Catholicism*, pp. 143–44. See "Dogmatic Constitution on Divine Revelation," in Abbott, *The Documents of Vatican II*, p. 116.

15. Cited in McSweeney, *Roman Catholicism*, p. 141. See "Dogmatic Constitution on Divine Revelation," in Abbott, *The Documents of Vatican II*, p. 119. On this general theme, see also David Wells, *Revolution in Rome* (London: Tyndale Press, 1973).

16. For an insightful discussion of some of these themes, see Gregory Baum, *Theology and Society* (New York: Paulist Press, 1987), ch. 1.

17. For a useful overview of the council's revolutionary capacity, see McSweeney, *Roman Catholicism*, ch. 6.

18. See James L. Franklin, "Contemporary Studies on the Priest Shortage," *Progressions: A Lilly Endowment Occasional Report* 1, 2 (June 1989), pp. 7–10; Richard A. Schoenherr and Lawrence A. Young, "Full Pews and Empty Altars: Demographics of U.S. Diocesan Priests, 1966–2005," in Helen Rose Ebaugh, ed., *Vatican II and U.S. Catholicism* (Greenwich, Conn.: JAI Press, 1991), pp. 85–104; and Dean Hoge, *Future of Catholic Leadership* (Kansas City: Sheed and Ward, 1987), p. 212.

19. Marie Augusta Neal, S.N.D., "American Sisters: Organizational and Value Changes," in Ebaugh, ed., *Vatican II and U.S. Catholicism*, p. 114; Martha Mary McGaw, C.S.J., "Nuns Face Up to Economic Crisis, New Ministries," *Progressions* 1, 2 (June 1989), pp. 15–18.

20. For sociological investigations of this phenomenon, see Helen Rose Fuchs Ebaugh, *Becoming an Ex: The Process of Role Exit* (Chicago: University of Chicago Press, 1988); Helen Rose Fuchs Ebaugh, *Women in the Vanishing Cloister* (New Brunswick, N.J.: Rutgers University Press, 1993); Patricia Wittberg, *The Rise and Decline of Catholic Religious Orders: A Social Movement Perspective* (Albany: State University of New York Press, 1994); and Joseph H. Fichter, "The Myth of Clergy Burnout," *Sociological Analysis* 45, 4 (1984): 373–82.

21. See Andrew M. Greeley, "The Demography of American Catholics: 1965–1990," in Ebaugh, ed., *Vatican II and U.S. Catholicism*, pp. 37–43; and Jane Redmont, "Melding a People, a Church and a Nation," *Progressions* 1, 2 (June 1989), p. 3.

22. See Andrew M. Greeley, *American Catholics Since the Council: An Unauthorized Report* (Chicago: Thomas More Press, 1985), pp. 50–51; and Greeley, "The Demography of American Catholics," p. 43. Of course, as Greeley has consistently pointed out, the defection rate among Hispanic Catholics has been considerably higher. See, for example, his *The Catholic Myth: The Behavior and Beliefs of American Catholics* (New York: Collier Books, 1990), pp. 120–24.

23. Greeley, *American Catholics Since the Council*, pp. 41–53.

24. Ibid., pp. 54–56. During a six-year stretch beginning in 1969, the proportion of American Catholics attending weekly Mass declined by approximately 16 percent. At least until quite recently, Greeley has attributed this decline to the appearance of the papal encyclical *Humanae Vitae*. See Greeley, *Religious Change in America* (Cambridge: Harvard University Press, 1989), pp. 50–52.

25. Greeley, *American Catholics Since the Council*, p. 98.

26. See, for example, Andrew M. Greeley, Kathleen McCourt, and William McCready, *Catholic Schools in a Declining Church* (Kansas City: Sheed and Ward, 1976); Joan Fee, Andrew M. Greeley, William McCready, and Teresa Sullivan, *Young Catholics* (New York: Sadlier, 1981); and Greeley, *American Catholics Since the Council*, pp. 83–84. For a highly nuanced discussion of the sociological research in this area, see James R. Kelly, "Catholic Sexual Ethics Since Vatican II," in Ebaugh, ed., *Vatican II and U.S. Catholicism*, pp. 139–54.

27. See Greeley, *American Catholics Since the Council*, p. 85; Andrew M. Greeley, *Crisis in the Church* (Chicago: Thomas Moore Press, 1979), p. 60; Andrew M. Greeley, William McCready, Teresa Sullivan, and Joan Fee, "A Profile of the American Catholic Family," *America* (September 27, 1980), pp. 155–60; David Moberg and Dean Hoge, "Catholic College Students' Religious and Moral Attitudes, 1961 to 1982: Effects of the Sixties and the Seventies," *Review of Religious Research* 28, 2 (1986): 104–17; Patrick H. McNamara, "Catholic Youth in the Modern Church," in Ebaugh, ed., *Vatican II and U.S. Catholicism*, pp. 57–65; and Patrick H. McNamara, *Conscience First, Tradition Second: A Study of Young Catholics* (Albany: State University of New York Press, 1991). For a breakdown of changing Catholic attitudes toward abortion, homosexuality, and other moral concerns, see Kelly, "Catholic Sexual Ethics Since Vatican II," pp. 145–48; and George Gallup, Jr., and Jim Castelli, *The American Catholic People: Their Beliefs, Practices, and Values* (Garden City, N.Y.: Doubleday, 1987).

28. On this point, see McSweeney, *Roman Catholicism*, pp. 146–47.

29. See Greeley, *American Catholics Since the Council*, p. 33; Greeley, "The Demography of American Catholics," pp. 43–48; and Andrew M. Greeley, *The American Catholic: A Social Portrait* (New York: Basic Books, 1977), ch. 3.

30. See Greeley, *Religious Change in America*, p. 91.

31. Greeley, *American Catholics Since the Council*, pp. 61–65; Greeley, *The Catholic Myth*, ch. 3.

32. This point is noted approvingly by McCann in *New Experiment in Democracy*, pp. 70–71.

Chapter 2

1. *Lay Witness*, Twentieth Anniversary Issue (September 1988), p. 2.

2. For his own account of the incident, see Charles Curran, "Growth (Hopefully) in Wisdom, Age and Grace," in Gregory Baum, ed., *Journeys* (New York: Paulist Press, 1975), pp. 87–116.

3. CUF had actually been founded in early September of 1968 at a hotel in downtown St. Paul by Stebbins, Michael Lawrence, L. Brent Bozell, Alphonse Matt, Sr., and his son Alphonse Matt, Jr. Bozell was the brother-in-law of William F. Buckley, Jr., and the founder, in 1966, of a short-lived but fairly influential Catholic conservative magazine called *Triumph*. For a discussion of the differences between the Catholic conservatism represented by Bozell and Stebbins (which is my chief interest here) and the political conservatism represented by Buckley and *National Review*, see Patrick Allitt, *Catholic Intellectuals and Conservative Politics in America, 1950–1985* (Ithaca: Cornell University Press, 1993), pp. 141–60.

4. On De Pauw, see William D. Dinges, "Roman Catholic Traditionalism in the United States," in Martin E. Marty and R. Scott Appleby, eds., *Fundamentalisms Observed* (Chicago: University of Chicago Press, 1991), pp. 70–72.

5. Ibid., pp. 71–72.

6. For a Catholic conservative defense of the new Mass, see James Likoudis and Kenneth D. Whitehead, *The Pope, the Council, and the Mass* (W. Hanover, Mass.: Christopher Publishing, 1981).

7. Personal interview, Yonkers, New York, 15 September 1991.

8. See James Hitchcock, *The Decline and Fall of Radical Catholicism* (New York: Herder and Herder, 1971), pp. 95, 130, 180; Dietrich von Hildebrand, *Trojan Horse in the City of God* (Chicago: Franciscan Herald Press, 1967), pp. 9, 39, 44; and *Lay Witness*, Twentieth Anniversary Issue (September 1988), pp. 2–3. This and especially the following paragraph draw upon my discussion in *Catholics Against the Church* (Toronto: University of Toronto Press, 1989), p. 190.

9. See, for example, John F. Kobler, *Vatican II and Phenomenology* (Dordrecht: Martinus Nijhoff Publishers, 1985).

10. Cited in *Lay Witness*, Twentieth Anniversary Issue (September 1988), p. 3.

11. The following discussion is distilled from my content analysis of some of Catholic conservatism's most prominent literary works, including James Hitchcock, *What Is Secular Humanism?* (Ann Arbor, Mich.: Servant Books, 1982); James Hitchcock, *The New Enthusiasts* (Chicago: Thomas More Press, 1982); James Hitchcock, *Catholicism and Modernity: Confrontation or Capitulation?* (New York: Crossroads, 1979); James Hitchcock, *Years of Crisis: Collected Essays, 1970–1983* (San Francisco: Ignatius Press, 1985); Msgr. George A. Kelly, *The Battle for the American Church* (Garden City, N.Y.: Doubleday, 1979); Msgr. George A. Kelly, *The Crisis of Authority* (Chicago: Regnery Gateway, 1982); Msgr. George A. Kelly, *Keeping the Church Catholic With John Paul II* (New York: Doubleday, 1990); Anne Roche, *The Gates of Hell* (Toronto: McClelland and Stewart, 1975); Anne Roche Muggeridge, *The Desolate City* (Toronto: McClelland and Stewart, 1986); Ralph Wiltgen, *The Rhine Flows into the Tiber* (New York: Hawthorn, 1967); Vincent P. Miceli, S.J., *The Antichrist* (Harrison, N.Y.: Roman Catholic Books, 1981); and Richard Cowden-Guido, *John Paul II and the Battle for Vatican II: Report from the Synod* (Manassas, Va.: Trinity Communications, 1986).

12. Anthony Kosnik, William Carroll, Agnes Cunningham, Ronald Modras, and James Schulte, *Human Sexuality: New Directions in American Catholic Thought* (New York: Paulist Press, 1977), p. 216; cited in Roche Muggeridge, *Desolate City*, p. 170.

13. I am using the term "progressive theology" as a schematic convenience; obviously, the sheer breadth and complexity of contemporary Catholic theologizing defies unilineal categorization. For insightful treatments, from a North American vantage point, of innovative Catholic theology in the post-conciliar era, see the following: David Tracy, *Blessed Rage for Order* (New York: Seabury Press, 1975); David Tracy, *The Analogical Imagination* (New York: Crossroad, 1981); Richard P. McBrien, *Do We Need the Church?* (London: Collins, 1969); Mary Jo Weaver, *New Catholic Women: A Contemporary Challenge to Traditional Religious Authority* (San Francisco: Harper & Row, 1985); and Andrew M. Greeley, *The New Agenda* (Garden City, N.Y.: Doubleday, 1973). In the last work, see especially the foreword by Gregory Baum, pp. 11–34. For a more extended discussion of this theme, see my *Conservative Catholicism in North America: Pro-Life Activism and the Pursuit of the Sacred* (Brussels: Pro Mundi Vita, 1987).

14. The remainder of this paragraph closely follows the argument in my *Catholics Against the Church*, p. 192.

15. Thomas Sheehan, "Revolution in the Church," *New York Review of Books* (14 June 1984), p. 35; cited in Roche Muggeridge, *Desolate City*, p. 120.

16. G. K. Chesterton, *The Catholic Church and Conversion* (New York: Macmillan, 1926), p. 93.

17. CUF has just recently moved its headquarters to Steubenville from New Rochelle, New York.

18. My discussion of CUF is based partly on three interviews I conducted with James Sullivan, former editor of *Lay Witness*, in New Rochelle in the autumn of 1991. See also M. Timothy Iglesias, "CUF and Dissent: A Case Study in Religious Conservatism," *America* (April 11, 1987), pp. 303–7; and James A. Sullivan, "Catholics United for the Faith: Dissent and the Laity," in Mary Jo Weaver and R. Scott Appleby, eds., *Being Right: Conservative Catholics in America* (Bloomington: Indiana University Press, 1995), pp. 107–37.

19. Among its several ongoing projects, CUF is currently preparing an extensive catechetical series called Faith and Life (see Sullivan, "Catholics United for the Faith," p. 131).

20. Telephone interview, 12 June 1992. The quotation attributed to James Likoudis in the penultimate paragraph of this section is taken from the same interview. .

21. Joseph Cardinal Ratzinger with Vittorio Messori, *The Ratzinger Report*, trans. by S. Attanasio and G. Harrison (San Francisco: Ignatius Press, 1985), pp. 36–37. For a fuller treatment of this topic, see my "Soldiers of Orthodoxy: Revivalist Catholicism in North America," *Studies in Religion/Sciences Religieuses* 17, 3 (1988): 347–63.

22. For background on CUF's long-running antagonisms with liberal bishops Raymond Hunthausen of Seattle and Rembert Weakland of Milwaukee, see Penny Lernoux, *People of God* (New York: Viking, 1989), ch. 8.

23. Most of this biographical information is based on an interview I conducted with James Hitchcock and Helen Hull Hitchcock in St. Louis on June 12, 1991.

24. The next several pages are my own distillation of themes that have stood out in Hitchcock's writings over the past twenty-five years. (I employ the present tense only as a stylistic convenience.) I have drawn particularly on *The Recovery of the Sacred* (New York: Seabury, 1974) and *Catholicism and Modernity* (New York: Crossroad, 1979). In addition to the works listed above (note 11), see *The Decline and Fall of Radical Catholicism* (New York: Herder and Herder, 1971); *On the Present Position of Catholicism in America* (New York: National Committee of Catholic Laymen, 1978); and *The Pope and the Jesuits: John Paul II and the New Order in the Society of Jesus* (New York: National Committee of Catholic Laymen, 1984). For Hitchcock's own overview of the Catholic conservative intellectual scene in the United States, see his "Catholic Activist Conservatism in the United States," in Marty and Appleby, *Fundamentalisms Observed*, pp. 101–41.

25. Hitchcock, *Catholicism and Modernity*, p. 35. For a similar sentiment, see Michael Novak, *Confession of a Catholic* (San Francisco: Harper & Row, 1983), pp. 114–15.

26. Hitchcock, *Catholicism and Modernity*, p. 13.

27. Personal interview, St. Louis, 12 June 1991.

28. Approximately fifty thousand American Catholic women have signed the Affirmation to date, and an additional twenty thousand women from outside the United States. For her own account, see Helen Hull Hitchcock, "Women for Faith and Family: Catholic Women Affirming Catholic Teaching," in Weaver and Appleby, *Being Right*, pp. 163–85.

29. The evils of American Catholic feminism are recounted in entertaining detail by Donna Steichen in *Ungodly Rage: The Hidden Face of Catholic Feminism* (San Francisco: Ignatius Press, 1991).

30. For the Fellowship's "Statement of Purpose," see James Hitchcock, "The Fellowship of Catholic Scholars: Bowing out of the New Class," in Weaver and Appleby, *Being Right*, pp. 203–4. See also Msgr. George A. Kelly, *Keeping the Church Catholic with John Paul II*, p. 153.

31. Personal interview, South Bend, Indiana, 18 June 1990; the quotations attributed to E.

Michael Jones and Ruth Jones at the end of the present section are also taken from this interview. For additional biographical information on Jones, see the three-part article by him ("How Catholic are Catholic Colleges?") that appeared in the 11 June 1981, 18 June 1981, and 25 June 1981 issues of *The Wanderer*. (*The Wanderer* was the publisher of *Fidelity* Magazine from 1981 to 1984.) See also Allitt, *Catholic Intellectuals and Conservative Politics in America*, pp. 300–303; and John H. Haas, "Conservative Catholic Periodicals," in Weaver and Appleby, *Being Right*, pp. 337–44.

32. E. Michael Jones, "Requiem for a Liturgist: Endgame Dissent at Notre Dame," *Fidelity* (January 1980), p. 29.

33. For several more telling examples of his characteristic approach, see E. Michael Jones, "The Many Faces of Cardinal Bernardin," *Fidelity* (March 1990), pp. 26–41; "Requiem for a Magazine: The Sodomization of the Catholic Press in Saskatchewan," *Fidelity* (February 1987), pp. 22–36; "Rationalized Lust," *Fidelity* (September 1989), pp. 43–45; and "The Pope and the Condom Worshippers," *Fidelity* (October 1987), pp. 32–44. Jones has also made a number of forays into broader cultural criticism with his sex-and-heresy thesis. See, for example, E. Michael Jones, "Samoa Lost: Margaret Mead, Cultural Relativism, and the Guilty Imagination," *Fidelity* (February 1988), pp. 26–37; "The Case Against Kinsey," *Fidelity* (April 1989), pp. 22–35; "Sigmund and Minna and Carl and Sabina: The Birth of Psychoanalysis out of the Personal Lives of its Founders," *Fidelity* (December 1989), pp. 31–40; and "Homosexual as Subversive: The Double Life of Sir Anthony Blunt," *Fidelity* (May 1988), pp. 18–31.

34. E. Michael Jones, "Medjugorje: The Untold Story," *Fidelity* (September 1988), pp. 18–41; (October 1988), pp. 20–39. The two-part article was published in book form in 1989 by Fidelity Press (South Bend, Ind.).

35. *Fidelity* (November 1988), p. 2; (January 1989), p. 4.

36. James Donovan, "Bayside Unveiled: The Blessed Mother Takes a Beating from Her 'Friends'," *Fidelity* (March 1988), pp. 34–42. For Donovan's specific broadsides against Gruner, see p. 36.

37. Fr. Paul Leonard, "Against the Wolves in Sheeps' Clothing," *Fatima Crusader* (August/September 1988), p. 23; E. Michael Jones, "You Toucha My Apparition, I Breaka You Face," *Fidelity* (December 1988), pp. 12–14.

38. Jones, "You Toucha My Apparition, I Breaka You Face," p. 13.

39. The most detailed study to date of *The Wanderer*, which I received rather too late to consult much here, is George Kendall's *"Watchman! What of the Night": THE WANDERER's Adventures in Public Witness* (Grand Marais, Mich.: St. George Press, forthcoming). A valuable source of historical information on the newspaper is *The Wanderer*'s 110th Anniversary Issue (October 6, 1977). For additional information, I am indebted to John Mulloy (telephone interview, 14 June 1991) and William Doino (telephone interview, 7 September 1994).

40. Personal interview, St. Paul, Minnesota, 14–16 June 1991.

41. In the early seventies, in fact, both Alphonse Matt, Jr., and his father were forced off CUF's board of directors for refusing to moderate their rhetoric against the American Catholic bishops; ibid.

42. For key resources on Vatican social teaching and liberation theology, see the following: Donal Dorr, *Option for the Poor: A Hundred Years of Vatican Social Teaching* (Maryknoll, N.Y.: Orbis Books, 1983); Joseph Gremillion, ed., *The Gospel of Peace and Justice* (Maryknoll, N.Y.: Orbis Books,

1976); J. Eagleson and P. Scharper, eds., *Puebla and Beyond* (Maryknoll, N.Y.: Orbis Books, 1979); Gregory Baum, *The Priority of Labor: A Commentary on Laborem Exercens* (New York: Paulist Press, 1982); Arthur F. McGovern, *Marxism: An American Christian Perspective* (Maryknoll, N.Y.: Orbis Books, 1981); Gustavo Gutierrez, *A Theology of Liberation* (Maryknoll, N.Y.: Orbis Books, 1973); and Jon Sobrino, *Christology at the Crossroads* (Maryknoll, N.Y.: Orbis Books, 1978).

43. National Conference of Catholic Bishops, *Economic Justice for All: Catholic Social Teaching and the U.S. Economy* (Washington, D.C., 1986); NCCB, *The Challenge of Peace: God's Promise and Our Response* (Washington, D.C., 1983).

44. Some of the people (and most notably Michael Novak, Richard John Neuhaus, and George Weigel) I am referring to as "mainstream Catholic conservatives" are sometimes (and sometimes among themselves) referred to as "Catholic neoconservatives." (See George Weigel, "The Neoconservative Difference: A Proposal for the Renewal of Church and Society," in Weaver and Appleby, *Being Right*, pp. 138–62.) Although there are clearly areas of ideological overlap, Catholic neoconservatives are considerably less antagonistic than "CUF" or "Wanderer" Catholics toward the democratic and pluralistic ethos of American culture, and considerably less single-minded (as a group) in their allegiance to Rome. In his *Catholicism and the Renewal of American Democracy* (New York: Paulist Press, 1989), for example, Weigel chastises "Wanderer" Catholics for having succumbed to a kind of "Tertullian" sectarianism (ch. 4). And in essays that they contributed to a symposium on the papal encyclical *Centesimus Annus* (National Review Special Supplement, *The Pope, Liberty, and Capitalism*, 1991), Novak, Neuhaus, and Weigel spend much of their time congratulating Pope John Paul II for finally having the good sense to see things their way (or the American way). Novak: "The encyclical *Centesimus Annus* does everything that many of us had hoped for from some Church authority; *viz.,* capture the spirit and essence of the American experiment in political economy. The Pope showed an extraordinary grasp of American ideas, achievements, and points of view. His vision of a free economy, within a culture moral and religious to its core, guided and energized by a democratic polity, is American in spirit and definition." And Neuhaus: "There were grim rumors about a new social encyclical that would harshly and unfairly attack the United States and democratic capitalism. Only nine months a Catholic, I was supposed to brace myself for a testing of my obedience to the Church's authority." Of course, whenever Rome has been slow in appreciating the virtues of Americanism, in economic matters or sexual matters or whatever, Catholic neoconservatives haven't hesitated in going on the attack. On Novak's dissent against *Humanae Vitae*, for example, see his *Confession of a Catholic*, pp. 118–30. (And for a "Wanderer" Catholic's response to Novak's apparent change of heart on the matter, which he announced in the June 1989 issue of *Crisis* Magazine, see John J. Mulloy's acerbic "Michael Novak's Acceptance of Humanae Vitae," *The Wanderer* [July 27, 1989], pp. 1–4.) The journals of record for Catholic neoconservatism in America today are *Crisis*, which was founded in 1982 by Novak and Notre Dame philosophy professor Ralph McInery, and *First Things*, which was founded in 1990 by Richard John Neuhaus. For admirable treatments of the conservative Catholic intellectual scene in the United States, see Allitt, *Catholic Intellectuals and Conservative Politics in America*; and Gene Burns, *The Frontiers of Catholicism: The Politics of Ideology in a Liberal World* (Berkeley: University of California Press, 1992).

45. In his "Liberation Philosophy and Catholic Social Teaching," which appeared in the August 1986 issue of *Fidelity* (pp. 36–42), Rupert Ederer takes direct aim at Michael Novak

and William F. Buckley, Jr., for their virtual deification of American-style market capitalism. See, for example, Novak's *The Spirit of Democratic Capitalism* (New York: Simon & Schuster, 1982).

46. Stephen M. Krason, *Liberalism, Conservatism, and Catholicism: An Evaluation of Contemporary American Political Ideologies in Light of Catholic Social Teaching* (Steubenville, Ohio: CUF Books, 1991). For a more impassioned critique of laissez-faire capitalism, once again from a "CUF"-Catholic perspective, see David M. Rooney, "A Commentary on Lamentations— Over Papal Social Teaching," *Lay Witness* (February 1990), pp. 1–6.

47. Personal interview, New Rochelle, New York, 15 October 1991. Many of the Catholic conservatives I interviewed for this study told me that they had turned to the GOP more out of disenchantment with the prevailing value liberalism of the Democratic Party establishment than out of affection for supply-side economics.

48. I am excluding, of course, mainstream conservative publications such as *National Review* from this equation. One of the reasons *The Wanderer* has succeeded in keeping its circulation up over the past decade is that it has been more careful than *Fidelity* about not alienating any of its readership constituencies. "We agree with E. Michael Jones right down the line, but we're more prudent than him," Matt, Jr., told me. "Jones attacks enemies on both the left and the right. He wants to separate the sheep from the goats. We don't feel the need to pick fights with everyone, or to take on crackpot apparitions such as Medjugorje" (personal interview, 15 June 1991).

49. *The Wanderer* has thus far attempted to avert stagnation by staging a conference called The Wanderer Forum, which has run annually at various sites around the country for almost thirty years now. The Forum, which attracts anywhere from 250 to six hundred participants at a time, is designed to promote a heightened sense of solidarity among Catholic conservatives and also to bring new blood into the conservative fold. On this latter count, however, it has mostly thus far proven unsuccessful.

50. Personal interview, Weston, Connecticut, 19 October 1991. For additional biographical information, see William Doino, Jr., "Eighteen-Inch Journey," *Messenger of the Sacred Heart, Canadian* (March 1986), pp. 14–19. For a broader sample of his writing, see William Doino, Jr., "Following Christ in a Secular World," *The Wanderer* (February 27, 1986), pp. 10–11; "Liberation Theology and the Lessons of Nicaragua," *The Wanderer* (January12, 1989), pp. 6–7; "The Darkened Mind of Andrew Greeley," *The Wanderer* (September 15, 1988), p. 4; "The Literary Art of J. F. Powers," *The Wanderer* (November 2, 1989), p. 6; and "Dinesh D'Souza Versus the Politically Correct," *The Wanderer* (November 14, 1991), pp. 6–7.

51. Telephone interview, 16 June 1991. Mr. Mulloy died on October 10, 1995, at the age of seventy-nine; his obituary appeared in the 19 October 1995 issue of *The Wanderer* (pp. 1, 11). In addition to contributing regularly to *The Wanderer*, he was the founding editor of *The Dawson Newsletter*. For a sample of his *Wanderer* pieces (including several critical of Pope John Paul II), see "Is the Spirit Speaking to the Catholic Church Through the Charismatic Movement?" (March 28, 1991); "The Charismatics, The Papacy, and St. John of the Cross" (June 13, 1991); "Why the Anarchy in the Catholic Church in America?" (February 25, 1993); "Laissez-Faire Economics and the Idolatry of Avarice" (July 1, 1982); and "Lack of Clarity Hinders Vatican II's Impact on Ecumenism" (June 7, 1990).

52. Telephone interview, 7 September 1994.

Chapter 3

1. The present chapter is a significantly revised version of my "Life Battles: The Rise of Catholic Militancy within the American Pro-Life Movement," in Mary Jo Weaver and R. Scott Appleby, eds., *Being Right: Conservative Catholics in America* (Bloomington: Indiana University Press, 1995), pp. 270–99. The opening section is based on interviews, both personal and telephone, that I conducted with Joseph Scheidler in June and July of 1993.

2. The Court declared abortion to be virtually an unfettered right during the first and second trimesters of pregnancy. For a more extensive discussion of the *Roe* opinion, see Lawrence H. Tribe, *Abortion: The Clash of Absolutes* (New York: W.W. Norton, 1992), pp. 11–13. For appraisals of *Roe* and of American abortion law more generally, see John T. Noonan, Jr., *A Private Choice* (New York: Free Press, 1979); Ronald Dworkin, *Life's Dominion* (New York: Knopf, 1993); and Mary Ann Glendon, *Divorce and Abortion in Western Law* (Cambridge: Harvard University Press, 1988).

3. For the movement's early history, see Faye D. Ginsburg, *Contested Lives* (Berkeley: University of California Press, 1989), ch. 2; Connie Paige, *The Right to Lifers* (New York: Summit Books, 1983); James R. Kelly, "Learning and Teaching Consistency: Catholics and the Right-to-Life Movement," in Timothy A. Byrnes and Mary C. Segers, eds., *The Catholic Church and the Politics of Abortion* (Boulder, Colo.: Westview Press, 1992), ch. 9; James R. Kelly, "Beyond the Stereotypes: Interviews with Right-to-Life Pioneers," *Commonweal* (November 1981), pp. 653–57; James R. Kelly, "Toward Complexity: The Right-to-Life Movement," in Monty L. Lynn and David O. Moberg, eds., *Research in the Social Scientific Study of Religion* (Greenwich, Conn.: JAI Press, 1989), ch. 5; and Kristin Luker, *Abortion and the Politics of Motherhood* (Berkeley: University of California Press, 1984). My historical account is based partly on these sources, partly on interviews I conducted with movement activists at the 1986 National Right to Life Committee convention in Denver, and partly on conversations with James R. Kelly of Fordham University, who is the movement's foremost social historian.

4. On Catholic stereotyping of the anti-abortion movement during the seventies and early eighties, see Bernard N. Nathanson, *The Abortion Papers* (New York: Frederick Fell, 1983), pp. 177–209.

5. Donald DeMarco, *The Contraceptive Mentality* (Edmonton: Life Ethics Centre,1982), p. 3. The Fr. Marx quotation is taken from Joseph Boyle, "Contraception and Natural Family Planning," *International Review of Natural Family Planning* 4, 4 (1980): 311–12.

6. Telephone interview, 10 August 1993. All subsequent quotations attributed to Judie Brown are derived from the same interview. (The American Life League is based in Stafford, Virginia.)

7. *HLI Reports*, the organization's principal informational organ, is published seventeen times annually, and the *Population Research Institute Review*, its most ambitious scholarly organ, is published bimonthly. See also Fr. Paul Marx, *The Death Peddlars* (Collegeville, Minn.: Saint John's University Press, 1971). For background information on HLI, I interviewed Vernon Kirby, the organization's public relations officer, in Gaithersburg, Maryland, on 17 June 1993. On HLI's alleged anti-Semitism, see Enzo Di Matteo, "Unholy Web," *Now* (Toronto) 14, 37 (May 1995), pp. 12–14.

8. Personal interview, Gaithersburg, Maryland, 18 June 1993. All subsequent quotations attributed to Fr. Paul Marx are from the same interview.

9. Personal interview, New Hope, Kentucky, 19 August 1995. In 1975 Stearns and her group became Third Order Dominicans, and since then they have been known as the St. Martin de Porres Community. As a complement to their ongoing street activism, community members sponsor a project called Free Speech Advocates, which is committed to defending the legal rights of nonviolent anti-abortion protesters, and also a national pro-life prayer crusade called Eternal Life. In addition to *Fidelity* Magazine, the community prints *Lay Witness* (and other CUF material) and a conservative Catholic monthly called *Inside the Vatican*. Over the past fifteen years, the community has suffered a steady decline in membership, and it currently consists of approximately fifteen adults and about the same number of children. For background on the community, see *St. Martin de Porres Dominican Community: Living a Life of Service to the Church* (New Hope, 1985). I am indebted to Hugh Pimentel (personal interview, New Hope, 20 August 1995) for informing me about some of the community's early history.

10. See Ginsburg, *Contested Lives*, p. 260. For an account of congressional testimony given by Archbishop John R. Roach and Cardinal Terence Cooke in support of the Hatch Amendment, see Patricia Beattie Jung and Thomas A. Shannon, eds., *Abortion and Catholicism: The American Debate* (New York: Crossroad, 1988), pp. 10–43.

11. Both Human Life International (with Fr. Paul Marx) and the Pro-Life Action League (with Scheidler) cultivate a kind of cult of personality. Displayed prominently on the face of *The Time For Action is NOW!*, an Action League promotional brochure, are the following words: "Joseph M. Scheidler is known across America as the pro-life leader in action on the streets, putting it all on the line to save even one little baby's life. He has been ostracised, mocked, arrested, and bullied. But Joe Scheidler has persevered in his holy mission to preserve the sanctity of human life." For additional information on the League, see the pamphlet *Pro-Life Action League: Because ACTION speaks louder than words.*

12. Personal interview, Laytonsville, Maryland, 17 June 1993. All subsequent quotations attributed to Cavanaugh-O'Keefe are from the same interview. For more extensive biographical information on Cavanaugh-O'Keefe, see his *Here I Am, Lord* (unpublished manuscript, 1993, author's files). Cavanaugh-O'Keefe has six children, which seems about average for militant Catholic pro-lifers.

13. The following lengthy (and literate) pamphlets serve as manifestos for the Prolife Nonviolent Action Project: *No Cheap Solutions* (1984) and *Nonviolence Is an Adverb* (1985), both written by John Cavanaugh-O'Keefe, and *Crypto-Eugenics: The Hidden Agenda of Planned Parenthood* (1991), which is written by his sister Katharine S. O'Keefe.

14. Quoted in E. Michael Jones, "Abortion Mill Rescue: Are Sit-ins the Answer?" *Fidelity* (July-August 1987), p. 34. On Prolifers for Survival, see the following brochures written by Juli Loesch, all published in Chapel Hill, North Carolina, in 1985: *Acts of Aggression*; *Imagining the Real*; and *On Nuclear Weapons*. See also the bimonthly newspaper *P.S. (Prolifers for Survival)*. PLS disbanded in March 1987.

15. It is unlikely that anyone is more admired by militant Catholic activists than Joan Andrews, who has spent five years in prison (mostly in solitary confinement) for acts of civil disobedience at abortion clinics. See Richard Cowden-Guido, ed., *You Reject Them, You Reject Me: The Prison Letters of Joan Andrews* (Manassas, Va.: Trinity Communications, 1988). For profiles of more than a dozen militant activists, see Joe Gulotta, *Pro-Life Christians: Heroes for the Pre-Born* (Rockford, Ill.: TAN Books, 1992).

16. By this point in time, the National Right to Life Committee had entered into a strategic

alliance with the Republican Party of then President Ronald Reagan, and the last thing the NRLC leadership wanted was to offend the law-and-order sensibilities of the GOP. The point, rather, was to portray the pro-life movement as a paragon of middle-class rectitude. For a provocative history of this alliance, see Michele McKeegan, *Abortion Politics: Mutiny in the Ranks of the Right* (New York: Free Press, 1992). For additional commentary, see James R. Kelly, "Learning and Teaching Consistency," 160; Michael W. Cuneo, "Life Battles," pp. 286–87; and Colin Francome, *Abortion Freedom* (Boston: Allen and Unwin, 1984).

17. Scheidler's remark, which was reported to me by several activists, has attained almost canonical status among militant Catholic pro-lifers.

18. John C. Willke, M.D., "From the President's Desk: A Place for Public Witness?" *National Right to Life News* (May 15, 1986), pp. 3, 8; John C. Willke, M.D. (NRLC President), *1986 Convention Hand-out* (Denver; May 27, 1986). I personally witnessed the events reported in this paragraph while doing field work at the convention. On the Pro-Life Direct Action League, see *The Unborn Speak... "Doesn't My Life Count for Something?"* (St. Louis, n.d.). For a more extensive discussion, see Cuneo, *Catholics Against the Church*, pp. 70–74.

19. See Joseph M. Scheidler, *Closed: 99 Ways to Stop Abortion* (Toronto: Life Cycle Books, 1985). On Operation Rescue, see Marian Faux, *Crusaders: Voices from the Abortion Front* (New York: Carol Publishing, 1990), pp. 116–72; and Susan Faludi, "Where Did Randy Go Wrong?" *Mother Jones* (November 1989), pp. 22–28, 61–65. For profiles of conservative Protestant activists, see Paul deParrie, *The Rescuers* (Brentwood, Tenn.: Wolgemuth and Hyatt, 1989). In addition to their street activism, conservative Protestant and Catholic pro-lifers have opened several thousand crisis pregnancy centers in the United States. For the most comprehensive listing of these centers, see *Life—What a Beautiful Choice: Resources* (Valley Forge, Pa.: Arthur S. DeMoss Foundation, 1993); and the *1991–92 Pro-Life Resource Directory* (Los Angeles: International Life Services, 1993). Mention should also be made of groups such as Women Exploited by Abortion (WEBA) and American Victims of Abortion, which provide counseling to women who have already undergone abortions. See Marshall Fightlin, "Post-Abortion Counselling: A Pro-Life Task," in Dave Andrusko, ed., *To Rescue the Future: The Pro-Life Movement in the 1980s* (Toronto: Life Cycle Books, 1983), pp. 273–79.

20. On Ireland, for example, see John A. Hannigan, "Containing the Luciferine Spark," in Roger O'Toole, ed., *Sociological Studies of Roman Catholicism* (Lewiston, N.Y.: E. Mellen Press, 1989), pp. 71–84. On Canada, see my "Keepers of the Faith: Lay Militants, Abortion, and the Battle for Canadian Catholicism," pp. 127–42 in the same volume.

21. For a more detailed discussion of these initiatives, see Timothy A. Byrnes, "The Politics of Abortion: The Catholic Bishops," in Byrnes and Segers, *The Catholic Church and the Politics of Abortion*, pp. 14–26.

22. Cardinal Joseph Bernardin, "A Consistent Ethic of Life: An American Catholic Dialogue," Fordham University Gannon Lecture, 6 December 1983.

23. Personal interview, Milwaukee, 30 June 1993. See Monica M. Migliorino, "Report from Rats' Alley: Down and Out with the Unborn in Chicago and Milwaukee," *Fidelity* (July-August 1987), pp. 38–45.

24. Personal interview, Chicago, 29 June 1993. The quotation attributed to Mary Anne Hackett in the final section of this chapter is taken from the same interview.

25. Letter from Committee of Pro-Life Catholics to Joseph Cardinal Bernardin, 17 February 1993; letter to Mrs. Hackett and Mrs. Quirke (Committee of Pro-Life Catholics) from Joseph

Cardinal Bernardin, 4 March 1993; letter from Mary Anne Hackett and Bonnie Quirke to Joseph Cardinal Bernardin, 26 March 1993; letter to Mrs. Hackett and Mrs. Quirke (Committee of Pro-Life Catholics) from Joseph Cardinal Bernardin, 12 May 1993.

26. See Timothy A. Byrnes, "The Cardinal and the Governor: The Politics of Abortion in New York State," in Byrnes and Segers, *The Catholic Church and the Politics of Abortion*, pp. 137–51. For Cuomo's position, see "Religious Beliefs and Public Morality: A Catholic Governor's Perspective," in Jung and Shannon, *Abortion and Catholicism*, pp. 45–96. For Cardinal O'Connor's perspective, see "Abortion: Questions and Answers," *Catholic New York* (Special Edition), 14 June 1990. See also Nat Hentoff, "Profiles (Cardinal O'Connor—Part II)," *New Yorker* (March 30, 1987), pp. 37–52, 73–92.

27. Needless to say, I am not suggesting that all (or even most) pro-lifers have committed themselves to street protest against abortion. Many have limited themselves to rather more pacific endeavors such as political lobbying and running crisis-pregnancy centers. Like any other complex social enterprise, the American pro-life movement defies simple characterization. My chief interest here is with the militant Catholic dimension of the movement.

28. For a fuller discussion of these themes, see my "Soldiers of Orthodoxy: Revivalist Catholicism in North America," *Studies in Religion/Sciences Religieuses* 17, 3 (1988): 347–63.

29. During the summer of 1993, I interviewed a total of twenty Catholic activists (all of whom were involved in militant forms of anti-abortion protest) in the metropolitan areas of New York City, Chicago, and Washington, D.C.; and in the spring of 1994, I interviewed an additional fifteen in the New York City/New Jersey area. The findings rehearsed in this concluding section are based almost entirely upon these interviews. For striking parallels between the American and Canadian cases, see my *Catholics Against the Church*, pp. 209–13.

30. Personal interview, Chicago, 29 June 1993. Julie and Steve McCreevy are pioneer leaders of Our Lady of Guadalupe Rosary Crusade for Life.

31. For a fuller discussion of this issue, see Philip F. Lawler, "Are We Really Losing?" *Catholic World Report* (March 1994), pp. 44–53.

32. Personal interview, Chicago, 28 June 1993.

33. In March 1993 Dr. David Gunn was slain outside a Pensacola, Florida, clinic; an activist named Michael Griffin was convicted and is now serving a life sentence. In July 1994 Dr. John Bayard Britton and his bodyguard, James Barrett, were also slain outside a Pensacola clinic; a former minister named Paul Hill was convicted of state murder charges and sentenced to death. (In a separate federal trial, Hill was sentenced to life without parole for violation of clinic-protection laws.) And in December 1994 two abortion-clinic receptionists, Shannon Lowney and Leanne Nichols, were shot to death in Brookline, Massachusetts; a freelance Catholic abortion foe named John C. Salvi III was convicted of murder in the shootings in March 1996. (See "Abortion Violence," *Toronto Star* [December 31, 1994], p. A10.) In the wake of the Salvi shootings, Bernard Cardinal Law, Archbishop of Boston, called for a moratorium on sidewalk protest outside Boston area clinics; the cardinal was mistaken, however, in apparently assuming that he possessed some sort of privileged moral authority over militant Catholic activists. (See Gustav Niebuhr, "Abortion Clinic Violence Stirs Debate Among Church Leaders," *New York Times* [January 9, 1995], pp. A1, A8.) In recent years, moreover, a small group of activists on the anti-abortion movement's extreme lunatic fringe have advanced the doctrine of "justifiable homicide," which upholds the killing of abortion practitioners as a moral imperative. Although most of these activists are conservative Protestants of various theological stripes, one of their spiritual leaders is a Catholic

priest based in Mobile, Alabama, named Fr. David C. Trosch. (See Gustav Niebuhr, "To Church's Dismay, Priest Talks of 'Justifiable Homicide' of Abortion Doctors," *New York Times* [August 24, 1994], p. A12.)

34. The theme of martyrdom plays an especially prominent role in the rhetoric of Fr. Norman Weslin, a Catholic convert and founder (in the early 1990s) of a militant anti-abortion organization called Mary's Lambs for Jesus. See, for example, the 1991 video *Mary's Lambs for Jesus: Fr. Doe Tells his Story* (Victim Souls for the Unborn Christ Child, Wichita, Kansas).

Chapter 4

1. Throughout much of the seventies Fr. Fancis Fenton was arguably one of the four or five most prominent traditionalist priests functioning in America. In January 1973 Fenton and several lay supporters founded the Orthodox Roman Catholic Movement, Inc. (ORCM) in Monroe (Stratford), Connecticut, and over the next several years the organization started up a string of chapels and Mass centers across the country. The chief objective of ORCM, according to Fenton, was to "preserve the Roman Catholic religion as it had existed historically up to and including the pontificate of Pope Pius XII" (Fenton, *Holding Fast*, 1977, p. 1). During the late seventies, however, a variety of factors (including dissension over Fenton's autocratic leadership style and his increasingly close ties with the John Birch Society) brought about a rupture within the organization, and in 1979 Fenton left ORCM and moved to Colorado Springs, where he established a rival organization called Traditional Catholics of America (CTA). Although the CTA was never able to develop into anything more than a bit player on the traditionalist scene, its quarterly newsletter, *The Athanasian*, played a significant role during the eighties in shaping traditionalist opinion. Following the departure of Fenton, a slightly more moderate priest named Fr. Robert McKenna took over the leadership reins of ORCM, but over the next ten years the organization fell into steady decline. In 1988 all of ORCM's remaining chapels outside of Connecticut became independent traditionalist Mass centers, and today the organization consists almost entirely of the 180-member Our Lady of the Rosary Chapel in Monroe (telephone interview, Fr. Robert McKenna, 15 June 1993). On Fr. Fenton and ORCM, see William D. Dinges, "Roman Catholic Traditionalism in the United States," in Martin E. Marty and R. Scott Appleby, eds., *Fundamentalisms Observed* (Chicago: University of Chicago Press, 1991), pp. 72–74; and Richard Cimino, "An Overview of Catholic Traditionalism in the United States," unpublished paper, author's files, 1993, pp. 6–7.

2. On December 8, 1864, Pope Pius IX published the encyclical *Quanta cura*, with the "Syllabus of Errors" attached, which denounced "the principal errors of our times," including the view that the pope "can or should reconcile himself to, or agree with, progress, liberalism, and modern civilization." Among Catholic traditionalists/separatists in the United States, the "Syllabus of Errors" is held up as a holy testament. See J. N. D. Kelly, *The Oxford Dictionary of Popes* (Oxford: Oxford University Press, 1986), pp. 309–11.

3. The "Siri theory" is also broached by Malachi Martin in *The Keys of This Blood* (New York: Touchstone, 1990), pp. 606–10. Martin is a best-selling author and former Jesuit whose books have served as a veritable mine of conspiracy for Catholic traditionalists in the United States.

4. Fr. Gruner, as we shall see in the next chapter, isn't a traditionalist in the rather strict sense intended here.

5. For a fairly comprehensive listing of traditionalist chapels in America, see *Our Lady of the Sun Mass Directory* (Peoria, Ariz., 1995).

6. Personal correspondence; Rev. Omer U. Kline, O.S.B., Archivist; Saint Vincent Archabbey and College Archives (Latrobe, Penn.); 27 February 1995. (Brother Joseph Natale passed away in the summer of 1995.)

7. For a more extensive discussion of De Pauw's traditionalist career, see William D. Dinges, "Roman Catholic Traditionalism in the United States," pp. 70–72.

8. Ibid., p. 70.

9. Rev. Dr. Gommar A. De Pauw, *The 'Rebel' Priest of the Catholic Traditionalist Movement* (New York: Catholic Traditionalist Movement, 1967), pp. 7, 9.

10. Dinges, "Roman Catholic Traditionalism in the United States," p. 71.

11. For a conservative Catholic rejoinder on this point, see James Likoudis and Kenneth D. Whitehead, *The Pope, the Council, and the Mass* (W. Hanover, Mass.: Christopher Publishing House, 1981), pp. 97–104. Of the many book-length critiques of the new Mass written from a traditionalist perspective, see in particular James Wathen, *The Great Sacrilege* (Rockford, Ill.: TAN Books, 1971); and Michael Davies, *Pope Paul's New Mass* (Dickinson, Texas: Angelus Press, 1980).

12. For some of the information reported in this paragraph, I am indebted to my research associate Richard Cimino, who undertook fieldwork at De Pauw's Ave Maria Chapel in Westbury, Long Island, during the summer of 1993. (De Pauw's congregation, and this is not entirely unusual within the world of Catholic traditionalism, is racially mixed. At a service Cimino visited on June 27, 1993, there were approximately seventy whites and thirty blacks in attendance.) For a brief period in 1967, De Pauw entered into an alliance with a controversial organization called the Sovereign Order of St. John (OSJ). Established in Shickshinny, Pennsylvania, in 1908, the OSJ claims to be the legitimate successor to the medieval Knights of Malta. The organization is opposed to both the council and the new Mass, and claims that the contemporary church has been "infiltrated by Freemasons, Jews, Marxists, homosexuals and radical feminists" (promotional brochure, Sovereign Order of St. John, n.d.). Currently based in Benton, Tennessee, the organization operates about fifty chapels (or traditionalist Mass centers) and three elementary schools across the country (Cimino telephone interview with Dr. John Grady, Grandmaster of the OSJ; 29 June 1993). For a fuller account of the OSJ, see Cimino, "An Overview of Catholic Traditionalism in the United States," pp. 7–8.

13. On Lefebvre, I am especially indebted to the following scholarly articles by William D. Dinges: "Catholic Traditionalism," in Joseph H. Fichter, ed., *Alternatives to American Mainline Churches* (New York: Rose of Sharon Press, 1983), pp. 137–58; "Quo Vadis, Lefebvre?" *America* (June 11–18, 1988), pp. 602–6; "The Quandary of Dissent on the Catholic Right," in Roger O'-Toole, ed., *Sociological Studies in Roman Catholicism* (Lewiston, N.Y.: Edwin Mellen, 1989), pp. 107–26; "'We Are What You Were': Roman Catholic Traditionalism in America," in Mary Jo Weaver and R. Scott Appleby, eds., *Being Right: Conservative Catholics in America* (Bloomington: Indiana University Press, 1995), pp. 241–69; and "Roman Catholic Traditionalism in the United States," pp. 74–78. Among Catholic traditionalists, the most prolific writer about Lefebvre and his movement is an Anglican convert to Catholicism named Michael Davies. Of his numerous works, see especially the following: *Liturgical Revolution: Cranmer's Godly Order* (New Rochelle, N.Y.: Arlington House, 1976); and *Apologia Pro Marcel Lefebvre*, 3 vols. (Dickinson, Texas: Angelus Press, 1979–83). For the clearest (and also the most accessible) statement of the traditionalist position by Lefebvre himself, see Archbishop Marcel Lefebvre, *Open Letter to Confused Catholics* (Kansas City: Angelus Press, 1986). And finally, for a relatively recent survey of the Vatican-

Lefebvre controversy from a traditionalist perspective, see Fr. Peter Scott, ed., *Is Tradition Excommunicated?: Where Is Catholicism Today?* (Kansas City: Angelus Press, 1993).

14. Dinges, "'We Are What You Were': Roman Catholic Traditionalism in America," p. 249; Cimino, "An Overview of Catholic Traditionalism in the United States," pp. 2–4.

15. Telephone interview, 28 June 1993.

16. During the fall of 1994, I made several research visits to SSPX chapels in Farmingdale, Long Island, and Salem, Connecticut.

17. *Catholic World Report* (February 1992), p. 36.

18. Personal interview, Oyster Bay, New York, 26 February 1995. During the winter and spring of 1995, I visited the chapel at Oyster Bay three times and the SSPV's Manhattan chapel once for research purposes. (The Oyster Bay chapel is located on the former Long Island estate of millionaire William Woodward, Jr.) For summary accounts of the SSPV, see Dinges, "'We Are What You Were': Roman Catholic Traditionalism in America," p. 250; and Cimino, "An Overview of Catholic Traditionalism in the United States," pp. 4–6.

19. On the Marisue Greve controversy, see E. Michael Jones, "The Kidnapping of Sister Mary Cecilia," *Fidelity* (March 1989), pp. 26–37. (See the May 1989 and June 1989 issues of *Fidelity*, "Letters to the Editor," for reader responses.) Charges of brainwashing and other atrocities are frequently raised against culturally deviant religious groups in America, and they should rarely (if ever) be taken at face value. For an insightful discussion of this issue in a somewhat different context, see David G. Bromley, Anson D. Shupe, Jr., and J. C. Ventimiglia, "Atrocity Tales, the Unification Church and the Social Construction of Evil," *Journal of Communication* 29, 3 (1979): 42–53.

20. Personal interview, Round Top, New York, 20 June 1995.

21. For an impassioned defense of this position, see Fr. Noël Barbara, "Episcopal Consecrations Without Papal Mandate," *Fortes in Fide* 12 (1993): 13–19. This was the final issue of *Fortes in Fide*, an occasional review published as *Forts dans la Foi* in Tours, France. Since its début in 1967, the review had been translated into English by Rama P. Coomaraswamy, M.D., a prominent traditionalist based in Greenwich, Connecticut, and distributed in the United States by William F. J. Christian of Saint Louis.

22. For a highly critical assessment of Thuc's liberal consecration policies, see Peregrinus [pseudonym], "Two Bishops in Every Garage," *The Roman Catholic* (January 1983), pp. 4–16. *The Roman Catholic* is a bimonthly journal published by the Society of St. Pius V. Peregrinus was actually Fr. Anthony Cekada, an SSPV priest who would later change his mind and become a Thuc supporter. (See Cekada's pamphlet *The First Stone*, Milwaukee, 1991.) For further information on Thuc, see "Autobiographie de Mgr. Pierre Martin Ngô-dinh-Thuc," in French, ed., *Einsicht* (August 1982), pp. 7–86.

23. On Fr. Robert McKenna, see note 1.

24. For background information on these and other traditionalist bishops, see Gary L. Ward, Bertill Persson, and Alan Bain, eds., *Independent Bishops: An International Directory* (Detroit: Apogee Books, 1990).

25. See Michael Glazier and Monika K. Hellwig, eds., *The Modern Catholic Encyclopedia* (Collegeville, Minn.: Liturgical Press, 1994); Karl Pruter and J. Gordon Melton, *The Old Catholic Sourcebook* (New York: Garland, 1983); and (less benignly) Fr. Anthony Cekada, "A Warning on the Old Catholics: False Bishops, False Churches," *The Roman Catholic* (January 1980), pp. 1–11.

26. Personal interview, Spokane, Washington, 11 October 1994. For additional information

on Dolan, see the pamphlet *Announcement of Episcopal Consecration*, Saint Gertrude the Great Church (Cincinnati), September 1993.

27. The story of Kelly's consecration is recounted at length in *The Roman Catholic* (Special Edition, 1995), pp. 1–40. (Bishop Alfred Mendez died on January 28, 1995.)

28. For some of the SSPV's rather more vigorous attacks against the Mount St. Michael's community, see the following: Fr. Clarence Kelly, "The Mount St. Michael's Issue," *The Bulletin* (February 1992), pp. 1–10; "Mount St. Michael's: Part II," *The Bulletin* (March 1992), pp. 1–5; "Mount St. Michael's: Part III," *The Bulletin* (April 1992), pp. 1–5; "The Mental State of Archbishop Thuc," *The Bulletin* (January 1994), pp. 1–4; "The Mental State of Archbishop Thuc: Part II," *The Bulletin* (February 1994), pp. 1–4; "The Mental State of Archbishop Thuc: Part III," *The Bulletin* (April—May 1994), pp. 1–4; and Fr. William W. Jenkins, *The Thuc Consecrations: An Open Appeal to Fr. Donald Sanborn* (Oyster Bay, New York, n.d.). (Fr. Sanborn was an SSPV priest who followed Dolan into Mount St. Michael's.) See also Kelly's undated broadsheet entitled "Caveat Emptor: Let the Buyer Beware of Mater Dei Seminary." (The reference here is to the Mount St. Michael's seminary in Omaha, Nebraska.)

29. For the early years of the TLRC, I have relied on interviews with current members of the Mount St. Michael's community and also on the following written sources: Bob Cubbage, *Tridentine Latin Rite Church* (Spokane: Inland Register, 1986); Thomas W. Case, "The Fatima Crusaders: Anatomy of a Schism," *Fidelity* (October 1988), pp. 37–42; Hazel Barnes, "Dissidents Leasing Mount St. Michael's," *Spokane Chronicle* (January 26, 1978); Mel Reisner, "Tridentine Rite Church Behind Investment Company," *Spokane Chronicle* (March 5, 1978); Tim Hanson, "A Bishop's Life on the Run," (Spokane) *Spokesman-Review* (August 26, 1984); Carla K. Johnson, "Mount St. Michael's Welcomes Visitors to Hilltop Parish," (Spokane) *Spokesman-Review* (October 6, 1991); and Fr. Clarence Kelly, "The Mount St. Michael's Issue."

30. Many members of the community sacrificed their life savings to come up with the down payment on the $1.5-million purchase price for the seminary.

31. Cubbage, *Tridentine Latin Rite Church*, pp. 22–23 (cited in Case, "The Fatima Crusaders," p. 43). See also Jim Sparks, "More Trouble on the Mount: Bishop Leaves Tridentines after Power Struggle," *Spokane Chronicle* (January 11, 1987).

32. Jim Sparks, "Former Tridentine Bishop in Drug Bust," *Spokane Chronicle* (May 14, 1987). I am also indebted for information in this paragraph to the Plymouth County (California) Probation Department.

33. On September 10, 1995, I spoke by telephone to Roy Horvath of Los Angeles, whose son Terence Fenton Horvath has been a staunch Schuckardt loyalist since 1979. The younger Horvath is forty-eight, single, and a Vietnam veteran. His father told me that the Oblates of Mary Immaculate are extremely secretive, and that he has no means of even contacting his son. He said that the order does a lot of street preaching, and that it probably numbers a bit less than a hundred people, including two or three priests who have been ordained by Schuckardt.

34. For background information on Bishop George Musey, see Cekada, "Two Bishops in Every Garage," pp. 9–10.

35. On the doctrine of sedevacantism, I have consulted the following Mount St. Michael's ephemera: Bishop Mark A. Pivarunas, "Sedevacantism," position paper, n.d.; Pivarunas, "Homily: Feast of Sts. Peter and Paul," 29 June 1994; Pivarunas, "Episcopal Letter to Community," Pentecost Sunday, 1994; Pivarunas, "Letter to Greg—," seven-page epistolic treatise, 18 October 1993; "Theological Position of the Congregation of Mary Immaculate Queen," community posi-

tion paper, 9 March 1990; "'Mass' Deception," twelve-page pamphlet produced by Americans for Public Morality (Norwood, Massachusetts), 16 June 1969; and Fr. Anthony Cekada, "Tradition-alists, Infallibility, and the Pope," thirty-three-page booklet, St. Gertrude the Great Roman Catholic Church (Cincinnati), 1995.

36. For Lefebvre's response to the council's new teaching on religious liberty, see *Open Letter to Confused Catholics*, ch. 11. See also Michael Davies, *The Second Vatican Council and Religious Liberty* (Long Prairie, Minn.: Neumann Press, 1992).

37. As additional warrant for his community's sedevacantist position, Pivarunas produced the following passage by the eighteenth-century Italian theologian St. Alphonsus de Liguori: "Some have sought to prove that certain Popes fell into heresy. . . . If, however, God were to permit any Pope to become a notorious and contumacious heretic, he would by such fact cease to be Pope, and the Pontificate would be vacant." (Cited in Rev. T. Livius, C.SS.R., *S. Peter, Bishop of Rome; or, The Roman Episcopate of the Prince of the Apostles* [London: Burns & Oates, 1888], p. 243.) The same passage, by the way, closes on a rather more awkward note for Mount St. Michael's: "But we ought, with good reason, to presume, as Cardinal Bellarmine says, that God will never allow any of the Roman Pontiffs, even as a private person, to become a heretic, either notorious or secret."

38. Nesta H. Webster, *World Revolution,* 2nd ed. (London: Constable, 1922); Eustace Mullins, *Secrets of the Federal Reserve* (Staunton, Va.: Bankers Research Institute, 1954). For a recent assess-ment of this genre of literature, see Jacob Heilbrunn, "On Pat Robertson: His Anti-Semitic Sources," *New York Review of Books* (April 20, 1995), pp. 68–71.

39. See Fr. Denis Fahey, *The Mystical Body of Christ in the Modern World* (Dublin: Regina Publi-cations, 1935). Fahey was Professor of Philosophy and Church History at Holy Ghost Missionary College, Kimmage, Dublin. His book has gone through eleven reprintings since its initial publi-cation, most recently in 1987. It should be noted that his views were widely denounced by Catholics in Ireland and elsewhere during the 1930s and forties. The major organ of Fahey's thought in the United States today is a traditionalist monthly called *All These Things*, which is published by Jim Condit, Jr., of the Cincinnatus Political Action Committee. A somewhat differ-ent, and decidedly less influential, source of traditionalist anti-Semitism are the homilies of Charles E. Coughlin, a Catholic priest who rose to national prominence in the 1930s as a radio preacher. For insightful accounts of Coughlin's career, see Jay P. Dolan, *The American Catholic Ex-perience* (Garden City, N.Y.: Doubleday, 1985), pp. 403–4; and David J. O'Brien, *American Catholics and Social Reform* (New York: Oxford University Press, 1968), pp. 150–81.

40. Two of the most popular diatribes against Freemasonry among American traditionalists are Paul A. Fisher's *Behind the Lodge Door* (Rockford, Ill.: TAN Books, 1991); and Monseigneur Du-panloup's *Study of Freemasonry* (Rochester, N.Y.: Kenek Books, n.d.). (The Dupanloup volume was originally published in France in 1876; the name of the translator is not given.) For an interest-ing (and mostly positive) appraisal of Freemasonry's role in eighteenth-century Europe, see Mar-garet C. Jacob, *Living the Enlightenment* (New York: Oxford University Press, 1991).

41. Personal interview with Joseph Berchtold, Spokane, 8 October 1994.

42. Personal interview, Spokane, 9 October 1994.

43. Personal interview, Spokane, 10–11 October 1994.

44. This apparent irony has previously been pointed out by William D. Dinges in several of his publications. See, for example, "The Quandary of Dissent on the Catholic Right," and "Ritual Conflict as Social Conflict: Liturgical Reform in the Roman Catholic Church," *Sociological Analysis* 48, 2 (1987): 138–57.

45. Personal interview, Cincinnati, 20 August 1995. See Cekada's interesting (and articulate) booklet *Welcome to the Traditional Latin Mass* (Troy, Mich.: Catholic Restoration, 1995).

46. Timothy Duff, "Private Revelation's Insights to the Future," Question and Answer Period, Fatima and World Peace Conference, Mount St. Michael's, Spokane, 11 October 1994.

47. Bishop Daniel Dolan, Question and Answer Forum, with Bishop Mark Pivarunas, Fatima and World Peace Conference, Mount St. Michael's, Spokane, 10 October 1994. (Although generally not activists, traditionalists almost universally oppose abortion, and some of them participate occasionally in public protest marches.) For a discussion of the *introversionist* sect, and also for a more general typology of sectarianism, see Bryan R. Wilson, "An Analysis of Sect Development," *American Sociological Review* 24, 1 (February 1959): 3–15; and *Patterns of Sectarianism* (London: Heinemann, 1967). As I shall suggest later, it may also be fruitful to regard separatist groups such as Mount St. Michael's as *utopian* sects.

48. Catholic traditionalists in France have sometimes allied themselves with the monarchist-nationalist movement of Jean-Marie Le Pen (see Dinges, "Roman Catholic Traditionalism in the United States," p. 91; and Gabriel A. Almond, Emmanuel Sivan, and R. Scott Appleby, "Examining the Cases," in Martin E. Marty and R. Scott Appleby, *Fundamentalisms Comprehended* [Chicago: University of Chicago Press, 1995], pp. 476–77). The theocratic aspirations of American traditionalists have not thus far given rise to any sort of concerted political action.

49. For the clearest traditionalist analysis of the aggrieved status of the contemporary priesthood, see Lefebvre, *Open Letter to Confused Catholics*, pp. 50–56. See also Dinges, "Ritual Conflict as Social Conflict."

50. For an unintentionally ironic theory of traditionalist dissent, see Scott, *Is Tradition Excommunicated?*, pp. 12, 18, 20, 23, 26, 72.

Chapter 5

1. Father John Gregory of the Trinity, *Questions and Answers* (St. Jovite, Quebec: Monastery of the Magnificat of the Mother of God, 1989), p. 23; Jean Côté, *Prophet Without Permit: Father John of the Trinity* (Montreal: Pro Manuscripto, 1991), p. 75. My account of Father John's life and the early history of his ministry is based primarily on these two works and also on interviews with members of the Infinite Love community (see below for interview citations). *Questions and Answers* consists of two lengthy (and apparently staged) interviews with Father John; *Prophet Without Permit* is mainly hagiographic, although the author is not himself a member of the Infinite Love community. (I am especially indebted to Jean-Guy Vaillancourt of the University of Montreal for providing me with both conceptual and contextual background on the community.)

2. Côté, *Prophet Without Permit*, p. 84; Father John Gregory, *Questions and Answers*, pp. 25–26.

3. On Fr. Michel Collin, see Côté, *Prophet Without Permit*, pp. 143–49; on La Salette, see Sandra L. Zimdars-Swartz, *Encountering Mary* (New York: Avon Books, 1992), pp. 27–43, 165–89. The Virgin apparently told Mélanie that the members of the eschatological community that she wanted established would be known as the "apostles of the last times" (Zimdars-Swartz, p. 184). This appellation (or its equivalent, "disciples of the latter days") has subsequently been claimed by a wide variety of groups on the Catholic right, including both the Infinite Love community and Bayside (see below, note 69).

4. On the "Pope chosen by God," which is allegedly mentioned in the so-called Fatima secret, see Father John Gregory, *Questions and Answers*, p. 26.

5. Côté, *Prophet Without Permit*, pp. 163–64.

6. Cited in *Father Jean de la Trinité and the Hidden Children of St. Jovite* (St. Jovite, Quebec: Magnificat Editions, 1971), p. 5. This work, whose production is credited to the entire Infinite Love community, contains extensive documentation on the "hidden children" saga.

7. *Father Jean de la Trinité and the Hidden Children of St. Jovite*, pp. 150–54. The following is merely a sample of the dozens of news articles that were generated by the saga: James K. Anderson, "How Priest Rescued 5 Children: Detroiter Quebec Story," *Detroit News* (January 19, 1967); Armand Gebert, "Freed Sect Children Better: Undernourished in Monastery," *Detroit News* (October 2, 1967); "Infinite Love: Dread and Reprisals," *Time* (January 27, 1967); "Hunt Quebec Monastery's 50 Missing Tots," *New York Post* (January 18, 1967); "Infinite Love Sect Split Over Children," *Cleveland Plain Dealer* (January 23, 1967); "Hunt for Children Secreted by Sect," (Wellington, New Zealand) *Evening Post* (January 19, 1967); Malcolm Daigneault, "Children Found—Safe and Sound," (Montreal) *Gazette* (January 19, 1967); "L'Interpol recherche le prieur," *La Presse* (Montreal) (February 13, 1967); Malcolm Daigneault, "Apostles Children Clean and Healthy: Doctor's Testimony," (Montreal) *Gazette* (January 28, 1967); "Monastery Hides Wanted Children," *Miami Herald* (January 18, 1967); Douglas Bradford, "Detroit Child Hunted After Monastery Raid," *Detroit News* (September 29, 1967); Dominique Clift, "Apostles of Infinite Love: They Want a Quick Return to the Church of the Past," *Toronto Star* (January 27, 1967); "Judge Tours Monastery to See Living Quarters," (Montreal) *Gazette* (December 30, 1967); and "Les Apôtres de l'Amour infini gagnent leur bataille juridique," *Montréal Matin* (February 17, 1968).

8. Letter from Michel Collin (Clement XV) to Good Father John of the Trinity, 9 May 1969; cited in Côté, *Prophet Without Permit*, p. 211. Father John, as Gregory XVII, is not to be confused with Clemente Dominguez Gomez of Palmar de Troya, Spain, who would name himself Pope Gregory XVII ten years later (see above, pp. 99).

9. See Laënnec Hurbon, "New Religious Movements in the Caribbean," in James A. Beckford, ed., *New Religious Movements and Rapid Social Change* (Beverly Hills, Ca.: Sage Publications, 1986), pp. 159–61.

10. Gregory XVII, *Peter Speaks to the World*, 2nd ed. (St. Jovite, Quebec: Editions Magnificat, 1993), pp. 211–12. See also the undated pastoral letter entitled "Exhortation to all Christians" (John Gregory XVII, Servant of the True Church of Jesus Christ by the election of God, St. Jovite).

11. See *"Justice" Put on Trial* (St. Jovite, Quebec: Editions Magnificat, 1984). This work, whose production is likewise credited to the entire Infinite Love community, contains extensive documentation on the Currier case. The following is just a selection of the numerous news pieces that were written about the case: Tom Hill and Donna Balkan, "Apostles Caught in Police Dragnet," (Ottawa) *Citizen* (May 2, 1978); Tom Harpur, "Fake Nuns Going Door-to-Door for Money, Catholics Warned," *Toronto Star* (March 1, 1978); Donna Balkan, "Mother Refuses to Agree on Turning Over Children," (Ottawa) *Citizen* (July 14, 1978); "Le 'pape' condamné à deux ans de prison," *Le Devoir* (Montreal) (October 14, 1978); and Lee Lester, "Sect Head Jailed, and Father Hopes Ordeal is Over," *Toronto Sun* (October 12, 1980).

12. See, for example, Monelle Saindon, "Des ramifications aussi étendues que LA MAFIA!" *Le Journal de Montréal* (April 2, 1982), p. 12; Anne Beirne, "The Sackcloth Adversity," *Macleans* (September 6, 1982), pp. 14–15; Paul Delean and Claudia Cattaneo, "Nun Says Runaways' Charges 'Grievous Injustice'," (Montreal) *Gazette* (April 3, 1984), p. A4; Maureen Peterson, "Life

with St. Jovite Apostles: Suffering is Key to Salvation," (Montreal) *Gazette* (May 12, 1984), p. B5; and Brian Bergman, "Parents Lost to a Cult," *Alberta Report* (July 23, 1984), p. 31.

13. In all likelihood (and here my information is spotty), there are no more than two or three thousand tertiaries worldwide.

14. For an interesting discussion (in a strikingly different vein) of this sort of hatred, see Paul Berman, "The Other and the Almost the Same," *New Yorker* (February 28, 1994), pp. 61–71.

15. In very recent years, in fact, two prominent traditionalist priests from the western United States, Fr. Paul Berchtold and Fr. Daniel Jones, have aligned themselves with the Infinite Love community. Fr. Berchtold (a younger brother of Joseph Berchtold) was formerly a member of the Mount St. Michael's community, and Fr. Jones was publisher (in Westcliffe, Colorado) of an influential traditionalist newsletter called *Sangre de Christo*. For a brief discussion of Fr. Jones and his "British Israelite" views, see Thomas W. Case, "The Tridentine Rite Conference and its Schismatic Cousins (Part 3)," *Fidelity* (April 1993), p. 39.

16. Personal interview, St. Jovite, Quebec, 25–28 September 1995.

17. See Jean-Marie Barette, *The Prophecy of the Apostles of the Latter Times* (St. Jovite, Quebec: Editions Magnificat, 1988), pp. 167–68. For a 950-page encyclopedia of legitimating prophecy recently produced by the Infinite Love community, see Catherine St-Pierre, *Thou Art Peter* (St. Jovite, Quebec: Editions Magnificat, 1994). And for a more general overview of Catholic apocalyptic scenarios, see Yves Dupont, *Catholic Prophecy: The Coming Chastisement* (Rockford, Ill.: TAN Books, 1973).

18. On Sr. Michelle's legal involvement with the Currier case, see *"Justice" Put on Trial*, pp. 255–59; personal interview (Sr. Michelle), St. Jovite, Quebec, 26–29 September 1995.

19. Father John Gregory, *Questions and Answers*, pp. 17–18. See also the pastoral letter entitled "How to Perceive Women Priests" (John Gregory XVII, 24 June 1994, St. Jovite).

20. For the Infinite Love community's critique of Paul VI, see Michel San Pietro [pseudonym], *Saul, Why Do You Persecute Me?*, 3rd ed. (St. Jovite, Quebec: Editions Magnificat, 1991). See also "Open Letters [13 January 1980, and 19 September 1984] to Pope John Paul II," from John Gregory XVII, Servant of the Holy Church of Jesus Christ by divine election (Sanctuary of the Keys of Saint Peter, St. Jovite). My personal interview with Father John (or Pope Gregory XVII) took place on September 26, 1995, in St. Jovite, Quebec.

21. Zimdars-Swartz, *Encountering Mary*, p. 197. For the most part, I follow Zimdars-Swartz's splendid account of Fatima here (ibid., pp. 67–91, 190–219). On a more pious note, see William T. Walsh, *Our Lady of Fatima* (Garden City, N.Y.: Image Books, 1954). And for a fascinating psychoanalytic interpretation, see Michael P. Carroll, *The Cult of the Virgin Mary: Psychological Origins* (Princeton: Princeton University Press, 1986), pp. 173–81.

22. Luis Kondor, ed., *Fatima in Lucia's Own Words*, trans. the Dominican Nuns of the Perpetual Rosary (Fatima, Portugal: Postulation Centre, 1976), pp. 104–5; cited in Zimdars-Swartz, *Encountering Mary*, pp. 199–200.

23. Cited in Fr. Joaquin Maria Alonso, "Meaning of the 'Consecration' of Russia," *Fatima Crusader*, Victory Issue (Autumn 1995), p. 13. See also Alonso's *The Secret of Fatima: Fact and Legend*, trans. the Dominican Nuns of the Perpetual Rosary (Cambridge, Mass.: Ravengate Press, 1979), p. 95.

24. The Vatican sent out letters requesting that all bishops participate from their home dioceses in the March 1984 consecration, but apparently not all bishops complied with the request (telephone interview, Bill Sockey, executive director of the Blue Army, 12 December 1995).

25. See *World Apostolate of Fatima Blue Army Manual* (Washington Township, Warren County, New Jersey, n.d.). The World Apostolate of Fatima operates the Blue Army National Shrine of the Immaculate Heart of Mary on the grounds of the National Blue Army Center in Washington Township, and also publishes a bimonthly journal called *Soul* Magazine. The organization's official position is that the consecration of Russia requested by the Virgin Mary at Fatima was properly carried out by Pope John Paul II on May 13, 1982 (*Blue Army Manual*, p. 2). For a provocative psychoanalytic analysis of the Brown Scapular, see Michael P. Carroll, *Catholic Cults and Devotions: A Psychological Inquiry* (Kingston, Ontario: McGill–Queen's University Press, 1989), ch. 7.

26. In the terms of Roman Catholic canon law, *incardination* refers to the attachment of a priest to a particular diocese, with correlative rights and duties under the local bishop; see John A. Hardon, S.J., *Modern Catholic Dictionary* (Garden City, N.Y.: Doubleday, 1980), p. 272.

27. Personal interview with Fr. Nicholas Gruner, Fort Erie, Ontario, 16 December 1995; telephone interview with Anne Cillis, 15 December 1995.

28. Hamish Fraser (now deceased) was founding editor of the right-wing, Scottish-Catholic *Approaches* Magazine. See "The Consecration Issue: A Debate between Hamish Fraser and John Haffert," *Approaches* (Summer 1982), pp. 3–15. (Haffert, at the time, was executive director of the Blue Army.) Fraser's position is set forth more succinctly in his "Pope John Paul II Fears Bishops' Open Rebellion," *Fatima Crusader* (February—April 1986), pp. 4, 13–14, 19.

29. On the Vatican-Moscow accord, see the following: Jean Madiran, "The Vatican-Moscow Agreement," *Fatima Crusader* (September–October 1984), pp. 5–8 (excerpted from the February 1984 issue of the right-wing French magazine *Itinéraires*); Fr. Paul Leonard, "The Plot to Silence Our Lady," *Fatima Crusader* (June—July 1986), pp. 9–13, 24–25, 27; Fr. Paul Leonard, "Up To Now—The Vatican Moscow Agreement Has Silenced Our Lady," *Fatima Crusader* (April–May 1987), pp. 12–15; and Arnaud de Lassus, "Conversion of Godless Portugal . . . A Foreshadowing of Russia's Future Conversion," *Fatima Crusader* (August–September 1988), pp. 10–13, 24–25, 41. In his *The Catholic Church in World Politics* (Princeton: Princeton University Press, 1987), it might be noted, Eric O. Hanson discusses relations between Pope John XXIII and Nikita Khrushchev but makes no mention of a clandestine Vatican-Moscow pact (pp. 9–11).

30. For a fairly representative selection of articles on the mounting communist menace, see the following: "Urgent! Communism is Advancing," Editorial, *Fatima Crusader* (November–December 1986), pp. 6–7, 21; Fr. Paul Leonard, "We Are on the Brink of Destruction," *Fatima Crusader* (August–September 1988), pp. 5, 8–9; Donald S. McAlvany, "The Expanding US/Soviet Military Gap," *Fatima Crusader* (Winter 1989), p. 31 (excerpted from the Fall 1989 issue of the *McAlvany Intelligence Advisor*); Donald S. McAlvany, "Mesmerized by the Bear: The Great Soviet Deception," *Fatima Crusader* (March—May 1990), pp. 18–25, 49–53 (reproduced from the Winter 1989 issue of the *McAlvany Intelligence Advisor*); and Frère Michel de la Sainte Trinité, "In Iraq: How Gorbachev is Following the Example of Stalin," *Fatima Crusader* (October–November 1990), pp. 16–17. Gruner has not been shy, the reader will note, about tapping into the broader (and frequently secular) anticommunist literature. In addition to printing excerpts from the *McAlvany Intelligence Advisor*, he has given full play in the *Crusader*'s pages to such right-wing screeds as Quentin Crommelin, Jr., and David S. Sullivan's *Soviet Military Supremacy: The Untold Facts About the New Danger to America* (Los Angeles, 1985) and Robert Conquest and Jon Manchip White's *What To Do When the Russians Come: A Survivor's Guide* (Briarcliff Manor, N.Y., 1984). See, for example, the article entitled "U.S.A. Prepares for Surrender?" in the March–May 1988 issue (p. 17).

31. For the complete text of this correspondence, see the February—April 1989 issue of the *Crusader*, pp. 27–33. The offending photograph of Cardinal Gagnon appeared on the cover of the March—May 1988 issue.

32. Michael McAteer, "Sincere but Misled or Self-Seeking Renegade?" *Toronto Star,* Saturday Magazine (August 25, 1990), p. M15. In addition to the McAteer piece, this paragraph is based on confidential ecclesiastical correspondence.

33. For the full text of Gruner's letter to Cardinal Innocenti, see the September–November 1989 issue of the *Crusader*, pp. 4, 34–39. See also, in the same issue (p. 4), Fr. Paul Leonard and Coralie Graham, "Some Vatican Officials Attempt to Silence and Suppress Our Lady of Fatima and Father Gruner."

34. See, for example, John Hauf, "The 1990 National Symposium: Fatima is Most Relevant Today," *Soul* Magazine (September–October 1990), pp. 12–13; and Fr. Robert J. Fox, "The Russian Consecration," *Soul* Magazine (March–April 1992), p. 13.

35. Fr. Nicholas Gruner, "Good News!" p. 43.

36. See page 4 of Gruner's "Dear Friend of Our Lady" insert letter, *Fatima Crusader* (Fall 1991).

37. "The Third Secret of Fatima Revealed- (Acts 2:40): 'Save Yourselves from this Perverse Generation'," *New York Times* (June 17, 1990), p. 37; reprinted in the Summer 1990 issue of the *Crusader*, pp. 20–23.

38. Frère Michel de la Sainte Trinité, *The Third Secret*, trans. John Collorafi (Buffalo: Immaculate Heart Publications, 1990); originally published as *Toute la vérité sur Fatima*, vol. 3: *Le troisième secret* (Saint-Parres-les-Vaudes: La Contre-Réforme Catholique, 1985). The first two volumes of Frère Michel's *Toute la vérité sur Fatima* series (*La science et les faits* and *Le secret et l'Église*, both originally published in 1984 by La Contre-Réforme Catholique) have also been translated by John Collorafi and issued by Immaculate Heart Publications under the titles, respectively, of *Science and the Facts* (1989) and *The Secret and the Church* (1989). (Immaculate Heart Publications is a division of Gruner's Fatima Crusader ministry.) In addition to *The Third Secret*, Gruner also sent the bishops copies of *World Enslavement or Peace . . . It's Up To the Pope* (Fort Erie, Ontario: Fatima Crusader, 1989), which is a compilation of articles most of which originally appeared in the *Crusader*. For the covering letter that accompanied this material, see the Summer 1991 issue of the *Crusader*, pp. 6–7. And for a provocatively evasive discussion of the Third Secret, see Joseph Cardinal Ratzinger with Vittorio Messori, *The Ratzinger Report*, trans. by S. Attanasio and G. Harrison (San Francisco: Ignatius Press, 1985), pp. 109–12.

39. Personal interview, Fort Erie, Ontario, 21 September 1992.

40. For the elaborate invitation that Gruner sent the bishops regarding the "Fatima Peace Conference," see the Summer 1992 issue of the *Crusader*, pp. 16–17; and for his assessment of the conference, see "A Great Success," *Fatima Crusader* (Winter 1993), pp. 2–3. Gruner ("A Great Success," p. 3) claims that "over sixty bishops" attended the conference, but this number seems grossly inflated: the Autumn 1992 *Crusader*, pp. 6–7, printed the responses of various bishops to the invitation, and very few actually indicated an intention to attend. The alleged assault against Gruner is reported in the Winter 1993 issue (p. 9).

41. Fr. Paul Leonard, "Has the Pope Fulfilled Our Lady of Fatima's Request?" *Fatima Crusader* (Winter 1993), p. 18.

42. See Brother François De Marie Des Anges, "A False Lucy Substituted for the True?" *Fatima Crusader* (Spring 1993), pp. 36–41.

43. In the terminology of the sociology of religion, Gruner's ministry may be characterized as an *audience cult* rather than a *cult movement*. On this distinction, see Rodney Stark and William Sims Bainbridge, *The Future of Religion* (Berkeley: University of California Press, 1985), pp. 27–30.

44. For the fundraising reference, see Fr. Nicholas Gruner, "The Devil is Mad as Hell!" *Fatima Crusader* (Spring 1993), p. 2. And for diatribes against Fatima competitors, see, for example, Coralie Graham, "We Must Defend Against Satan's Attack on Fatima," *Fatima Crusader* (Spring 1992), p. 3; and Fr. Paul Leonard, "Paving the Way for Antichrist: The Fatima Consecration Hoax Continues," *Fatima Crusader* (Summer 1992), pp. 18–23. Next to the Blue Army, Gruner's most hated foe on the international Fatima scene is an American priest named Fr. Robert J. Fox. The founding director of the Mid-America Fatima Shrine in Alexandria, South Dakota, and the publisher (through his Fatima Family Apostolate) of a quarterly magazine called the *Immaculate Heart Messenger* (formerly the *Fatima Family Messenger*), Fr. Fox claims to have received a personal letter from Sr. Lucia in July 1990 stating explicitly that the consecration of Russia was accomplished by Pope John Paul II on March 25, 1984 (telephone interview with Fr. Fox, 13 February 1996). Gruner and his team, needless to say, are unconvinced that such is the case. "Clearly we are not dealing with mere stupidity, but with a lack of honesty on Father Fox's part," Fr. Paul Leonard writes in the Summer 1992 *Crusader* (p. 19). For a compilation of some of his more relevant writings, see Fr. Robert J. Fox, *The Collegial Consecration of Russia Is Accomplished* (Chulmleigh-Devon, England: Augustine Publications, 1991). And for additional background on the Fatima wars, see Gustav Niebuhr, "Fatima Fever: Did Mary Prophesy Soviet Goings-On?" *Wall Street Journal* (September 27, 1991), pp. A1, A4.

45. From the Autumn 1993 issue of the *Crusader*, for example, see Kirk Kidwell, "Satan Stalks Your Children: The Crime of the Nineties," pp. 27–28; and Fr. Paul Leonard, "The Nazi-Communist Takeover is Under Way in America," pp. 40–47. On page 46 of "The Nazi-Communist Takeover," Fr. Leonard writes: "The Waco Massacre was intended to make an example of what treatment awaits those who constitute a threat to the New World Order simply because they do not intend to meekly give up their constitutional rights to keep and bear arms or their exercise of religious freedom."

46. For reports by Gruner and his staff on the debacle in Mexico City, see the Autumn 1995 issue of the *Crusader* (Victory Issue), pp. 2–31.

47. "Lettera aperta a S.S. Giovanni Paolo II," *Il Messaggero* (July 12, 1995), pp. 12–13; reprinted in the Autumn 1995 issue of the *Crusader* (Victory Issue), pp. 23–24, 26–31.

48. Supremum Signaturae Apostolicae Tribunal, CITTA DEL VATICANO (Congregatio pro Clericis), 15 May 1995.

49. According to Gruner's calculations, approximately 70 percent of his ministry's supporters are American, and 30 percent are Canadian. And of the 500,000 magazines that are produced per issue, anywhere from 300,000 to 400,000 go to the United States. In recent years, moreover, Gruner's ministry has quietly taken control of a monthly newspaper called *Catholic Family News*. Published out of Buffalo, and edited by John Vennari (formerly Brother John of the Holy Family Monastery), *CFN* currently comes across as a sort of staid cousin of the *Fatima Crusader*.

50. Personal interview, Fort Erie, Ontario, 16 December 1995.

51. Field observations; Our Lady of the Roses Shrine, Flushing Meadow Park (Queens, New York); 7 December 1995.

52. My account of Veronica's life is based mainly on interviews with former and current mem-

bers of her movement (see below for interview citations) and also on the following written sources: Roberta Grant, "War of the Roses," *Rolling Stone* (February 21, 1980), pp. 43–46; Philip Nobile, "Our Lady of Bayside," *New York* (December 11, 1978), pp. 57–60; James Donovan, "Bayside Unveiled: The Blessed Mother Takes a Beating from Her 'Friends'," *Fidelity* (March 1988), pp. 34–42; and Richard Cimino, "Our Lady of the Roses Shrine and the Bayside Movement," unpublished paper, author's files, 1993. I have also consulted two prominent movement publications: *Roses from Heaven* (Orange, Texas: Children of Mary, Inc., 1990), pp. 13–14; and *Our Lady of the Roses, Mary Help of Mothers: A Book about the Heavenly Apparitions to Veronica Lueken at Bayside, New York {Blue Book}* (Lansing, Mich.: Apostles of Our Lady, Inc., 1993), pp. 14–18, 28–31.

53. For information on some of the earlier messages, I have relied on Richard P. Gill's "An Inquiry into the Alleged Apparitions of Veronica Lueken," an unpublished investigative document prepared for the Roman Catholic Diocese of Brooklyn in 1983 (author's files).

54. Telephone interview with Melvin Sickler, Pilgrims of Saint Michael, 19 February 1996; personal interviews with Isabel Mikolainis and Pierre Marchildon, Pilgrims of Saint Michael, Toronto, 19 February 1996. On the belief system of the White Berets, see, for example, Louis Even, "The Monster's Tentacles on America," *Michael Journal* (March–April 1982), pp. 5–6; and Myron Fagan, "A Satanic Plot for a One World Government—The World Conspirators: the Illuminati," *Michael Journal* (September–October 1994), pp. 8–9.

55. On the miraculous photographs, see Daniel Noel Wojcik, "Approaching Doomsday: Fatalism in Contemporary American Apocalyptic Beliefs" (Unpublished Ph.D. dissertation, University of California at Los Angeles, 1992), ch. 4; on the "JACINTA 1972" photograph, see *An Introductory Booklet on the Apparitions of Bayside* (Bayside, N.Y.: Our Lady of the Roses, Mary Help of Mothers Shrine, n.d.), p. 12.

56. Gill, "An Inquiry into the Alleged Apparitions of Veronica Lueken," p. 12; Msgr. Anthony J. Bevilacqua, "Critique of News Article by Anne McGinn Cillis," unpublished and undated document, Roman Catholic Diocese of Brooklyn's Bayside files (prepared in response to Anne McGinn Cillis, "Investigation of Veronica by Church Officials, a Sham," *Sancta Maria* [Winter 1978]).

57. Richard Cimino, "Our Lady of the Roses Shrine and the Bayside Movement," p. 3; Jim Greene, "Bayside Church Statue Removed to Curb Spurious Marian Rites," *The Tablet* (December 6, 1973); and Jo-Ann Price, "Church Removes Statue in Dispute over Visions," *New York Times* (December 2, 1973), p. 7.

58. *Blue Book*, p. 29.

59. David M. White, "Messenger of the Madonna: A Sociological Examination of Marian Apparitions in Bayside Hills, New York," unpublished paper, author's files, 1994, pp. 16–25; St. Robert Bellarmine Roman Catholic Church Bulletin (Bayside Hills, Queens), 18 April 1975; Thomas Collins, "Veronica Will Move Vigils in a Pact with Homeowners," *New York Daily News* (May 23, 1975), p. 53; and *Blue Book*, p. 17.

60. *Blue Book*, p. 29; Grant, "War of the Roses," p. 45. To this day, the Pilgrims of Saint Michael uphold the authenticity of all of Veronica's revelations that took place prior to the "beret fiasco."

61. Gill, "An Inquiry into the Alleged Apparitions of Veronica Lueken," pp. 14–16, 22–26, 28. On Veronica's fascination with "Son of Sam," see Maury Terry, *The Ultimate Evil* (Garden City, N.Y.: Doubleday, 1987).

62. *Blue Book*, pp. 128–29; "The Imposter Pope," *Directives from Heaven* 3, 50 (August 6, 1993). (The *Directives* are thematic breakdowns of the divine messages published by the shrine on an occasional basis.)

63. For photographs of the imposter Paul VI and the real Paul VI, see *Blue Book*, pp. 128–29.

64. "Remain in Parish Church," *Directives from Heaven* 2, 11 (February 7, 1992). See the same *Directive* for similar messages from Jesus.

65. "Communion in the Hand?" *Directives from Heaven* 1, 3 (October 18, 1991); "The Mass," *Directives from Heaven* 1, 1 (September 20, 1991). In 1982, six Baysiders in Stellarton, Nova Scotia, were actually charged under section 172 (3) of Canada's Criminal Code with "wilfully disturbing an assemblage of persons met for religious worship" when they insisted upon kneeling for communion at Our Lady of Lourdes Roman Catholic Church. They were convicted and sentenced to probation, the conviction was upheld by the Nova Scotia Supreme Court, and finally, in March 1985, the Supreme Court of Canada ruled that the six communicants should not have been found guilty of criminal activity. See "From Church to Court," Editorial, *Globe and Mail* (March 22, 1985), p. 6.

66. With the idea of a "celestial miracle" especially, but in other respects as well, there is an obvious link between Bayside and the apparitions that took place at Garabandal, Spain, during the early 1960s (see *Blue Book*, p. 37). For fascinating discussions of the Garabandal apparitions, see Zimdars-Swartz, *Encountering Mary*, pp. 124–56; and John Cornwell, *Powers of Darkness, Powers of Light* (New York: Viking, 1991), ch. 20.

67. "The Great Chastisement," *Directives from Heaven* 3, 57–62 (November 12, 1993—January 21, 1994); *An Introductory Booklet on the Apparitions of Bayside*, pp. 1–4; *Blue Book*, pp. 36–46. See also "New York City—'That Great City Babylon'," *Directives from Heaven* 4, 64 (February 18, 1994).

68. "The Great Chastisement, Part 6," *Directives from Heaven* 4, 62 (January 21, 1994).

69. "Disciples of Latter Days, Part 1," *Directives from Heaven* 2, 22 (July 10, 1992); "Disciples of Latter Days, Part 2," *Directives from Heaven* 2, 30 (October 30, 1992).

70. *An Introductory Booklet on the Apparitions of Bayside*, p. 2. This notion of a "miraculous rapture" seems (at the very least) an indirect borrowing from John Nelson Darby and Protestant dispensationalism; see Ernest R. Sandeen, *The Roots of Fundamentalism: British and American Millenarianism, 1800–1930* (Chicago: University of Chicago Press, 1970), pp. 62–64.

71. I am indebted to Dan Callegari for this information (see below, note 72).

72. Telephone interview with Dan Callegari, 7 February 1996. (Callegari's wife eventually left Bayside, and they remarried five years ago.)

73. Telephone interview with Ben Salomone, 7 February 1996. For a more extensive discussion of Salomone's personal experiences with Bayside, see Donovan, "Bayside Unveiled," pp. 38–41. (The drowning story may be apocryphal; there are several variants of it currently circulating in Bayside circles, none of which I have thus far been able to confirm.)

74. Telephone interviews with Anne Cillis, 15 December 1995, 27 January 1996; *Bayside Backstage* (Ottawa: Archangel Press, 1986). For additional information on Anne Cillis and *Bayside Backstage*, see Donovan, "Bayside Unveiled," pp. 39–41; and E. Michael Jones, "The Cult, the Statue, and the Fall of the *Canadian Layman*," *Fidelity* (May 1989), pp. 30–44.

75. On the purported Necedah connection, see Carroll, *The Cult of the Virgin Mary*, pp. 138–40; and Marlene Maloney, "Necedah Revisited: Anatomy of a Phony Apparition," *Fidelity* (February 1989), p. 25. (See the May 1989 issue of *Fidelity*, p. 8, for a Bayside response to Mal-

oney's allegations.) For a superb discussion of the Necedah apparitions, see Zimdars-Swartz, *Encountering Mary*, pp. 259–67. In July 1992 I spent six days undertaking fieldwork at Necedah and the diocesan headquarters in La Crosse but was unable to establish a certain connection between Mary Ann Van Hoof and Veronica. (Mrs. Van Hoof died in 1984.)

76. Francis John Mugavero (Bishop of Brooklyn), "Declaration Concerning the 'Bayside Movement'," 4 November 1986; Ari L. Goldman, "Bishop Rejects Apparition Claims," *New York Times* (February 15, 1987), p. 67.

77. *Roses from Heaven* is a chronological compilation of messages up to October 1990; the *Directives from Heaven* series is the best source for more recent messages.

78. *Roses* (June 18, 1993), p. 2.

79. Personal interview, Manhattan, 15 October 1993.

80. The crowd was racially mixed; there were about three hundred Asians in attendance (most of whom seemed either Filipino or East Indian) and forty to fifty blacks. Although roughly two-thirds of the crowd looked middle-aged or older, there were also dozens of young families with children. Women outnumbered men by approximately six to four.

81. See "Cure and Conversion," *Directives from Heaven* 3, 51 (August 20, 1993).

82. Our Lady of the Roses Silver Anniversary field notes, 18 June 1995. (Several weeks after the anniversary celebration, the shrine sent me a copy of *Waco, The Big Lie*, a video produced by the Indianapolis-based American Justice Federation.)

83. Personal interview, Queens, New York, 26 July 1995. Baysiders in general seem to regard their ministry and Gruner's as complementary. Indeed, some of the Bayside messages refer directly to the eschatological importance of consecrating Russia. See "Consecrate Russia," *Directives from Heaven* 2, 10 (January 24, 1992).

84. "Veronica of the Cross," Our Lady of the Roses Shrine (letter sent to Veronica's followers several weeks after her death on August 3, 1995).

85. These (uncorroborated) numbers were given to me by shrine personnel in December 1995. The shrine survives entirely on private donations; it has no corporate sponsorship. A small percentage of its private donors, however, seem particularly generous. According to Michael Mangan, the current shrine director, "There is a very successful private businessman in Connecticut who helps us out enormously" (personal interview, 8 December 1995). Thus far, the shrine has succeeded in holding on to these generous donors.

86. Personal interview, Queens, New York, 8 December 1995. For several years now, in fact, the shrine has advertised itself as "The Lourdes of America."

Conclusion

1. For admirably insightful discussions of the cultural conflicts that have arisen within American society in recent years over issues such as abortion and school prayer, see Robert Wuthnow, *The Restructuring of American Religion: Society and Faith Since World War II* (Princeton: Princeton University Press, 1988); James Davison Hunter, *Culture Wars: The Struggle to Define America* (New York: Basic Books, 1991); and Stephen L. Carter, *The Culture of Disbelief: How American Law and Politics Trivialize Religious Devotion* (New York: Basic Books, 1993). Mainly because of its immense symbolic, moral, and ideological importance to Catholic conservatism, I have quite deliberately given the abortion issue narrative pride of place in the present study. This is not of course to suggest, however, that there aren't other topics also worthy of serious consideration. A differ-

ently focused study would do well, for example, to investigate more systematically than I have here the complex relationship between Catholic conservatism and the broader religio-political right in recent American political history. Indeed, it would likely take a book in itself simply to come to terms with the religious discourses and political orbits of such right-wing operatives as Pat Buchanan and Paul Weyrich. For helpful pointers in this direction, see Michele McKeegan, *Abortion Politics: Mutiny in the Ranks of the Right* (New York: Free Press, 1992); Thomas Byrne Edsall and Mary D. Edsall, *Chain Reaction: The Impact of Race, Rights, and Taxes on American Politics* (New York: Norton, 1992); and Dallas A. Blanchard, *The Anti-Abortion Movement and the Rise of the Religious Right* (New York: Twayne, 1994). For a marvelously insightful comparative discussion, see Raymond Tatalovich, *The Abortion Controversy in Canada and the United States* (Orono, Maine: Canadian-American Center, 1996).

2. From the voluminous literature on utopianism in America, see Frank E. Manuel, ed., *Utopias and Utopian Thought* (Boston: Beacon Press, 1965); Robert S. Fogarty, *American Utopianism* (Itasca, Ill.: F.E. Peacock Publishers, 1972); and Lawrence Foster, *Religion and Sexuality* (New York: Oxford University Press, 1981). And for an investigation of the Feeneyite movement, which may be viewed as another precursor of sorts to the separatist groups discussed here, see George B. Pepper, *The Boston Heresy Case in View of the Secularization of Religion* (Lewiston, N.Y.: Edwin Mellen, 1988). It might also be noted that Catholic separatists (or traditionalists) have played a significant role, sometimes despite themselves, in keeping the issue of the Tridentine liturgy alive within the broader world of American Catholicism. For evidence of the old Latin Mass's continuing popularity within the American church, see Peter Steinfels, "New York to Hear Mass in Latin, Language of Catholic Discontent," *New York Times* (May 12, 1996), pp. 1, 16. And for a distinctly conservative Catholic defense of the Tridentine liturgy, see *The Latin Mass*, a quarterly magazine published in Ridgefield, Connecticut, and edited by Roger A. McCaffrey.

3. See, for example, Ernest R. Sandeen, *The Roots of Fundamentalism: British and American Millenarianism, 1800–1930* (Chicago: University of Chicago Press, 1970).

4. On the new conservative Catholic colleges, see Mary Jo Weaver, "Self-Consciously Countercultural: Alternative Catholic Colleges," in Weaver and R. Scott Appleby, eds., *Being Right: Conservative Catholics in America* (Bloomington: Indiana University Press, 1995), pp. 300–24. During the spring of 1992, I visited two of the new colleges, Thomas More in New Hampshire and Christendom in Virginia, and was enormously impressed by both their sense of close community and their intellectual vigor.

5. For a provocative discussion of the contemporary militia movement, see Garry Wills, "The New Revolutionaries," *New York Review of Books* (August 10, 1995), pp. 50–55. It would be wrong, I think, to underestimate the survival prospects of separatist groups such as Mount St. Michael's. As Rodney Stark and Roger Finke have persuasively argued in their *The Churching of America, 1776–1990* (New Brunswick, N.J.: Rutgers University Press, 1992), smaller commitment-intensive religious groups have frequently emerged (and sometimes prospered) in America whenever more established religious bodies have grown soft and accommodating.

6. On the most recent allegations of abuse against Father John and the Infinite Love community, see Guy Roy, "'J'ai été violé au monastère': Les Apôtres de l'Amour Infini au cœur d'une vaste enquête policière," *Journal de Montréal* (February 28, 1996), pp. 1–3. And on some recent sightings of the Virgin (and related matters), see Sandra L. Zimdars-Swartz, "The Marian Revival in American Catholicism: Focal Points and Features of the New Marian Enthusiasm," in Weaver and Appleby, eds., *Being Right*, pp. 213–40.

7. See, for example, Lionel Caplan, ed., *Studies in Religious Fundamentalism* (Albany: State University of New York Press, 1987), p. 21; and Bruce B. Lawrence, *Defenders of God: The Fundamentalist Revolt Against the Modern Age* (San Francisco: Harper and Row, 1989), p. 15. For a highly sophisticated (if somewhat tendentious) conceptual discussion of *fundamentalism*, see Gabriel A. Almond, Emmanuel Sivan, and R. Scott Appleby, "Fundamentalism: Genus and Species," in Martin E. Marty and Appleby, eds., *Fundamentalisms Comprehended* (Chicago: University of Chicago Press, 1995), pp. 399–424.

8. The three categories (or types) of right-wing Catholicism that I have defined here should be regarded as *analytically* but not necessarily *empirically* distinct: as the cases of both Gruner and the Infinite Love community suggest, there may occasionally be empirical overlap. And finally, there may perhaps be a compelling reason after all for resisting the *fundamentalist* designation in the present context. In much of the popular and scholarly literature on religion, *fundamentalism* is employed not as a term of description and analysis but rather as one of opprobrium. For examples of relatively recent writings in which the term has clearly *not* been disinfected of bias, see Patrick M. Arnold, S.J., "The Rise of Catholic Fundamentalism," *America* (April 11, 1987), pp. 297–302; and John A. Coleman, S.J., "Who are the Catholic 'Fundamentalists'?" *Commonweal* (January 27, 1989), pp. 42–47.

INDEX